# Police, Firefighter, and Paramedic Stress

**Recent Titles in**
**Bibliographies and Indexes in Psychology**

Psychosocial Research on American Indian and Alaska Native Youth: An Indexed Guide to Recent Dissertations
*Spero M. Manson, Norman G. Dinges, Linda M. Grounds, and Carl A. Kallgren, compilers*

Research on Suicide: A Bibliography
*John L. McIntosh, compiler*

Books for Early Childhood: A Developmental Perspective
*Jean A. Pardeck and John T. Pardeck, compilers*

Family Therapy: A Bibliography, 1937-1986
*Bernard Lubin, Alice W. Lubin, Marion G. Whiteford, and Rodney V. Whitlock, compilers*

States of Awareness: An Annotated Bibliography
*John J. Miletich, compiler*

# *POLICE, FIREFIGHTER, AND PARAMEDIC STRESS*

## An Annotated Bibliography

***Compiled by***
**John J. Miletich**

Bibliographies and Indexes in Psychology, Number 6

***GREENWOOD PRESS***
New York • Westport, Connecticut • London

**Library of Congress Cataloging-in-Publication Data**

Miletich, John J.
Police, firefighter, and paramedic stress : an annotated bibliography / compiled by John J. Miletich.
p. cm.—(Bibliographies and indexes in Psychology, ISSN 0742-681X ; no. 6)
Includes bibliographical references.
ISBN 0-313-26682-4 (lib. bdg. : alk. paper)
1. Emergency medical technicians—Job stress—Bibliography.
2. Police—Job stress—Bibliography. 3. Fire fighters—Job stress—Bibliography. I. Title. II. Series.
Z6675.E45M54 1990
[RA645.5]
016.1587—dc20 89-28649



Library of Congress Catalog Card Number: 89-28649
ISBN: 0-313-26682-4
ISSN: 0742-681X

First published in 1990

Greenwood Press, Inc.
88 Post Road West, Westport, Connecticut 06881

Printed in the United States of America

The paper used in this book complies with the Permanent Paper Standard issued by the National Information Standards Organization (Z39.48-1984).

10 9 8 7 6 5 4 3 2 1

To Gordon I. Wilson
Edmonton, Alberta

# Contents

# Preface

It is routine, especially in urban areas, for police officers, firefighters, and paramedics to respond to many of the same calls for assistance. At motor vehicle accidents, fires, industrial accidents, and incidents involving weapons these public safety professionals work together in life-and-death situations. Earthquakes, hurricanes, tornadoes, and transportation disasters—including airplane crashes and train derailments—are examples where police officers, firefighters, and paramedics assist both the injured and the uninjured and maintain law and order. They, in addition, standby to assist the public at certain athletic events, recreation areas, and political and social gatherings. These professionals are often not only interesting to the news media, but are also romanticized in television series and motion pictures.

Tasks that are unsuitable to be filmed and shown to a general audience, however, are performed by real-life public safety professionals. These men and women pick up body parts at airplane crashes, remove homicide and suicide victims from death scenes, restrain violent individuals, console sexually-abused people, search burned-out buildings for human remains, handle hazardous materials, and, in effect, deal with many individuals who are covered with various amounts of blood, vomit, feces, or urine. To make matters worse, it is common for some people to become hostile and to verbally abuse and to assault police officers, firefighters, and paramedics—even when they prevent injury or death. The efforts of these professionals are often criticized by some strangers or family members of the injured or deceased as having been too slow or too careless. Sometimes, there is resentment that a certain person did not die!

This bibliography consists of over 700 references, covering the time period 1945 to the first quarter of 1989. Source publications, all of which are annotated, include books, articles, conference proceedings, theses, government publications, and dissertations. Information on obtaining government publications is available from the: National Technical Information Service; 5285 Port Royal Road, Springfield, Virginia, 22161. Information on obtaining dissertations is available from: University Microfilms International, 300 North Zeeb Road, Ann Arbor, Michigan, 48106.

Six chapters comprise the bibliography, in which references are arranged alphabetically by author. The chapters are: Chapter One, "Psychological Aspects;" Chapter Two, "Physiological Factors;" Chapter Three, "The Family;" Chapter Four, "Substance Abuse;" Chapter Five, "Accidents;" and Chapter Six, "Suicide." There are also separate author and subject indexes. The numbers in these indexes refer to entries, not to pages. There is also a list of acronyms.

This bibliography, in addition to being of interest to police officers, firefighters, and paramedics—and their colleagues, families, and friends—will also be of interest to legislators, physicians, nurses, social workers, psychiatrists, psychologists, and sociologists. Librarians at university, college, special, and public libraries can consult this publication as a reference work.

For those professionals who face daily job stress, this book aims to remind them that a certain amount of stress is healthy and, therefore, they should not strive to be completely stress-free. Although stress can be harmful—even fatal—police officers, firefighters, and paramedics can have more productive and satisfying lives, when they learn to positively control stress, rather than when stress controls them. It is hoped this book can help these and other professionals manage stress more effectively.

I want to express my gratitude to the individuals mainly responsible for providing me with information regarding this book. The individuals include: Janice Broverman (Librarian, Edmonton Police Department); Alan Gale (Research Associate, Faculty of Engineering, University of Alberta); and Bradley T. Guthrie (Inspector, Edmonton Fire Department). I am also grateful to staff at two provincial government libraries in Edmonton: Advanced Education (especially, Linda Harris), and Hospitals and Medical Care. Thanks to University of Alberta interlibrary loan staff, who provided me with numerous articles and other publications. Thank you to Diane Spalding, Assistant Production Editor. And a special thank you to Loomis Mayer, Editor, Social and Behavioral Sciences, for feeling the book was worth researching and writing.

# Acronyms

| | |
|---|---|
| AA | Alcoholics Anonymous |
| AFD | Alexandria Fire Department |
| AIDS | Acquired Immune Deficiency Syndrome |
| AKS | Attitude, Knowledge, Skill |
| CADS | Computer Assisted Dispatch System |
| CDF | California Department of Forestry |
| CGA | Compressed Gas Association |
| CHD | Coronary Heart Disease |
| CHOL | Cholesterol |
| CHP | California Highway Patrol |
| CIPS | Clinical Index of Potential Suicide |
| CIS | Critical Incident Stress |
| CISD | Critical Incident Stress Debriefing |
| CO | Carbon Monoxide |
| COPS | Concerns of Police Survivors |
| CPJSD | Coulson Police Job Stress Discussionnaire |
| CRF | Coronary Risk Factors |
| CSV | Crew Safety Vehicle |
| DBP | Diastolic Blood Pressure |
| DPD | Dallas Police Department |
| DPOWA | Detroit Police Officers' Wives' Auxiliary |
| EAP | Employee Assistance Program |

| | |
|---|---|
| ECG | Electrocardiogram |
| EKG | Electrocardiogram |
| EMIT | Enzyme Multiplied Immunoassay Technique |
| EMS | Emergency Medical Services |
| EMT | Emergency Medical Technician |
| ERT | Emergency Response Team |
| EVADE | Emergency Vehicle Advanced Driver Education |
| FEV | Forced Expiratory Volume |
| FMPG | Ford Motor Proving Grounds |
| FVC | Forced Vital Capacity |
| GSPA | Greater St. Louis Police Academy |
| HDL | High Density Lipoproteins |
| HELP | Health Evaluation and Longevity Planning |
| HPPP | Health and Physical Performance Program |
| HRE | High Resolution Electrocardiography |
| HSPH | Harvard School of Public Health |
| IACP | International Association of Chiefs of Police |
| IAD | Internal Affairs Division |
| IAFC | International Association of Fire Chiefs |
| IAFF | International Association of Fire Fighters |
| IBS | Interpersonal Behavior Survey |
| IHD | Ischemic Heart Disease |
| JDI | Job Descriptive Index |
| JDS | Job Diagnostic Survey |
| JSQ | Job Satisfaction Questionnaire |
| KPRST | Kasch Pulse Recovery Step Test |
| LA | Los Angeles |
| LAFD | Los Angeles Fire Department |
| LAI | Life Assets Inventory |

| | |
|---|---|
| LAPD | Los Angeles Police Department |
| LBDQ | Leader Behavior Description Questionnaire |
| LCU | Life Change Unit |
| LEAA | Law Enforcement Assistance Administration |
| MAS | Manifest Anxiety Scale |
| MBI | Maslach Burnout Inventory |
| MCMI | Millon Clinical Multiaxial Inventory |
| MDMTA | Multi-Dimensional Measure for Trait Anxiety |
| MEDIC | Medical Emergency Defense and Incident Control |
| MERV | Multiple Emergency Response Vehicle |
| MIAPS | Motoric Ideational Activity Preference Scale |
| MIT | Maximal Treadmill Time |
| MIT CSDL | Massachusetts Institute of Technology Charles S. Draper Laboratory |
| MMPI | Minnesota Multiphasic Personality Inventory |
| MOR | Mortality Odds Ratio |
| MPSS-R | Medical Personnel Stress Survey-Revised |
| MSP | Massachusetts State Police |
| NBS | National Bureau of Standards |
| NE | Norepinephrine |
| NFPA | National Fire Protection Association |
| NIJ | National Institute of Justice |
| NIOSH | National Institute of Occupational Safety and Health |
| NMJC | New Mexico Junior College |
| NOAA | National Oceanic and Atmospheric Administration |
| NT | Northern Territories |
| NTSB | National Transportation Safety Board |

| | |
|---|---|
| NYPD | New York Police Department |
| OSHA | Occupational Safety and Health Administration |
| PADI | Professional Association of Diving Instructors |
| PASS | Personal Alert Safety System |
| PCB | Polychlorinated Biphenyl |
| PHI | Personal History Index |
| PMR | Progressive Muscle Relaxation |
| POMS | Profile of Mood States |
| PSA | Pacific Southwest Airlines |
| PSI | Police Stress Inventory |
| PSS | Perceived Stress Scale |
| PSU | Psychological Services Unit |
| PTSD | Posttraumatic Stress Disorder |
| PVC | Polyvinyl Chloride |
| PWC | Physical Work Capacity |
| RCMP | Royal Canadian Mounted Police |
| RPD | Respiratory Protective Device |
| SAS | Situation Anxiety Scale |
| SCBA | Self-Contained Breathing Apparatus |
| SCE | Sister Chromatid Exchange |
| SCR | Skin Conductance Response |
| SD | Social Desirability |
| SDPD | San Diego Police Department |
| SFPD | San Francisco Police Department |
| SOS | Sources of Stress |
| SRLC | Schedule of Recent Life Changes |
| SSQ | Social Support Questionnaire |
| STAI | State Trait Anxiety Inventory |
| STPI | State Trait Personality Inventory |

| | |
|---|---|
| SUNY | State University of New York |
| SWAT | Special Weapons and Tactics |
| TAIS | Test of Attentional and Interpersonal Style |
| TAT | Thematic Apperception Test |
| TJTA | Taylor-Johnson Temperament Analysis |
| TM | Transcendental Meditation |
| TRI | Texas Research Institute |
| | Triglycerides |
| TSCS | Tennessee Self-Concept Scale |
| UCI | University of California at Irvine |
| UMBC | University of Maryland Baltimore County |
| USAF | United States Air Force |
| USDA | United States Department of Agriculture |
| VPD | Vancouver Police Department |

# *Police, Firefighter, and Paramedic Stress*

# 1

# Psychological Aspects

1.001 Ackerley, Diana Guarnera. "The Effects of a Stress Management Program on Police Personnel." **Dissertation Abstracts International** 48: 1114A-1115A. Ph.D. dissertation, University of Missouri, Columbia, 1986. Order No. DA8716685.

Forty-nine police personnel were divided into two groups: a treatment group and a control group. The Social Readjustment Rating Scale, Maslach Burnout Inventory, Police Officer's Questionnaire, and Rotter 1-E Scale were the major research instruments used. Burnout, aspects of the quality of family life, and perceived control over events were of special interest to the author.

1.002 Ainsworth, Peter B. and Ken Pease. "Stress and the Police Officer." Chapter in **Police Work,** by Peter B. Ainsworth and Ken Pease, 143-162. London: British Psychological Society and Methuen and Co. Ltd., 1987.

Police officer stress in Britain and the U.S. A table ranks, in descending order, forty-five situations described as stressful by British police officers. Being held hostage by terrorists was listed as most stressful. Covering up for a colleague was tenth most stressful. Having to pass exams was twentieth, while inadequate training was thirtieth on the list. Fortieth was rivalry with colleagues of the same rank. The table was based on information provided by police officers at the Bramshill Police College. Another table lists 144 situations perceived as stressful by U.S. police officers. 9 references.

1.003 "Air Crash Haunts Rescue Workers." **Canadian Emergency Services News** 1 (November/December 1978): 20-21.

The psychological effects on police officers,

firefighters, and other personnel of the September 25, 1978 crash of a Pacific Southwest Airlines (PSA) jet in San Diego, California. Dr. Allan Davidson, President, Academy of San Diego Psychologists, talks about the counseling services available to rescue workers, who were at the scene of the crash. 1 illustration.

1.004 Aldag, Ramon J. and Arthur P. Brief. "Supervisory Style and Police Role Stress." **Journal of Police Science and Administration** 6 (1978): 362-367.

The Job Diagnostic Survey (JDS); Porter, Steers, Mowday, and Boulian Organizational Commitment Questionnaire; the Job Descriptive Index (JDI); and the Leader Behavior Description Questionnaire (LBDQ) were the main research tools used in this study. The subjects were ninety-nine members of a police force in the U.S. midwest. Author biographical information. 3 tables. 19 footnotes.

1.005 "The Alienated Cop." **Human Behavior** 5 (July 1976): 62-63.

Tom Denyer, Robert Callender, and Dennis L. Thompson—State University of New York (SUNY) at Binghamton, New York—recommend more effective training as a way to reduce police officer alienation, especially cynicism. 1 photograph.

1.006 Alkus, Stephen and Christine Padesky. "Special Problems of Police Officers: Stress-Related Issues and Interventions." **Counseling Psychologist** 11, No. 2 (1983): 55-64.

This article consists of two main parts. The first part is about sources of stress and maladaptive reactions; the second part is about potentially effective interventions. There are performance-related stressors (patrol duty and self-image and role expectation conflicts); organization-related stressors (structural stressors and supervisory stressors); external, duty-related stressors (the courts and legal system, public attitudes and the media); and personal stressors (marital/family and social networks). Special subpopulations (administrators, women and other minorities, and rural officers) are discussed. The effects of stress are dealt with in terms of physical, cognitive-emotional, and behavioral effects. Work-related and marital programs can help manage stress. Special issues in individual and marital counseling are covered.

Author biographical information. 73 references.

1.007 Anson, Richard H., J. Dale Mann and Dale Sherman. "Niederhoffer's Cynicism Scale: Reliability and Beyond." **Journal of Criminal Justice** 14 (1986): 295-305.

An empirical assessment of a modified version of Arthur Niederhoffer's police officer cynicism scale. The researchers, using a sample of forty police officers, learned the scale was an unstable instrument, and had little predictive validity. Furthermore, cynicism is positively reinforced by superiors and peers. Author biographical information. Abstract. 5 tables. 3 notes. 33 references.

1.008 Axelberd, Mark M. "The Effects of Family Crisis Intervention Training on Police Behavior and Level of Anxiety in Response to a Domestic Dispute." **Dissertation Abstracts International** 38: 5536B. Ph.D. dissertation, Georgia State University, 1977.

There was a treatment group and two comparison groups in this study involving fifty police officers, who participated in a forty-hour, simulated domestic dispute. The Behavioral Scale for Measuring Police Effectiveness in a Domestic Dispute was developed for and used in this research. The author concluded that police officers can be trained to successfully intervene in domestic disputes.

1.009 Ayotte, Thomas E. "Chaplaincy Program." **Fire Command** 51 (December 1984): 13-14.

A fire department chaplain talks about his work with the Grand Rapids Fire Department in Grand Rapids, Michigan. Author biographical information. 2 photographs. Includes a profile of the Grand Rapids Fire Department.

1.010 Babin, Michael. "'Killed in the Line of Duty.'" **RCMP Gazette** 44, No. 3 (1982): 5-7.

Covers: the normal grieving process, sudden death, psychological dangers of repressed grief, helping the survivors, and four guidelines for peer support. Author biographical information.

1.011 Baker, Mark. **Cops: Their Lives in Their Own Words.** New York, NY: Pocket Books, 1986.

Based on interviews with over one hundred police officers—urban and rural—in a dozen states.

1.012 Barker, Bruce B. "Methods for Reducing Stress in a Small Police Department." in **Proceedings of Symposium, Job Stress and the Police Officer: Identifying Stress Reduction Techniques,** Cincinnati, Ohio, May 8-9, 1975, edited by William H. Kroes and Joseph J. Hurrell, Jr., 157-162. Washington, DC: U.S. Government Printing Office, 1975.

Discusses what constitutes a small police department and how the small department is different from larger ones in terms of personal characteristics, organization, and community attitudes. Author biographical information.

1.013 Barrett, Robert Francis. "The Effectiveness of a Cognitive Behavioral Intervention Program in Remediating Symptoms of Stress in a Police Communication Center." **Dissertation Abstracts International** 46: 2054B. Ph.D. dissertation, California School of Professional Psychology, San Diego, 1985. Order No. DA8517920.

Seventy-four police communication center personal, from the San Diego Police Department, were the volunteer subjects in this study. Anxiety, burnout, and physiological symptoms of stress were studied. The author used the State-Trait Anxiety Inventory, Maslach Burnout Inventory, and Health and Daily Living Form B. The cognitive behavioral intervention program did not appear to significantly reduce symptoms of stress.

1.014 Baum, Lisa and Steven K. Baum. "Fear of Death in Ontario Police." **Ontario Psychologist** 17 (October 1985): 9-10.

A Canadian study in which the subjects were twenty-three, Caucasian police officers, whose mean age was forty-seven years. The subjects completed a battery of tests, including the Death Anxiety Scale and the Multi-Dimensional Measure for Trait Anxiety (MDMTA). It could not be concluded, within the parameters of this study, that the police officers were more death anxious than the general population. Author biographical information. 12 references.

1.015 Behrend, Kenneth R. "Police Cynicism: A Cancer in Law Enforcement?" **FBI Law Enforcement Bulletin** 49 (August 1980): 1-4.

Defines and elaborates on police cynicism, then talks about ways of preventing and managing it. The criminal justice system and obstacles to career advancement contribute to police cynicism. Training bulletins or sessions can be vehicles with which to address this problem topic. Author biographical information. 3 photographs.

1.016 Bennett-Sandler, G., Robert L. Frazier, Donald A. Torres and Ronald J. Waldron. "Mental Health and Stress." in **Law Enforcement and Criminal Justice: An Introduction**, by G. Bennett-Sandler, Robert L. Frazier, Donald A. Torres and Ronald J. Waldron, 289. Boston, MA: Houghton Mifflin Co., 1979.

Emphasizes the importance of the psychological testing of police applicants, in order to select the best individuals. Also emphasizes the importance of all police employees having access to a psychiatrist. States that **The Onion Field**, a novel by Joseph Wambaugh, illustrates the psychological implications of dangerous police situations. Claims the suicide rate for law enforcement personnel is at least twice the national average.

1.017 Bennett-Sandler, G., Robert L. Frazier, Donald A. Torres and Ronald J. Waldron. "Stress and Tension." in **Law Enforcement and Criminal Justice: An Introduction**, by G. Bennett-Sandler, Robert L. Frazier, Donald A. Torres and Ronald J. Waldron, 207-208. Boston, MA: Houghton Mifflin Co., 1979.

Police officers encounter, daily, individuals and situations which are an outright threat or, at the very least, a potential threat. Officers are threatened with lawsuits and physical violence. They are also tempted by offers of tax-free bribes. Police officers are expected to maintain a professional detachment under circumstances which produce tension and nausea in most other people—a serious automobile accident or suicide by shotgun. Yet police officers, like people everywhere, have marital problems, sick children, and financial worries. All this causes officers stress and tension.

1.018 Bergmann, Lawrence H. and Timothy R. Queen. "Critical

Incident Stress: Part 1." **Fire Command** 53 (April 1986): 18-20.

Seven indicators of critical incident stress (CIS): numbing and withdrawal; reliving the event; depression; sleep difficulties; substance abuse; guilt; and family and marital problems. Author biographical information. 2 photographs. 1 figure.

1.019 Bergmann, Lawrence H. and Timothy R. Queen. "Critical Incident Stress: Part 2." **Fire Command** 53 (May 1986): 52 and 55-56.

Covers: critical incident stress (CIS) debriefing; individual and family counseling; and organizing a CIS program. Author biographical information. 2 photographs. 4 references.

1.020 Berting, Randi. "Conference Addresses Stress and Crisis Management." **Canadian Emergency Services News** 9 (October/November/December 1986): 50-52.

Brian Larson, Wascana Institute, Regina, Saskatchewan, spoke about job stress associated with emergency medical services (EMS) workers. Larson spoke at Interphase Saskatchewan, a conference which had 300 registrants in 1986. 2 photographs.

1.021 "The Bitter World of the Policeman." **Nation's Business** 55 (October 1967): 84-86.

Unpleasant surroundings, charges of brutality, lenient court decisions, and lack of support from the press all contribute to police officer frustrations. Includes comments by Quinn Tamm, Executive Director, International Association of Chiefs of Police; Senator Robert C. Byrd, Democrat, West Virginia; and Frank Hogan, District Attorney, New York. 1 illustration.

1.022 Blackmore, John. "Are Police Allowed to Have Problems of Their Own?" **Police Magazine** 1 (July 1978): 47-55.

Reports on counseling services available to police officers across the U.S. Individuals associated with the development of these services are mentioned. Examples include: Dr. Martin Reiser and Dr. William Kroes, Los Angeles, California; Dr. Harvey Schlossberg, New York; Joe Ravino and John Gouthro, Boston,

Massachusetts; and Dr. Michael Roberts, San Jose, California. Differences between the Boston Police Stress Program and other programs are outlined. A report about police officers by the National Institute of Occupational Safety and Health (NIOSH) is previewed. More than 2300 officers across the U.S. were studied. 5 illustrations.

1.023 Blackmore, John. '"I Feel Useless.'" **Police Magazine** 1 (July 1978): 54.

A thirty-year-old officer of the New York Police Department (NYPD), who wants to leave police work, discusses: pay; the public; nature of police calls; liability; feelings of uselessness; and arrests and court time.

1.024 Blackmore, John. '"I Pride Myself on Control.'" **Police Magazine** 1 (July 1978): 52.

A twenty-nine-year-old officer of the Detroit Police Department comments on: police work and divorce; hanging out and drinking; the street; assault on an officer; court leniency; public abuse; fear; and home life.

1.025 Blackmore, John. "'I Want to Be Loved...'" **Police Magazine** 1 (July 1978): 50.

A twenty-eight-year-old officer—New York Police Department (NYPD)—talks about: money; general frustration; the street criminal; police and social class; police and the public; boredom; and what can be done to alleviate police frustration.

1.026 Bolz, Frank and Edward Hershey. **Hostage Cop: The Story of the New York City Police Hostage Negotiating Team and the Man Who Leads It.** New York, NY: Rawson, Wade Publishers, Inc., 1979.

Although the focus of the book is on the hijacking of a bus, and two murders at Kennedy Airport in July 1977, the book also examines incidents such as Attica and the massacre of Israelis at the Olympic Games.

1.027 Breen, Lawrence. "Riding With the Redcoats: A

Psychologist on Patrol in 'D' Division." **RCMP Quarterly** 43, No. 2 (1978): 29-33.

Dr. Lawrence Breen, a psychologist and consultant to the Royal Canadian Mounted Police (RCMP) 'D' Division, talks about his experiences, while on patrol with RCMP officers in Emerson, Manitoba. Dr. Breen describes his stress as a combination of vague fear and exhilaration. 2 photographs. Author biographical information.

1.028 Bridgwater, Carol Austin. "'Hill Street' Burnout Blues." **Psychology Today** 18 (May 1984): 70.

Reports on research which found that police officer burnout was more often associated with limited advancement opportunities than with physical danger.

1.029 Brodsky, Stanley L. "Situation-Specific Stressors and Training for Police." in **Proceedings of Symposium, Job Stress and the Police Officer: Identifying Stress Reduction Techniques,** Cincinnati, Ohio, May 8-9, 1975, edited by William H. Kroes and Joseph J. Hurrell, Jr., 50-59. Washington, DC: U.S. Government Printing Office, 1975.

Situation specific training and differential vulnerability of police officers to stress. Police officers from Illinois and Alabama participated in this research. 4 tables. 5 references. Author biographical information.

1.030 Browdy, Jennifer. "Dr. Roger M. Solomon: Colorado Springs Police Psychologist and Trauma Specialist." **Law Enforcement News** 10 (February 27, 1984): 11-12, 14 and 16.

According to this interview, nightmares, flashbacks, and fear of loss of emotional control are three common reactions to critical incident trauma. A heightened sense of danger and anger, or hatred toward an assailant, are the two most common reactions noted by Dr. Solomon. 3 photographs.

1.031 Burden, Ordway P. "Post-Shooting Stress, A Serious Problem." **Police Stress** 6 (Spring 1983): 30.

Describes how stress is managed at the Marion County

Sheriff's Department, where the chaplain is J. Patrick Sheehy. In addition to handling post-shooting stress, the department also has a six-session seminar for new officers and their families. Author biographical information. 1 illustration.

1.032 Burgin, A. Lad. "The Management of Stress in Policing." **Police Chief** 45 (April 1978): 53-54.

Major topics covered and examples: uncontrollable stressors (handling drunks and shift work); controllable stressors (poor supervisory practices and inadequate training); impact of stress on police officers (diabetes and alcoholism); and impacts of stress on police organizations (workmen's compensation claims and disability retirements). Also covers stress management programs, including seminars for police spouses. Author biographical information. 1 photograph. 12 references. 4 footnotes.

1.033 Burke, Ronald J. and Eugene Deszca. "Correlates of Psychological Burnout Phases Among Police Officers." **Human Relations** 39 (1986): 487-501.

A Canadian study in which the sample consisted of 828 police officers, who completed questionnaires anonymously. Burnout, as a process, develops over time, and, in, this study, the phase model of burnout was examined. A number of work setting variables were studied, work load, institutional goals, autonomy, and social isolation being four of the variables. Research results were reported in terms of: burnout phases and total Maslach Burnout Inventory (MBI) scores; covariants of phases of progressive burnout; demographic characteristics; physical health and life style; and incidence of burnout by phases. Author biographical information. Abstract. 4 tables. 16 references.

1.034 Burke, Ronald J., Eugene Deszca and Jon Shearer. "Career Orientations and Burnout in Police Officers." **Canadian Journal of Administrative Sciences** 1 (1984): 179-194.

Four career orientations—self-investors, social activists, careerists, and artisans—were related to burnout in police work. The orientations were proposed by C. Cherniss in 1980. Respondents were 426 men and women. This research was supported by York University and the Ontario Police College. Author biographical information. English abstract. 8 tables. 11 references.

French abstract.

1.035 Cannon, Gerald A. "Spreading the Wealth: A Theoretical Rotation to Relieve Burnout." **JEMS** 13 (March 1988): 37-39.

Describes the Paramedic Triad System in San Diego, California. The system, a rotating schedule, arose because of high turnover for paramedic personnel. The turnover was associated with discontent regarding pay, benefits, and burnout. The goal of the system: have personnel stay in their jobs for several years. Author biographical information. 2 figures.

1.036 Caretti, Richard and Aubrey E. Green. "Improving Psychological Services to Police Officers: A Management Problem." **Police Stress** 1 (Fall 1978): 15-16.

Avoiding the use of stereotyped descriptions, when referring to police officers with psychological problems, is one aspect of improving psychological services to this occupational group. Author biographical information. 1 photograph. 5 references.

1.037 Chard, Philip S. "Grief: Handling Theirs and Yours." **Emergency Medical Services** 16 (January/February 1987): 36-38 and 40-43.

Emergency medical services (EMS) personnel must learn to deal with acute grief reactions. These reactions are exhibited most often in relatives or close friends of someone who has died suddenly and unexpectedly or who has had a severe injury. Anger, denial, and shock are associated with acute grief reactions. EMS personnel can experience their own delayed or pathological grief reactions, as a result of daily contact with physical and emotional traumas. 1 illustration. 5 references. Author biographical information.

1.038 Cheek, Frances E. "Coping Techniques—Negative and Positive." Chapter in **Stress Management for Correctional Officers and Their Families**, by Frances E. Cheek, 17-22. College Park, MD: American Correctional Association, 1984.

Suppression of feelings, withdrawal, irritability, projection, and overeating are examples of negative coping techniques regarding stress. Daily goals, delegating responsibility, taking breaks, proper diet, sufficient exercise, and relaxing hobbies are examples of positive coping. 3 photographs.

1.039 Cheek, Frances E. "Desensitization Exercise." Appendix in **Stress Management for Correctional Officers and Their Families**, by Frances E. Cheek, 84-85. College Park, MD: American Correctional Association, 1984.

This exercise should be preceded by the muscle-relaxant exercise.

1.040 Cheek, Frances E. "Handling Tense Situations With Correct Assertiveness." Chapter in **Stress Management for Correctional Officers and Their Families**, by Frances E. Cheek, 57-64. College Park, MD: American Correctional Association, 1984.

Talks about the underassertive personality, the overassertive personality, and six guidelines pertaining to correct assertiveness. 3 photographs.

1.041 Cheek, Frances E. "How I See Myself in My Job." Appendix in **Stress Management for Correctional Officers and Their Families**, by Frances E. Cheek, 87. College Park, MD: American Correctional Association, 1984.

A ten-item rating technique. 1 photograph.

1.042 Cheek, Frances E. "How to Change Behavior." Chapter in **Stress Management for Correctional Officers and Their Families**, by Frances E. Cheek, 53-56. College Park, MD: American Correctional Association, 1984.

By making reference to B.F. Skinner, this chapter contends it is better to change people by rewarding desirable behavior than by punishing undesirable behavior. 1 photograph.

1.043 Cheek, Frances E. "Introduction." in **Stress Management for Correctional Officers and Their Families**, by Frances E. Cheek, xi-xiv. College Park, MD: American Correctional Association, 1984.

Comments on the personal costs of correctional stress, organizational costs of correctional stress, and stress and correctional administration. 1 photograph.

1.044 Cheek, Frances E. "Managing Tension in the Correctional Setting." Chapter in **Stress Management for Correctional Officers and Their Families,** by Frances E. Cheek, 33-46. College Park, MD: American Correctional Association, 1984.

Stress management through desensitization, as described by J. Wolpe and A. Lazarus (1966). 1 figure. 5 photographs.

1.045 Cheek, Frances E. "Muscle-Relaxant Technique." Appendix in **Stress Management for Correctional Officers and Their Families,** by Frances E. Cheek, 81-82. College Park, MD: American Correctional Association, 1984.

An exercise adapted from E. Jacobsen (1938).

1.046 Cheek, Frances E. "Positive Self-Image Exercise." Appendix in **Stress Management for Correctional Officers and Their Families,** by Frances E. Cheek, 86. College Park, MD: American Correctional Association, 1984.

This exercise should be preceded by the muscle-relaxant exercise.

1.047 Cheek, Frances E. "Self-Relaxation Exercise." Appendix in **Stress Management for Correctional Officers and Their Families,** by Frances E. Cheek, 83-84. College Park, MD: American Correctional Association, 1984.

An exercise which can be used as a person is preparing for sleep or as he wakes up.

1.048 Cheek, Frances E. "Sources of Stress in Corrections." Chapter in **Stress Management for Correctional Officers and Their Families,** by Frances E. Cheek, 9-16. College Park, MD: American Correctional Association, 1984.

Abraham Maslow's hierarchy of basic needs is expressed in five rather than seven categories: physiological (food and warmth); safety and an orderly environment; emotional (affection and sense of belonging); ego (status and esteem); and self-actualization (sense of purpose and accomplishment). Stress can block the satisfaction of these needs. Sources of stress for managers and the stresses of top versus middle managers are also discussed. 2 photographs. 1 cartoon illustration.

1.049 Cheek, Frances E. "Stress and Burnout Self-Evaluation." Appendix in **Stress Management for Correctional Officers and Their Families,** by Frances E. Cheek, 88-102. College Park, MD: American Correctional Association, 1984.

Burnout, the Selye Health Score, nutrition, physical exercise, vulnerability to stress, and sources of stress are covered in this appendix. 2 photographs. 1 figure.

1.050 Cheek, Frances E. "Stress and Burnout—Their Nature and Consequences." Chapter in **Stress Management for Correctional Officers and Their Families,** by Frances E. Cheek, 1-8. College Park, MD: American Correctional Association, 1984.

What is stress?; the limits of adaptive energy; the adaptive process; the sustained stress response and illness; life changes, everyday "hassles," and illness; employee burnout; organizational symptoms of burnout; characteristics of burnout-prone jobs; characteristics of burnout-prone workers; and the five stages of burnout. 1 photograph.

1.051 Cheek, Frances E. "Stress and Irrational Thinking." Chapter in **Stress Management for Correctional Officers and Their Families,** by Frances E. Cheek, 65-70. College Park, MD: American Correctional Association, 1984.

Applies the rational-emotive therapy of Albert Ellis to the correctional setting, then describes five types of irrational thinking: dichotomous thinking, overgeneralization, stereotyping, excessive reliance on other people's judgement, and enculturation and oversocialization. 2 photographs.

1.052 Cheek, Frances E. "Stress and Self-Image Improvement."

Chapter in **Stress Management for Correctional Officers and Their Families,** by Frances E. Cheek, 47-52. College Park, MD: American Correctional Association, 1984.

Includes a positive self-image exercise and a self-image improvement exercise. 1 photograph.

1.053 Cheek, Frances E. "'Turning Off the Stress Alarm' With Deep Relaxation." Chapter in **Stress Management for Correctional Officers and Their Families,** by Frances E. Cheek, 23-32. College Park, MD: American Correctional Association, 1984.

Elaborates on progressive muscle relaxation developed by E. Jacobsen in the 1930s. This technique involves the tightening and relaxing of muscles. The body rids itself of toxins. Progressive muscle relaxation can be used in controlling anxiety and hypertension. A few minutes of this type of relaxation is apparently of more value to a person than hours of deep sleep. 2 photographs. 1 illustration.

1.054 Cheek, Frances E. and Marie Di Stefano Miller. "The Experience of Stress for Correction Officers: A Double-Bind Theory of Correctional Stress." **Journal of Criminal Justice** 11 (1983): 105-120.

The subjects were 143 New Jersey correction officers, who were administered a questionnaire. Physical illnesses and high divorce rates were objective indicators the subjects were in a stressful occupation. Officer-inmate interaction was identified as the major stressor. The officers felt they were in a double-bind predicament, in terms of their macho self-image and their powerlessness, in dealing with inmates. Bureaucracy was perceived as the cause of the double-bind situation. Author biographical information. Abstract. 6 tables. Acknowledgements. 1 note. 43 references.

1.055 Clark, David F. "Debriefing to Defuse Stress." **Fire Command** 55 (November 1988): 33-35.

The work of Dr. Jeffrey Mitchell. Mitchell, who is affiliated with the University of Maryland, is a pioneer in dealing with critical incident stress (CIS). Emergency services personnel who were associated with the Pacific Southwest Airlines (PSA) crash in San Diego, California in 1978, and the skywalk collapse at the Hyatt Regency Hotel in Kansas City, Kansas in 1981, experienced CIS. This type of stress was also associated with the Air Florida crash in Washington, DC and the Baltimore, Maryland Amtrak disaster. Author biographical information. 6 illustrations.

1.056 Cohen, Lori Robin. "Occupational Stress, Personality Styles, and Somatic Symptoms in Police Officers." **Dissertation Abstracts International** 48: 259B. Ph.D. dissertation, California School of Professional Psychology, Los Angeles, 1987. Order No. DA8704341.

Eighty-two male patrol officers, the subjects in this study, were divided into two groups: histrionic police officers and avoidant police officers. The officers were compared to four comparison groups regarding six variables. The Millon Clinical Multiaxial Inventory (MCMI) and the Somatic Reactions Scale were used in this research.

1.057 Colegrove, Susan Carol Barnett. "Personality and Demographic Characteristics As Predictors of Burnout in Female Police Officers." **Dissertation Abstracts International** 44: 1232B-1233B. Ph.D. dissertation, California School of Professional Psychology, Berkeley, 1983. Order No. DA8317074.

The subjects were 196 female police officers in California, Arizona, and Texas. The Maslach Burnout Inventory, Internal-External Control Scale, and State-Trait Anxiety Inventory were three of the research instruments used. Anxiety, emotional exhaustion, depersonalization, self-acceptance, and education were some of the variables examined.

1.058 "Consultant Says Stress Increasing Police Job Dissatisfaction." **Criminal Justice Newsletter** 13 (July 5, 1982): 4-5.

Reports on research by Dr. Mimi H. Silbert, a California police department consultant. The subjects of her research were male and female members of the San Francisco Police Department (SFPD). She learned that psychological problems on the job are more stressful to the officers than the prospects of physical danger. She also learned that female officers demonstrated more work stress than male officers. A total of 267 police officers participated in the study.

1.059 Cooper, Cary L., M.J. Davidson and P. Robinson. "Stress in the Police Service." **Journal of Occupational Medicine** 24 (January 1982): 30-36.

Approximately 200 supervisory police officers—in a police department in the United Kingdom—were the subjects for this research. Sex, age, marital status, length of service in years, rank, and average age by rank were some of the demographic characteristics of the subjects studied. Work stressors examined: work overload; lack of personal recognition and frustrated ambition; perceived unnecessary obstacles which inhibit the police function; autocratic management consequences; the effect of perceived police/public relations; work function/environment interface; short term high intensity police stressors; responsibility for a police unit; and complaints against police. Author biographical information. Abstract. 7 tables. 14 references.

1.060 "Cop Who Saved MOVE Child Resigning Due to Stress." **Jet** 71 (October 27, 1986): 32.

Concerns the resignation of James P. Berghaier, a police officer in Philadelphia, Pennsylvania.

1.061 "Coping With Death: First Experiences." **Emergency Medical Services** 16 (January/February 1987): 20, 22, and 32-34.

Six emergency medical services (EMS) personnel talk about their first experiences with death. The EMS personnel are: Tim Butcher (Chalmette, Louisiana); Lisa Dubnoff (Benicia, California); Lowell V. Ackerman (Minneapolis, Minnesota); Christopher P. Koesterer (Perryville, Missouri); Danny Harbinson (Newton, North Carolina); and James A. Koehn (Lake Oswego, Oregon). 1 illustration.

1.062 **Coping With Stress.** Gaithersburg, MD: International Association of Chiefs of Police, Inc., 1978.

Fifteen indicators of stress, including: rapid mood changes, excessive use of alcohol, overhostility, excessive nervous habits, sleep disturbances, and depression. Repression of emotion, displacement of anger, isolation, and unspoken fears are discussed as reactions to stress. A section on the female officer is included. Nine suggestions for reducing stress. Abstract. Acknowledgement.

1.063 "Coping With Stress." **Emergency Medical Services** 17 (March 1988): 11-12, 14, 16 and 48.

Seven emergency medical services (EMS) personnel discuss coping with stress. The personnel are: Gary T. Ohler (Danvers, Illinois); Gretchen Norton (Park Forest, Illinois); Stephen R. Kruft (Aberdeen, New Jersey); J.B. deSaulles (Youngstown, Ohio); Charles A. Aquilla (Baltimore, Maryland); Margaret Franckowiak (Flint, Michigan); and Lynda Parker (Lapeer, Michigan).

1.064 Coulson, Jesse Edward. "The Effectiveness of a Stress Reduction Program for Police Officers." **Dissertation Abstracts International** 48: 872A. ED.D. dissertation, North Texas State University, 1987.

This research involved three groups of police officers. Two of the groups were control groups. The Coulson Police Job Stress Discussionaire (CPJSD) and the Profile of Mood States (POMS) were used. Each group was pretested and posttested. This research questions the validity of the POMS.

1.065 Cowardin, David H. "Stress and the Command Officer." **Current Municipal Problems** 13 (1986/1987): 475-477.

Examines the reduction of internal and external stress experienced by the fire service incident commander. Lists four ways of reducing internal stress. Discusses seven methods of dealing with external stress—stress imposed by a situation. The seven methods are: increasing activity, queuing or stacking, increasing channels, filtering, chunking, trading errors, and variations of omissions. Abstract. Author biographical information. This article also appeared in the June 1986 issue of **American Fire Journal**.

1.066 Cox, Jackie. "The PCB/PVC Confusion Continues to Spell Caution for Fire Fighters." **Fire Engineering** 136 (December 1983): 46, 49 and 51.

Firefighters must exercise caution when dealing with PCBs (polychlorinated biphenyls) and PVC (polyvinylchloride). Both constitute a hazardous chemical environment. PCBs are found in hydraulic systems, natural gas pipeline compressors, and electromagnets. PVCs are found in electrical cable, house siding, and food packaging. Both PCBs and PVCs release toxic gases. PVCs have been associated with tragic fires, including the Beverly Hills Supper Club fire (1977) near Cincinnati, Ohio, and the MGM Hotel fire (1980) in Las Vegas, Nevada. 1 illustration.

1.067 Crawford, Thomas J. "Police Overperception of Ghetto Hostility." **Journal of Police Science and Administration** 1 (1973): 168-174.

Compares police prediction of public response to fire survey questions, regarding ghetto hostility, and actual public response to survey questions. This survey, conducted in an industrial city in California, revealed that police officers overestimated antipolice sentiment. Author biographical information. 2 tables. 10 footnotes.

1.068 Danish, Steven J. and Stanley L. Brodsky. "Training of Policemen in Emotional Control and Awareness." **American Psychologist** 25 (1970): 368-369.

Professional actors appeared in films and expressed four emotions—of varying intensity of feeling—to a sample of police officers. Each officer imagined the actor was addressing him personally. The films simulated realistic situations pertinent to police work. Author biographical information. 6 references.

1.069 Danto, Bruce L. and Loren M. Pittman. "A Study of Politically Induced Stress in Officers of the Wayne County Sheriff's Department." **Police Stress** 5 (Winter 1982): 18-29.

In this research into politically induced stress in officers of the Wayne County Sheriff's Department in Wayne County, Michigan, which includes the city of Detroit, questionnaires were distributed to the police officers. Officer-respondents returned the questionnaires anonymously. The response rate for the male officer-respondents was 44%; the response rate for the female officer-respondents was 100%. A total of 226 officers participated in the research. Results were compared and reported in terms of: race, sex, and rank change. Author biographical information. 7 illustrations. 4 references. 1 appendix.

1.070 Davidson, Alan D. "Air Disaster: Coping With Stress A Program That Worked." **Police Stress** 1 (Spring 1979): 20-22

On September 25, 1978, a Boeing 727 and a Cessna 172 collided in midair over San Diego, California. A total of 144 people died in the collision, which was also referred to as the Pacific Southwest Airlines (PSA) disaster. Members of the San Diego Police Department (SDPD), who were at the crash scene, and who sought and received confidential counseling because of what they saw—for example, body parts—reported a number of distressing symptoms, including nightmares, anxiety, and loss of appetite. Physical exercise, self-hypnosis, and deep muscle relaxation were three types of treatment used. Author biographical information. 3 photographs.

1.071 Davidson, Marilyn J. and Arthur Veno. "Police Stress in Australia: A Current Perspective." **Australian and New Zealand Journal of Criminology** 12 (1979): 153-161.

Data from Australia, the U.S., and England is used in a discussion of cross-cultural police role and community relations; stress and job dissatisfaction; and stress indicators. Author biographical information. 46 references.

1.072 Davis, Goliath John, III. "Work Group Cohesion and Job Stress Among Police Officers." **Dissertation Abstracts International** 45: 1535A. Ph.D. dissertation, Florida State University, 1984. Order No. DA8416698.

The sample in this investigation consisted of 289 police officers—265 male and twenty-four female—from the St. Petersburg Police Department, St. Petersburg, Florida. The mean age was 32.75 years, with a mean educational level of 13.6 years, and mean length of service 8.76 years. Five substantive hypotheses were tested.

1.073 Davis, James A. "Perspectives of Policewomen in Texas and Oklahoma." **Journal of Police Science and Administration** 12 (1984): 395-403.

This research revealed female police officers to be more authoritarian than male police officers. It also revealed female officers to be more cynical about human nature regarding obedience to the law. Also, danger was more important to female officers than to their male counterparts. Females, furthermore, rated their self-confidence lower than did males. Author biographical information. 4 tables. 3 footnotes. Acknowledgement. 26 references.

1.074 DeLey, Warren W. "American and Danish Police 'Drop-out' Rates: Denmark's Force As a Case Study in High Job Satisfaction, Low Stress, and Low Turnover." **Journal of Vocational Behavior** 25 (1984): 58-69.

In this comparative study of U.S. and Danish police officers, a number of key topics are addressed, including the following: danger of physical assault or other bodily harm; role conflict and ambiguity; job security and compensation; career advancement and diversification; and education, training, and pride. The author conducted research while in Denmark and later in the U.S. Part of his research in Denmark consisted of riding in police cars. In the U.S., he surveyed via questionnaire 126 police departments. Author biographical information. Abstract. 1 table. 38 references.

1.075 Delprino, Robert P. and Charles Bahn. "National Survey of the Extent and Nature of Psychological Services in Police Departments." **Professional Psychology: Research and Practice** 19 (1988): 421-425.

A national survey of psychological services in 232 police departments in the U.S. Although questionnaires were sent to 336 police agencies, 193 municipal and thirty-nine state police departments replied. A table summarizes current use, perceived need, and future use of psychological services. Author biographical information. Abstract. 1 table. 26 references.

1.076 Deoma, Joseph M. "Stress in Policing: A Command Problem." **Police Stress** 7 (Autumn 1984): 27-30.

Nine steps employers can take, according to Dr. Carol Boggs, to prevent employee job burnout. Two breathing exercises which bring about relaxation. Time management as a means of stress reduction. Author biographical information. 1 illustration.

1.077 Depue, Roger L. "Turning Inward: The Police Officer Counselor." **FBI Law Enforcement Bulletin** 48 (February 1979): 8-12.

Stress regarding a number of police departments is discussed, including departments in Seattle, Washington; Los Angeles, California; Salt Lake City, Utah; Tacoma, Washington; San Jose, California; Baltimore, Maryland; and Chicago, Illinois. Police officer stress is frequently associated with marriage, situational crises (for example, shootings), and organizational factors, poor equipment being one of them. Attempts to deal with these and other problems is discussed in relation to police departments in Dallas, Texas; Oakland, California; and Kansas City, Missouri. Author biographical information. 31 footnotes.

1.078 Dernocoeur, Kate. "Total Self-Care: Basic Stress Management—And More." **Emergency Medical Services** 18 (March 1989): 29, 32, 37 and 38.

Self-understanding, recognizing trouble, and healthy habits for total self-care for emergency medical services (EMS) personnel. Author biographical information. 1 table. 1 photograph.

1.079 Dick, Thom. "Anxiety in the Street: Understanding Yourself and Relating to Your Patients." **JEMS** 5 (June 1980): 29-31.

How the paramedic can manage his own anxiety and that of his patient. Sources of anxiety are discussed. Mild and severe anxiety are compared. Seven techniques for dealing with relatives and friends of the patient are given. Author biographical information. 1 photograph. 1 figure. 2 references.

1.080 Diskin, Susan D., Michael J. Goldstein and Judith M. Grencik. "Coping Patterns of Law Enforcement Officers in Simulated and Naturalistic Stress." **American Journal of Community Psychology** 5 (1977): 59-73.

The subjects were 135 deputies of the County of Los Angeles Sheriff's Department. They were administered the Coper-Avoider Sentence Completion Test, and the Trait-State Anxiety Scale. Psychophysiological and self-report measures were noted when the subjects were shown a stressful film. The authors were interested in standards of physical and emotional fitness for individuals in law enforcement. Author biographical information. Abstract. 4 footnotes. 3 tables. 2 figures. 9 references.

1.081 Dobson, Clifford B. "Stress in the Police." in **Stress: The Hidden Adversary**, by Clifford B. Dobson, 304-310. Lancaster: MTP Press Ltd., 1982.

Compares stress in police in Britain, Australia, and the United States. The following are some of the stressors discussed: high-density urban areas, amount of time spent in court, social isolation, and light sentences received by criminals.

1.082 Dolphin, Ric. "Patrolling the Night." **Maclean's** 102 (January 9, 1989): 34-35.

A magazine writer's observations during a Saturday night, with police officers of the Toronto Police Department's 51 Division. There were 15,000 criminal offenses committed in this division in 1988. The officers and the public they deal with represent a variety of racial and ethnic groups. About two-thirds of the police officers in 51 Division are separated, divorced, or remarried. 3 photographs.

1.083 Donahue, Michael J. "Peer Counseling for Police Officers: A Program for Skill Development and Personal Growth." **Dissertation Abstracts International** 38: 1992A-1993A. ED.D. dissertation, Boston University School of Education, 1977. Order No. DA7721637.

Twenty-two Massachusetts police officers comprised a sample study population, consisting of an experimental (eleven officers) and a control (eleven officers) group. The researcher used the Carkhuff Empathy Scale and the Loevinger Sentence Completion Form. Two hypotheses were tested.

1.084 Donovan, Ed. "Receptivity Is Key to Recovery." **Police Stress** 6 (Spring 1983): 42-45.

Describes the behavior of a police officer involved in trauma, explains police department procedures in dealing with this type of officer, and states how the trauma can be overcome. 2 illustrations.

1.085 Donovan, Edward C. "'Need Some Help, Doc?'" **Police Stress** 1 (Fall 1978): 25 and 30.

Value of peer counseling to police officers with psychological and other problems. Why the peer counselor is likely to be trusted by the officer with a problem. Type of setting in which to do peer counseling. Author biographical information. 1 photograph.

1.086 Drabek, Thomas E. "Theory and Methods in the Study of Organizational Stress." **Government Reports Annoucements and Index** 69 (February 10, 1969): 36. NTIS AD-678 929.

This research, about stress in simulated police communication teams, was discussed in January 1968, at the Symposium on Organizational Stress held at the University of Denver.

1.087 Drabek, Thomas Edward. "Laboratory Simulation of a Police Communication System Under Stress." **Dissertation Abstracts International** 26: 6218. Ph.D. dissertation, Ohio State University, 1965. Order No. DA66-1771.

Lists five major methodological conclusions and four specific hypotheses supported by the research. The central hypothesis supported was that organizational stress will be followed by a change in organizational performance structure.

1.088 Droge, Edward F., Jr. **The Patrolman: A Cop's Story.** Scarborough: New American Library of Canada Ltd., 1973.

The everyday police work of Edward F. Droge, Jr., of the New York Police Department (NYPD), and his work for the Knapp Commission, which investigated police corruption in New York.

1.089 Dubinsky, Steven and Leo Standora. **Decoy Cop.** New York, NY: Ace Books, 1974.

Five police officers assigned to an anti-crime unit which fights street crimes in New York.

1.090 Duncan, J.T. Skip, Robert N. Brenner and Marjorie Kravitz. "Police Stress Training Films." Appendix in **Stress and Police Personnel**, by Leonard Territo and Harold J. Vetter, 319-330. Boston, MA: Allyn and Bacon, Inc., 1981.

Discusses thirty-three police stress training films made between 1970 and 1976. "Perception of Danger" (1974); "Interview With George Kirkham: The Professor Who Became a Cop " (1976); "Officer Stress Awareness" (1976); and "Behavioral Simulation Modules:

Hostility" (1975) are some of the films.

1.091 Dunne, Joseph A. "Police Officers Should Know About Compulsive Gambling." **Police Stress** 1 (Fall 1978): 21.

The answers to five questions can help determine if a person who gambles requires the help of Gamblers Anonymous. A profile of the addicted gambler is included. The compulsive gambler, in the final stages of his addiction, will turn to crime to help finance his gambling. Treatment is similar to that provided by Alcoholics Anonymous. Author biographical information. 1 photograph.

1.092 Durham, Thomas W., Susan L. McCammon and E. Jackson Allison, Jr. "The Psychological Impact of Disaster on Rescue Personnel." **Annals of Emergency Medicine** 14 (1985): 664-668.

Psychological impact of disaster on rescue personnel at an apartment building explosion on March 2, 1983 in Greenville, North Carolina. One person died, one was comatose, eleven were hospitalized, and more than one hundred were homeless as a result of the explosion. Eighty percent of rescue personnel who helped victims of the explosion exhibited evidence of posttraumatic stress disorder (PTSD). This and other information was obtained from a questionnaire administered to seventy-nine subjects. Author biographical information. Abstract. 3 tables. 10 references. Acknowledgements.

1.093 Dustow, Sue. "Firefighters Under Constant Stress." **Canadian Emergency Services News** 11 (September/October 1988): 41.

Reports on the Canadian Association of Fire Chiefs meeting in Kitchener, Ontario. Wayne Corneil (Health and Welfare Canada); Joe Scanlon (Carleton University); and Lowell Jenkins (Edmonton Fire Department) were three of the attendees. To firefighters too few calls, and the resulting boredom, is stressful, just as are the variety of incidents firefighters deal with. Airplane crashes, car collisions, hazardous material spills, and natural disasters are some of the incidents. The Edmonton, Alberta tornado on July 31, 1987 in which twenty-eight people died is an example of the latter. Dealing with people who have Acquired Immune Deficiency Syndrome (AIDS) or hepatitis B is also stressful. 3 photographs.

1.094 Earle, Howard H. **Police Recruit Training: Stress vs. Non-Stress.** Springfield, IL: Charles C. Thomas, 1973.

Examines a three-year field experiment in the Los Angeles County Sheriff's Department—August 1968 to June 1971—which analyzed the effect of authoritarian input (stress) on the field performance of newly trained officers.

1.095 Egan, Cy. **Some Very Special Men: The Emergency Service to the Rescue.** New York, NY: Harper and Row, Publishers, 1974.

The Emergency Service is a branch of the New York Police Department (NYPD). Its members talk would-be suicides out of taking their own lives, respond to airplane crashes, face armed criminals, and engage in a number of other dangerous tasks. Having quick reactions, being expert swimmers, and having a knowledge of artificial respiration are three of a number of qualities members of the Emergency Service must have. Before beginning work on this book in 1971, the author spent almost a decade making notes.

1.096 Eisenberg, Terry. "Job Stress and the Police Officer: Identifying Stress Reduction Techniques." in **Proceedings of Symposium, Job Stress and the Police Officer: Identifying Stress Reduction Techniques,** Cincinnati, Ohio, May 8-9, 1975, edited by William H. Kroes, and Joeseph J. Hurrell, Jr., 26-34. Washington, DC: U.S. Government Printing Office, 1975.

A look at thirty-three sources of psychological stress in police work. They range from poor supervision to excessive paper work, from unfavorable court decisions to unfavorable minority attitudes, from role conflict to the female officer. 2 footnotes. Author biographical information.

1.097 Elder, Rob. **Chiodo 2: The Decoy Man.** Chicago, IL: Playboy Press, 1975.

Additional accounts about the undercover work of Dan Chiodo, a police officer, New York Police Department (NYPD).

1.098 Ellison, Katherine W. and John L. Genz. "The Nature of Stress." Chapter in **Stress and the Police Officer,** by Katherine W. Ellison and John L. Genz, 3-39.

Springfield, IL: Charles C. Thomas, 1983.

Some of the key areas in this chapter: defining stress; stress and coping; individual personality factors; stressful life events; influence of organizational factors; burnout; influence of sociocultural factors; universal stressors; physical responses to stressful events; psychological responses to stressful events; and reactions in crisis. There are five case studies included. 12 notes.

1.099 Ellison, Katherine W. and John L. Genz. "Organizational and Supervisory Strategies for Stress Management." Chapter in **Stress and the Police Officer**, by Katherine W. Ellison and John L. Genz, 87-105. Springfield, IL: Charles C. Thomas, 1983.

Examines: stress and organizational style; progressive discipline; the department psychologist; prevention and crisis intervention (physical fitness, retirement planning, posttraumatic incidents counseling); chronic problems (alcoholism, suicide); supervisory strategies for stress management; progressive discipline for supervisors; interviewing and counseling; and counseling for acute crisis. Includes 3 case studies. 12 notes.

1.100 Ellison, Katherine W. and John L. Genz. "The Police Officer As Burned-Out Samaritan." **FBI Law Enforcement Bulletin** 47 (March 1978): 1-7.

Burnout, as described by Dr. Christina Maslach, a psychologist, is related to stress in police officers. The injury or death of a fellow officer or child is particularly stressful to police officers. Ventilation of feelings with colleagues, physical exercise, biofeedback, and meditation can help prevent burnout. Author biographical information. 2 photographs. 3 illustrations. 21 footnotes.

1.101 Ellison, Katherine W. and John L. Genz. "Recognizing Stress Reactions." Chapter in **Stress and the Police Officer**, by Katherine W. Ellison and John L. Genz, 76-86. Springfield, IL: Charles C. Thomas, 1983.

How to recognize stress reactions in others and in oneself. Personality changes, physical changes, and changes in work patterns are major indicators. Depression, agitation, trembling hands, and insomnia are symptoms of stress. Lists approximately forty warning signs of stress. 3 tables. 1 figure.

1.102 Ellison, Katherine W. and John L. Genz. "Stress in Policing." Chapter in **Stress and the Police Officer**, by Katherine W. Ellison and John L. Genz, 40-75. Springfield, IL: Charles C. Thomas, 1983.

Compares how male and female police officers differ in their perception of what is most stressful to them. Talks about stressors external to the police organization, one of them being the criminal justice system. Examines stressors inherent in the police role. An example of the latter is an officer involved in a fatal shooting. Covers the special stress problems of minority group officers. Views the family as a mediator of police officer stress reactions. 18 notes.

1.103 Ellison, Katherine W. and John L. Genz. "Techniques for Individual Stress Management I." Chapter in **Stress and the Police Officer**, by Katherine W. Ellison and John L. Genz, 106-134. Springfield, IL: Charles C. Thomas, 1983.

There are nine techniques for individual stress management in this chapter: goal setting; time management; financial planning; physical fitness; requirements for a physical fitness program (nutrition, exercise, rest); meditation; progressive relaxation; biofeedback; and support from other police officers, family, and nonpolice friends. 6 exercises. 2 figures. 13 notes.

1.104 Ellison, Katherine W. and John L. Genz. "Techniques for Individual Stress Management II: Cognitive Strategies." Chapter in **Stress and the Police Officer**, by Katherine W. Ellison and John L. Genz, 135-159. Springfield, IL: Charles C. Thomas, 1983.

Main topics here are about irrational thought patterns, guidelines for a low stress life style, and five exercises for changing thoughts and behaviors. 1 case study. 1 figure. 12 notes.

1.105 Ellison, Katherine W. and John L. Genz. "Training." Chapter in **Stress and the Police Officer**, by Katherine W. Ellison and John L. Genz, 160-182. Springfield, IL: Charles C. Thomas, 1983.

Talks about: training methods; curriculum core; command personnel; first-line supervisors, particularly stressful assignments; patrol officers; recruit training; the family; training aids (films, case materials);

and development of policy statements. 4 sample class schedules. 7 case examples. 8 notes.

1.106 "Emergency Personnel Encounter Increasing Violence and Vandalism on Runs: What Are Some Solutions?" **Emergency Medical Services** 12 (January/February 1983): 9 and 11-13.

The comments of five emergency medical services (EMS) personnel: Robert Freeman (Newark, New Jersey); Jerald Birt (Seattle, Washington); Michael L. Hampton (Little Rock, Arkansas); Robert G. Nixon (Fort Lauderdale, Florida); and Ronald A. Smith (Chicago, Illinois).

1.107 Esbeck, Edward S. and George Halverson. "Stress and Tension-Teambuilding for the Professional Police Officer." **Journal of Police Science and Administration** 1 (1973): 153-161.

Some of the areas dealt with in the stress seminar: principles of perception, self-image, the self-disclosure model, effects of stress on self-image, stress and the disclosure process, team experience with disclosure; characteristics of interpersonal stress, team process feedback, and crisis events. Author biographical information. 2 tables. 3 footnotes.

1.108 Eszterhas, Joe. **Nark!** San Francisco, CA: Straight Arrow Books, 1974.

The author uses three case examples in criticizing the actions of selected narcotics agents, claiming this criticism is not directed at police officers in general. The author is a former police reporter who spent two years professionally and socially with police officers, and liked most of them.

1.109 Everly, Jeff. "Debriefings Defuse Stress." **Fire Command** 51 (November 1984): 34-35.

If a firefighter becomes frustrated at the scene of a fire or other disaster, and cannot save as many lives as he would like to save, he may become overly self-critical, and experience unusually strong emotions. This may be the case, even though he realistically may not be at fault, since there may be circumstances over which he has no control. Confidential debriefings—group or individual—can help firefighters or other rescue personnel deal with critical incident stress (CIS). Author biographical information.

1.110 Fagan, M. Michael and Kenneth Ayers, Jr. "The Life of a Police Officer: A Developmental Perspective." **Criminal Justice and Behavior** 9 (1982): 273-285.

Twenty-three police officers in a city in Kentucky were interviewed and the interviews were taped. Some of the questions the officers were asked related to ethnic, religious, and socioeconomic matters. The age of the officers was between twenty-seven and fifty-five years; the mean age was 33.9 years. Data about the officers is discussed in terms of five stages, each stage representing a range of years: the early adult transition (19-22); entering the adult world (22-28); the age thirty transition (28-33); settling down (33-40); and the midlife transition (40-45). Six suggestions are given for helping improve police morale and efficiency. Author biographical information. Abstract. 1 figure. 17 references.

1.111 Fain, Dawn B. and George M. McCormick, II. "Use of Coping Mechanisms As a Means of Stress Reduction in North Louisiana." **Journal of Police Science and Administration** 16 (1988): 21-28.

Officers from six police departments in Louisiana were the subjects in this study. The departments are: the Alexandria Police Department, Bossier City Police Department, Bossier Parish Sheriff's Office, Monroe Police Department, Ouachita Parish Sheriff's Office, and Rapides Parish Sheriff's Office. The subjects were between twenty-one and sixty years of age. They were administered the Jalowiec Coping Scale and the Critical Life Events Scale for Law Enforcement. Six hypotheses were tested. Author biographical information. 2 tables. 19 references.

1.112 Farland, Gary R. "'All I Could Do Was Cry With Her.'" **Fire Command** 52 (September 1985): 24-25.

An account by a firefighter/paramedic from the Portland Fire Bureau, Portland, Oregon, and his reaction to the death, in a fire, of a three-year-old boy. The firefighter/paramedic had to comfort the child's family and also deal with his own emotions. Author biographical information. 1 photograph. Profile of the Portland Fire Bureau.

1.113 Farmer, Richard E. "Cynicism: A Factor in Corrections Work." **Journal of Criminal Justice** 5 (1977): 237-246.

The author states that cynicism in some correctional officers may be a defense mechanism used to cope with strain or conflict in the correctional role. A twenty-question cynicism test was administered to subjects in three county houses of corrections. The test was based on a test used by Arthur Niederhoffer. Author biographical information. Abstract. 4 tables. 3 footnotes. 28 references.

1.114 Farmer, Richard E. and Lynn H. Monahan. "The Prevention Model for Stress Reduction: A Concept Paper." **Journal of Police Science and Administration** 8 (1980): 54-60.

A look at psychosocial and physiological consequences of stress, the intervention model of stress management, and the stress prevention model (individual control techniques, peer group interaction, and family support). The intervention model used by the New York Police Department (NYPD) is critiqued. Reasons are given why the prevention model is preferable to the intervention model. Author biographical information. 1 figure. 23 footnotes.

1.115 Fennell, John T. "Psychological Stress and the Peace Officer or Stress—A Cop Killer." Chapter in **Police Human Relations,** edited by George Henderson, 170-179. Springfield, IL: Charles C. Thomas, 1981.

Stress defined, consequences of stress, causes of stress, and defending against stress. Includes a thirty-item stress quiz. 2 figures. 19 references.

1.116 Fenster, C. Abraham and Bernard Locke. "Neuroticism Among Policemen: An Examination of Police Personality." **Journal of Applied Psychology** 57 (1973): 358-359.

Subjects consisted of male police officers and male civilians in New York. Research instruments included the Eysenck Personality Inventory and the Rokeach Dogmatism Scale. Neuroticism was not a major characteristic of the police officers studied. Author biographical information. Abstract. 17 references.

1.117 Fenster, C. Abraham and Harvey Schlossberg. "The Psychologist As Police Department Consultant." Chapter in **The Psychological Consultant,** edited by Jerome J. Platt and Robert J. Wicks, 135-156. New York, NY: Grune and Stratton, 1979.

Relationship of the consulting psychologist to the police department; providing direct services (counseling, psychotherapy, and police personality); selection and placement of police officers; setting up training programs; and research roles of consulting psychologists. 123 references.

1.118 Ferguson, Janet K. and James E. Gerspach. "Stress Reduction: Taking Responsibility for Your Emotional Stability." **Current Municipal Problems** 11 (1984/1985): 476-480.

An imaginary conversation between the mind and body is used to describe stress in firefighters. This article was also published in the September 1984 issue of **American Fire Journal.**

1.119 Fink, Kenneth. "Breaking the News." **Emergency Medical Services** 16 (January/February 1987): 37.

Dr. Spencer Eth, Veterans Administration Medical Center, Los Angeles, California, addressed the 139th. Annual Meeting, American Psychiatric Association. Eth spoke about personnel who deliver death notifications. He found—in a study of homicide detectives—that the task of death notification became worse rather than better, the more often the detectives carried out the task. Kevin Nida, Paramedic Coordinator, Los Angeles Fire Department, is quoted extensively.

1.120 Fischman, Joshua. "Trauma Junkies." **Psychology Today** 18 (February 1984): 79.

Trauma junkies are emergency medical technicians (EMTs) and paramedics, who thrive on the excitement and challenge associated with certain aspects of their work. They exhibit anxiety, moodiness, and work dissatisfaction when they respond to a call, and learn the situation is not literally a matter of life and death. Trauma junkies experience considerable stress when they experience too few (fewer than 200) or too many (greater than 600) serious runs a year. 1 photograph.

1.121 Fitzgerald, R.E. "Management of Occupational Stress in Prison Officers." in **The Role of Psychologists in the Criminal Justice System**, edited by Grant Wardlaw, 53-69. Canberra: Australian Institute of Criminology, 1983.

Defining occupational stress, sources of work stress, studies of occupational stress in corrections, methods of stress prevention, program for increasing awareness of occupational stress. 23 references.

1.122 Fjelstad, Margaret Ann. "A Study of the Relationship Between the Firefighter Occupational Role and Dyadic Adjustment." **Dissertation Abstracts International** 39: 1135A. Ph.D. dissertation, Oregon State University, 1978. Order No. DA7811982.

Spanier's Dyadic Adjustment Scale and the Tennessee Self-Concept Scale (TSCS) were two research instruments used in this investigation. The subjects were sixty-one male firefighters and forty-four dyad partners. Perceived job stress, off-duty moonlighting, self-concept, and decisionmaking were some of the variables studied.

1.123 Floren, Therese M. "Impact of Death and Dying on Emergency Care Personnel." **Emergency Medical Services** 13 (March/April 1984): 43-47.

A female paramedic writes about the desensitization of paramedics to death, and elaborates on three types of reactions to losing a patient. Author biographical information. 7 references.

1.124 French, John R.P., Jr. "A Comparative Look At Stress and Strain in Policemen." in **Proceedings of Symposium, Job Stress and the Police Officer: Identifying Stress Reduction Techniques**, Cincinnati, Ohio, May 8-9, 1975, edited by William H. Kroes and Joseph J. Hurrell, Jr., 60-71. Washington, DC: U.S. Government Printing Office, 1975.

Job stress in police officers is compared to job stress in twenty-two other occupations—blue collar and white collar. Train dispatcher, air traffic controller, engineer, and family physician are some of the other occupations. 2 tables. 3 figures. Author biographical information.

1.125 Fuehrer, Ann Elizabeth. "Occupational Stress, Social

Support and Job Satisfaction Among Police Recruits." **Dissertation Abstracts International** 43: 3073B. Ph.D. dissertation, University of Illinois at Chicago Circle, 1982. Order No. DA8304233.

Effects of professional socialization, during an eight-month period, on 176 police recruits, and an examination of role stresses, support from significant others, and job satisfaction.

1.126 Gaines, Jeannie and John M. Jermier. "Emotional Exhaustion in a High Stress Organization." **Academy of Management Journal** 26 (1983): 567-586.

Police officers in a U.S. southern community were the sample in this investigation. The Maslach Burnout Inventory, Job Diagnostic Survey (JDS), and Minnesota Satisfaction Questionnaire were three research instruments used. Changing administrative practices is the way to significantly reduce police stress within the police department. An earlier version of this paper was presented at the Academy of Management, New York, 1982. Author biographical information. Abstract. 1 figure. 4 tables. 61 references.

1.127 Gardner, Ralph, Jr. "Guard Stress." **Corrections Magazine** 7 (October 1981): 6-10 and 12-14.

The focus is on the work of Dr. Frances Cheek, Director, Behavior Modification Training Programs, New Jersey Department of Corrections. Cheek, a sociologist, has, since 1977, trained several thousand correction officers regarding stress management. Stress and corrections work in New Mexico, Oregon, Florida, California, Colorado, and South Carolina is also covered. Some of the individuals who comment are: Rich Johnson (Michigan Department of Corrections), James Dahl (National Institute of Justice), Lieutenant James Tolantino (Middlesex County Jail, New Jersey), Roger Crist (New Mexico Commissioner of Corrections), and Albert Scheckenbach (U.S. Bureau of Prisons). Author biographical information. 4 photographs.

1.128 Geiss, Robert John. "Stress Factors in Suburban Female Police Officers." **Dissertation Abstracts International** 46: 3592B. Ph.D. dissertation, Union for Experimenting Colleges, University Without Walls and Union Graduate School, 1985. Order No. DA8528135.

Fifteen female police officers, representing suburbs

of Chicago, Illinois, were interviewed between November 1983 and September 1984. Other data regarding police stress was obtained from a fifty-item questionnaire administered to police administrators and mental health professionals. This study found that female officers perceive stress based on their gender. Examples of this included lack of acceptance from male officers and unfair promotional policies.

1.129 Gelzinis, Peter. "Stress Drives Smart Cop to the Couch." **Police Stress** 6 (Spring 1983): 31.

A police officer talks about stress and the assistance provided by the stress unit of the Boston Police Department. The unit was established in 1973 by two Boston, Massachusetts police officers, Eddie Donovan and Joe Ravino.

1.130 Glander, B. "A Cry for Help." **Police Stress** 6 (Spring 1983): 36-40.

Details the events in the life of a police officer involved in a shooting, resulting in death, and the officer's subsequent psychological and other problems. The shooting took place on September 19, 1980 in a motel in Stamford, Connecticut. The officer felt he needed counseling, but was not quite sure how to obtain it. Later, he committed a felony, half-hoping he would go to jail. Although the officer received a jail term in Florida, the governor of that state granted him clemency, after police officers and other individuals declared their support for the officer, stating it was completely out of character for him to have committed the felony. 3 illustrations.

1.131 Glatzle, Mary. **Muggable Mary: My Life As a Decoy Cop.** New York, NY: Berkley Books, 1982.

Experiences of Mary Glatzle, a New York Police Department (NYPD) detective, who combats street criminals.

1.132 Goodin, Carl. "Opening Remarks." in **Proceedings of Symposium, Job Stress and the Police Officer: Identifying Stress Reduction Techniques,** Cincinnati, Ohio, May 8-9, 1975, edited by William H. Kroes and Joseph J. Hurrell, Jr., 1-2. Washington, DC: U.S. Government Printing Office, 1975.

Conference opening remarks by the Chief, Cincinnati

Police Department.

1.133 Goodman, Alan Mitchell. "A Model for Police Officer Burnout." **Dissertation Abstracts International** 44: 1237B. Ph.D. dissertation, California School of Professional Psychology, San Diego, 1983. Order No. DA-8319163.

Approximately 200 male police officers in five police departments in San Diego County, California were the sample. The Staff Burnout Scale for Police and Security Officers and the State-Trait Anxiety Inventory were the two most important research tools used. The author was interested in events—precareer and after the officers were on the police force—which would indicate burnout. Shootings, moonlighting, age, and marital status were variables studied.

1.134 Gordon, Thomas James. "The Organization As Stressor: A Police Perspective." **Dissertation Abstracts International** 42: 2599B. Ph.D. dissertation, University of Michigan, 1981. Order No. DA8125115.

In a survey of 114 police officers, in three suburban police departments, the police organization was perceived, by the officers, as a primary source of stress. This research indicated a constancy of organizational problems and a commonality of organizational experience.

1.135 Graf, Francis A. "The Relationship Between Social Support and Occupational Stress Among Police Officers." **Journal of Police Science and Administration** 14 (1986): 178-186.

The research sample consisted of 105 police officers, who were members of the Saanich Police Department, located on Vancouver Island, British Columbia. The Social Support Questionnaire (SSQ) and the Perceived Stress Scale (PSS) were used. The questionnaire response rate was approximately 73%. A multi-dimensional intervention strategy for assisting stressed police officers is discussed. Author biographical information. 4 tables. Acknowledgement. 28 references.

1.136 Graham, Nancy K. "Done In, Fed Up, Burned Out: Too Much Attrition in EMS." **JEMS** 6 (January 1981): 24-29.

Nancy K. Graham, a paramedic instructor and psychotraumatologist in Los Angeles, California gives an overview of burnout and attrition in emergency medical services (EMS). 2 photographs. 5 footnotes.

1.137 Graham, Nancy K. "Part 2: How to Avoid a Short Career." **JEMS** 6 (February 1981): 25-31.

Emergency medical technicians (EMTs) and other emergency medical services (EMS) personnel can do various things to minimize stress and burnout. These things range from sharing troublesome feelings with others to spending time with people not in the health professions. Employers can help by reducing the size of districts or the length of the work day. Employers can also rotate parademic teams regularly, in order that the teams experience both heavy and light work loads. Author biographical information. 5 photographs. 20 footnotes.

1.138 Gravel, Dick. "Rescue Workers Learn to Manage Stress." **Canadian Emergency Services News** 6 (December 1983): 57.

Jeff Mitchell, of the University of Maryland Baltimore County (UMBC), conducts stress management workshops for police, firefighters, and paramedics. After the Air Florida crash into the Potomac River, he held a workshop for some of the rescue personnel who responded to the crash. The workshop was held at the request of the Federal Aviation Administration. 1 photograph.

1.139 Greene, Donald Joseph. "The Enhancement of the Performance and Judgement of SWAT Officers Involved in Stress-Shooting." **Dissertation Abstracts International** 45: 3320B. Ph.D. dissertation, United States International University, 1984. Order No. DA8429679.

Fifty-four police officers, who belonged to a SWAT (Special Weapons and Tactics) unit, took part in this research. They were randomly assigned to three groups: attention control training, progressive relaxation training, and no-treatment control. Two weeks later all the SWAT members participated in a stress-shooting course. They were evaluated regarding shooting accuracy, course competition, time, and target selection.

1.140 Greene, Robin Lea. "Psychological Well-Being, Physical Health and Coping Responses in a Police Population." **Dissertation Abstracts International** 46: 1875A. Ph.D. dissertation, University of California, Los Angeles, 1985. Order No. DA8519098.

A survey instrument (common belief attitude measure, coping resource inventory, and a psychological distress symptom checklist) and a narrative form were used in this research, involving 197 male police officers. Supervisory conflicts, internal affairs investigations, and frustrations with the promotional system were some of the stressful events revealed.

1.141 Grencik, Judith M. "Toward an Understanding of Stress." in **Proceedings of Symposium, Job Stress and the Police Officer: Identifying Stress Reduction Techniques**, Cincinnati, Ohio, May 8-9, 1975, edited by William H. Kroes and Joseph J. Hurrell, Jr., 163-181. Washington, DC: U.S. Government Printing Office, 1975.

Theoretical background of stress, the experience of stress, the nature of police stress, and coping with stress. Author biographical information. 28 references.

1.142 Grier, Kenneth Scott. "A Study of Job Stress in Police Officers and High School Teachers." **Dissertation Abstracts International** 43: 870B-871B. Ph.D. dissertation, University of South Florida, 1982. Order No. DA8216880.

The subjects—police officers and teachers—were employed in Houston, Texas. The police subjects were 142 male sergeants from the Houston Police Department. The 138 teachers worked in public high schools. The Police Stress Survey, Teacher Stress Survey, Job Descriptive Index, State-Trait Personality Inventory, Biodata Questionnaire, and Stress-Satisfaction Questionnaire were the research tools used by the author. This investigation raised questions about the degree of stress of police work relative to other occupations.

1.143 Griggs, Dee Franklin. "Police Stress and Management Style." **Dissertation Abstracts International** 46: 1094A. ED.D. dissertation, University of La Verne, 1985. Order No. DA8511741.

In a study of 293 police officers, representing ten separate police departments, it was learned that of the top ten harmful stressors measured, 50% of the stressors involved management. The author made five recommendations regarding police stress.

1.144 Guttmann, E. and A.A. Baker. "Neuroses in Firemen." **Journal of Mental Science** 91 (1945): 454-457.

A British study of neuroses in firefighters admitted to Mill Hill Emergency Hospital during World War II. Anxiety state, hysteria, and depression were the three most common diagnoses. Six case histories are used in this article. Author biographical information. 3 tables.

1.145 Hale, Charles D. "Fatigue." in **Police Patrol: Operations and Management,** by Charles D. Hale, 74-75. New York, NY: John Wiley and Sons, 1981.

The routine of uneventful random patrol can create job fatigue, making certain officers a serious liability in emergency situations, which arise suddenly and unexpectedly. If officers exhibit diminished readiness, they or others can experience serious injury—even death. Shift rotation has been suggested as one way of dealing with job fatigue. 1 footnote.

1.146 Hale, Charles D. "Psychological Hazards." in **Police Patrol: Operations and Management,** by Charles D. Hale, 59-65. New York, NY: John Wiley and Sons, 1981.

Police officers must perform their duties objectively, must remain calm in the face of adversity, and must be cool and professional in times of sorrow and tragedy. They must respond to critical situations, knowing that lives, including their own, can be at stake. If officers are found to be negligent in their protection of the lives and property of others, they can be subject to legal action. Officers involved in violent confrontations are expected to take the right action—meaning that too little or too much action can jeopardize innocent lives. 9 footnotes.

1.147 Hale, Charles D. "Stress Control Program for Police Officers, Miami Police Department." in **Police Patrol: Operations and Management,** by Charles D. Hale,

80-83. New York, NY: John Wiley and Sons, 1981.

Three aspects—psychological, physiological, and nutritional—are associated with stress control for officers of the Miami Police Department, Miami, Florida. Specific examples of what the program entails: decreasing absenteeism, reducing accidents, reducing number of citizen complaints against officers, improving eating habits, controlling blood pressure, and alleviating sleeping problems. 1 footnote.

1.148 Hammer, Jeffrey S., James J. Mathews, John S. Lyons and Nancy J. Johnson. "Occupational Stress Within the Paramedic Profession: An Initial Report of Stress Levels Compared to Hospital Employees." **Annals of Emergency Medicine** 15 (1986): 536-539.

A total of 374 paramedics—average age 29.7 years—were studied. The high level of stress found in this profession can be categorized in four ways: organizational, job dissatisfaction, attitude regarding patients, and somatic distress. The Medical Personnel Stress Survey-Revised (MPSS-R) was used in this research. Author biographical information. Abstract. 1 figure. 2 tables. 23 references.

1.149 Hasek, John. "Stress in the Halton Regional Police Force." **RCMP Gazette** 47, No. 3 (1985): 13-14.

The Halton Regional Police Force is responsible for policing an area of 381 square miles located near Toronto and Hamilton, Ontario. The force employs 417 individuals. The beginnings of a program to deal with stress at Halton Regional date back to October 1981. An employee assistance program was established later, as a result of the concern and support of Chief W.I. James Harding. Author biographical information. 1 photograph. 3 footnotes.

1.150 Haynes, William D. "The Nature of Police Work." Chapter in **Stress Related Disorders in Policemen**, by William D. Haynes, 15-35. San Francisco, CA: R. and E. Research Associates, Inc., 1978.

Professional demands, personal demands, and social isolation.

1.151 Haynes, William D. "The Nature of Stress." Chapter

in **Stress Related Disorders in Policemen,** by William D. Haynes, 4-14. San Francisco, CA: R. and E. Research Associates, Inc., 1978.

The conceptual structure of stress research, components of stress, models of stress, and factors determining stress response.

1.152 Haynes, William D. "Psychological Factors: Preparation to Meet Any Situation At Any Time." Chapter in **Stress Related Disorders in Policemen,** by William D. Haynes, 36-45. San Francisco, CA: R. and E. Research Associates, Inc., 1978.

Uncertainty and tedium, boredom and self-control, continuous awareness of surroundings, and frustration all contribute to tension experienced by police officers. At any moment, a police officer can encounter one or more of the following: an overdosed junkie, a raped woman, an elderly person robbed and beaten, an abused child, a violent drunk, a suicidal individual, a potential murderer armed with a gun.

1.153 "Helping Yourself." **Emergency Medical Services** 18 (March 1989): 36.

Eleven suggestions from the U.S. Department of Health and Human Services regarding stress management.

1.154 Helrich, Karen L. "The Use of Hardiness and Other Stress-Resistance Resources to Predict Symptoms and Performance in Police Academy Trainees." **Dissertation Abstracts International** 46: 2063B. Ph.D. dissertation, California School of Professional Psychology, San Diego, 1985. Order No. DA8517932.

The Hassles Scale, Supportive Relationship Index, and Coping Response Indices were used in this study involving 106 police academy trainees.

1.155 Hempel, Linda S. "Wellness Programs for EMS Personnel." **Emergency Medical Services** 16 (March 1987): 48-49 and 51-53.

Management support and an employee steering committee are essential elements in wellness programs for emergency medical services (EMS) personnel. These programs save employers money—reduced absenteeism being one reason—and improve the health and overall well-being of employees. Nutrition, stress management, and safety are three areas of concern in wellness programs. Author biographical information.

1.156 Henderson, Bruce. **Ghetto Cops.** Chatsworth, CA: Major Books, 1975.

Policing Compton, California, a suburb of Los Angeles. Compton was part of the Watts riot of 1965.

1.157 Henderson, George. "Police Need People." Chapter in **Police Human Relations**, edited by George Henderson, 149-169. Springfield, IL: Charles C. Thomas, 1981.

Covers: results of psychological stress; coping with stress; importance of communication; friends and spouses; and the healthy police officer. 28 references.

1.158 Herrick, Neal Q. "A Process for Reducing Occupational Stress." in **Proceedings of Symposium, Job Stress and the Police Officer: Identifying Stress Reduction Techniques**, Cincinnati, Ohio, May 8-9, 1975, edited by William H. Kroes and Joseph J. Hurrell, Jr., 203-216. Washington, DC: U.S. Government Printing Office, 1975.

The Ohio Quality of Work Project, developed by Ohio business and labor leaders, is a process for reducing occupational stress. It is suggested this process be applied to reducing police officer stress. Author biographical information. 1 table. 7 footnotes.

1.159 "Highlights From the 2nd. International Symposium on the Management of Stress." **Police Stress** 1 (Spring 1980): 24-27.

Eight photographs and comments about the Second International Symposium on the Management of Stress.

1.160 Hillgren, James S., Rebekah Bond and Sue Jones. "Primary Stressors in Police Administration and Law Enforcement." **Journal of Police Science and Administration** 4 (1976): 445-449.

The subjects in this research were twenty police

chiefs and sheriffs from seven southeastern U.S. states. Thirteen major stressors were identified by the subjects. Six stressors pertained to line personnel; seven stressors pertained to the administrative function of the subjects. Author biographical information. 2 tables. 6 footnotes.

1.161 Hinds, Charles. "The Heat of Burnout: How to Reduce Stress." **Emergency Medical Services** 17 (November 1988): 52-54.

Distress, eustress, and cognitve therapy are discussed in relation to emergency medical services (EMS) personnel. 1 illustration. 1 table. 2 figures. 2 references. Author biographical information.

1.162 Hirsch, Marc Robert. "The Experience of Stress Associated With the Interaction Between Ideational and Motorically Oriented Personality Styles and Differential Role Demands in Police Work." **Dissertation Abstracts International** 48: 3711B. Ph.D. dissertation, University of Detroit, 1987. Order No. DA88-03357.

The sample in this study consisted of 102 police officers, who completed the Motoric Ideational Activity Preference Scale (MIAPS), and the Perceived Sources of Stress Inventory for Police Officers (a revised version). The author did not find any statistically significant differences among the groups.

1.163 Hoge, Michael A. and Richard Hirschman. "Psychological Training of Emergency Medical Technicians: An Evaluation." **American Journal of Community Psychology** 12 (1984): 127-131.

The subjects were college students enrolled in emergency medical technician (EMT) courses in Ohio. The mean age of the seventeen females and nineteen males was 19.8 years. Selected subjects were randomly assigned to either a psychologically trained condition or to a psychologically untrained condition. The EMTs who completed the eight-hour training program enhanced their style of handling psychological problems. Author biographical information. 1 table. 2 footnotes. 2 reference notes. 3 references.

1.164 Holt, Francis X. "Assessing Risk-Taking Behavior in Firefighters." **Fire Engineering** 141 (November 1988): 30 and 32-33.

Analyzes positive and negative risk-taking behavior in firefighters. On the positive side, some of the reasons for risk taking are: saving lives, advancement in the job, and awards. On the negative side, risk taking can be associated with guilt, machismo, and substance abuse. Author biographical information.

1.165 Holt, Francis X. "Post-Traumatic Stress Disorder and the Firefighter." **Fire Engineering** 138 (November 1985): 24-27.

Some of the indicators of posttraumatic stress disorder (PTSD) are: repeated and intrusive memories of a traumatic event, recurrent dreams of the event, emotional withdrawal, hyperalertness or exaggerated startle response, difficulty sleeping, guilt, and impaired memory or difficulty concentrating. Author biographical information.

1.166 Hooke, James F. and Herbert H. Krauss. "Personality Characteristics of Successful Police Sergeant Candidates." **Journal of Criminal Law, Criminology and Police Science** 62 (1971): 104-106.

Subjects were thirty-seven officers of the Kansas City Police Department, Kansas City, Missouri. The Minnesota Multiphasic Personality Inventory (MMPI), Allport-Vernon-Lindzey Study of Values, and Gough Adjective Check List were the research instruments used. Successful police sergeant candidates were found to be psychologically normal, and well-suited for leadership and disciplinary roles. This article is based on a paper presented at the Southeastern Psychological Association Meeting, New Orleans, Louisiana, 1968. Author biographical information. 1 table. 6 references.

1.167 Horn, William G. "Stress Training for Federal Police." **Police Stress** 1 (Fall 1978): 18-20.

A description of stress management training at the Federal Law Enforcement Training Center, located near Brunswick, Georgia. Secret service agents, capitol police, border patrol agents, and deputy marshals are some of the U.S. federal law enforcement personnel trained at the center. Role playing, peer critiques, and videotape equipment are used in the training. Author biographical information. 4 photographs.

1.168 Horne, Peter. "Policewomen and Stress." in **Women in Law Enforcement,** Second Edition, by Peter Horne, 169-176. Springfield, IL: Charles C. Thomas, 1980.

Focuses on unique stresses and unique strengths of policewomen. There is, for example, the peer group influence in a dominantly male profession. On the other hand, a woman is not expected to know many technical things. For this reason, she can readily ask for assistance, as a recruit in training, how to load and unload a shotgun. A male recruit could be looked down upon by male instructors, if he were to ask for the same assistance. Also, it would be more acceptable for a woman to call for help over the radio than for a man, since a male officer would be expected to be more adept in a conflict situation. Although it becomes common practice for male officers not to discuss their work with their wives, female officers tell their husbands about work.

1.169 Hou, Charles, Andrew Miracle, Eric D. Poole and Robert M. Regoli. "Assessing Determinants of Police Cynicism in Taiwan." **Police Studies** 5 (Winter 1983): 3-7.

Out of 400 police officers in Taiwan, representing both urban and rural officers, 325 responded to a questionnaire regarding cynicism. The police officers represented three precincts. A revised form of A. Niederhoffer's (1967) twenty-item index was used to measure cynicism. The three major findings reported were: relationship between officer rank and police cynicism, relationship between police locality and cynicism, and relationship between length of police service and cynicism. Author biographical information. Abstract. 4 tables. 3 notes. 11 references. 1 appendix.

1.170 Hoyt, Darlene Prandine. "The Role of Mediators in Attenuating Stress in Police Officers." **Dissertation Abstracts International** 45: 2311B. Ph.D. dissertation, California School of Professional Psychology, San Diego, 1984. Order No. DA8418806.

This research involved police officers from the San Diego Police Department, San Diego, California. Five of the research tools used were: the Personal Data Questionnaire, the Coping Response Index, the Test of

Attentional and Interpersonal Style (TAIS), the Police Events Scale, and the Social Readjustment Rating Scale. The research identified two types of officers.

1.171 Huder, Roger C. "Burnout: The Preventable Disease." **JEMS** 12 (March 1987): 50-52 and 54.

Venting feelings, maintaining contact with friends, having a balanced diet, exercising, and getting adequate rest can help prevent burnout. Author biographical information. 1 photograph. 6 references.

1.172 Hurrell, Joseph J., Jr. and William H. Kroes. "Stress Awareness." in **Proceedings of Symposium, Job Stress and the Police Officer: Identifying Stress Reduction Techniques**, Cincinnati, Ohio, May 8-9, 1975, edited by William H. Kroes and Joseph J. Hurrell, Jr., 234-246. Washington, DC: U.S. Government Printing Office, 1975.

Defining job stress; sources of stress in policing; job stress and heart attacks; consequences of shift-work in policing; effects on homelife of the police officer's job; alcoholism and work; concept of a police subculture and job stress; exercise and stress; proposes solutions to the problem of police stress. Author biographical information. 2 tables. 19 references.

1.173 Hurrell, Jospeh J., Jr., Anthony Pate and Robert Kliesmet. "Stress Among Police Officers." **Government Reports Announcements and Index** 83 (August 5, 1983): 3768. NTIS PB83-195321.

Self-report questionnaires were sent to police officers in nineteen police departments. The response rate was 37%. Attitudinal, behavioral, and health problems were studied. The authors were interested in, among other things, examining job elements perceived by police officers as stressors.

1.174 Hyder, Joe. "Memories of My Dad the Cop." **Police Stress** 6 (Spring 1983): 28.

The life of a police officer in Newport, Rhode Island in the 1930s and 1940s, and the effect on that police officer of having shot and killed a burglary suspect. 1 photograph.

1.175 Ianni, Francis A.J. and Elizabeth Reuss-Ianni. "'Take This Job and Shove It!' A Comparison of Organizational Stress and Burnout Among Teachers and Police." Chapter in **Stress and Burnout in the Human Service Professions,** edited by Barry A. Farber, 82-96. New York, NY: Pergamon Press, 1983.

Discusses teachers, stress, and the social order of the school; organizational stress, burnout, and the two cultures of urban policing; organizations and the management of stress; and adolescence and the internalization of structure. 22 references.

1.176 Jacobi, Jerome H. "Reducing Police Stress: A Psychiatrist's Point of View." in **Proceedings of Symposium, Job Stress and the Police Officer: Identifying Stress Reduction Techniques,** Cincinnati, Ohio, May 8-9, 1975, edited by William H. Kroes and Joseph J. Hurrell, Jr., 85-116. Washington, DC: U.S. Government Printing Office, 1975.

A paper based on the author's experiences, as a psychiatrist, with approximately fifty disabled police officers of the Los Angeles Police Department (LAPD). Author biographical information. 34 references. An appendix includes a transcript of comments between the author/psychiatrist and a police officer/patient.

1.177 James, Alma E.C. "Stress in the Ambulance Service: An Investigation Into the Sources of Occupational Stress Perceived by Managerial, Control and Operational Staff of the Devon Ambulance Service." **Dissertation Abstracts International** 49: 1513A. Ph.D. dissertation, University of Bradford, 1988. Order No. BRDX82502.

During a two-and-a-half-year period, data was obtained from 518 ambulance personnel employed by the Devon Ambulance Service. At least nine major categories of stressors were identified. Some employees were attracted to the work by certain stressors. Employees with longer service, more experience, and an internal locus of control experienced less stress.

1.178 James, Pat and Martha Nelson. "He's Going to Need Your Tender Lovin' Care." Chapter in **Police Wife: How to Live With the Law and Like It,** by Pat James and Martha Nelson, 26-35. Springfield, IL: Charles C. Thomas, 1975.

Indicators of emotional and physical demands of police work: the "John Wayne" syndrome, suspicion, prejudice, latent hypochondria, alcoholism, and cynicism.

1.179 James, Pat and Martha Nelson. "It's All a Part of the Job." Chapter in **Police Wife: How to Live With the Law and Like It**, by Pat James and Martha Nelson, 13-25. Springfield, IL: Charles C. Thomas, 1975.

Stress related to undercover work, court duty, routine patrolling, domestic calls, and other police work.

1.180 Jermier, John M. "Ecological Hazards and Organizational Behavior: A Study of Dangerous Urban Space-Time Zones." **Human Organization** 41 (1982): 198-207.

The sample for this investigation were 256 urban patrol officers, who were administered a questionnaire. Variables measured by the researcher were: danger, work performance, organizational commitments, participative leader behavior, task interdependence, formalization, career stage, and perceived job expertise. The Ohio State University Small Grants Program supported this study. Author biographical information. Abstract. 3 tables. 2 notes. 59 references.

1.181 Jirak, Milton. "Alienation Among Members of the New York City Police Department on Staten Island." **Journal of Police Science and Administration** 3 (1975): 149-161.

Over 700 police officers—patrolmen, detectives, and superiors—working at three patrol precincts on Staten Island, New York were the study sample. They were administered a questionnaire designed to measure alienation. The questionnaire, designed by Dr. Dwight Dean of Iowa State University, specifically measures: powerlessness, normlessness, and social isolation. A copy of the twenty-four item questionnaire is included as an appendix. Author biographical information. 9 footnotes. 4 figures. 6 tables.

1.182 **Job Stress in Police Work.** Gaithersburg, MD: International Association of Chiefs of Police, Inc., 1978.

Twenty-eight sources of psychological stress, divided into five categories, are related, in point form, to police work. Abstract. Acknowledgement.

1.183 Johnson, Edward E. "Psychological Tests Used in Assessing a Sample of Police and Fire Fighter Candidates." **Journal of Police Science and Administration** 11 (1983): 430-433.

Two hundred and ten police and firefighter candidates in New Jersey were the subjects. They were rejected as future police officers and firefighters on the grounds they were not mentally fit to do the job effectively. They later appealed to the New Jersey Civil Service Commission Medical Review Board. Some of the psychological tests used in assessing the candidates: Minnesota Multiphasic Personality Inventory (MMPI), Thematic Apperception Test (TAT), Edwards Personal Preference Schedule, Guilford-Zimmerman Temperament Survey, Wide Range Achievement Test, Police Information Questionnaire Test, Drawings Personality Test, Sixteen Personality Factor Questionnaire, and the Szondi Test. Author biographical information. 4 tables. 8 references.

1.184 Johnson, Kenneth E. "Missing Link in Police Education: Retirement Counseling." Chapter in **Stress and Police Personnel**, by Leonard Territo and Harold J. Vetter, 314-318. Boston, MA: Allyn and Bacon, Inc., 1981.

Retirement as a problem for police officers is discussed with reference to Joseph Wambaugh's book, **The New Centurions** (1970), and the work of police psychologists, Harold E. Russell and Martin Reiser. Suicide is a common way for police officers to deal with the change and stress associated with retirement. A career-guidance program can help counter this by including a section on retirement preparation. 9 end notes.

1.185 Jones, Robert Clayton. "Relationship of Selected Training Characteristics to Stress Management in Police Field Operations." **Dissertation Abstracts International** 48: 2913B. Ph.D. dissertation, Oklahoma State University, 1987. Order No. DA8729602.

Community service officers, who were the treatment group, and apprentice police officers, who were the comparison group, were given a pretest and posttest. The community service officers were exposed to simulated dangerous situations. Pretest scores were significantly related to posttest scores in terms of perceived stress and vulnerability.

1.186 Kankewitt, Bill. **The Shattered Badge: The Story of Ed Donovan, Stress Cop.** Toronto, Methuen, 1986.

Formerly a drunk and potential suicide, Ed Donovan, of the Boston Police Department, turned his life around, and established the Boston Police Stress Program, which helps police officers afflicted with stress disorders.

1.187 Kelling, George and Mary Ann Pate. "The Person-Role Fit in Policing: The Current Knowledge and Future Research." in **Proceedings of Symposium, Job Stress and the Police Officer: Identifying Stress Reduction Techniques,** Cincinnati, Ohio, May 8-9, 1975, edited by William H. Kroes and Joseph J. Hurrell, Jr., 117-129. Washington, DC: U.S. Government Printing Office, 1975.

This paper focuses on the Dallas Police Department, Dallas, Texas. Author biographical information. 2 figures. 10 references.

1.188 Kirkham, George. **Signal Zero.** Philadelphia, PA: J.B. Lippincott Co., 1976.

George Kirkham, Assistant Professor of Criminology, worked as a street patrolman for several months in a large U.S. city. His book describes how his preconceived ideas about crime and police work changed. After he left the university to work the streets, he realized that he gradually became increasingly like his fellow officers. He also realized that there is a great disparity between the knowledge one reads about, and the knowledge one obtains in real-life situations.

1.189 Kirkham, George L. and Laurin A. Wollan, Jr. "Pressures on the Thin Blue Line: Stress in Policing." Chapter in **Introduction to Law Enforcement,** by George L. Kirkham and Laurin A. Wollan, Jr., 367-389. New York, NY: Harper and Row, Publishers, 1980.

This chapter consists of six main parts: shift work; economic pressure; work load; the police administration; the law and the courts; and danger and trauma. Real-life police officers are portrayed differently than are those in many motion pictures. Real-life police officers are people with human strengths and weaknesses. Real-life police are much more likely and frequently to experience stress brought about by daily time pressure and daily emotional demands than by occasional high-speed chases and infrequent shootouts. 45 notes. 6 references.

1.190 Kirmeyer, Sandra L. "Observing the Work of Police Dispatchers: Work Overload in Service Organizations." **Applied Social Psychology Annual** 5 (1984): 45-66.

A National Science Foundation grant supported this research, in which the author observed, for three years, police dispatchers at work. 5 tables. 53 references.

1.191 Kirmeyer, Sandra L. and Thomas W. Dougherty. "Work Load, Tension, and Coping: Moderating Effects of Supervisor Support." **Personnel Psychology** 41 (1988): 125-139.

Subjects were sixty police officers and civilians, who were police radio dispatchers at twelve rural and urban police stations. A trained observer observed each dispatcher, during the dispatcher's eight-hour work shift. The effects of work load were moderated by support from superiors. The greater the social support, the lower the tension-anxiety experienced by dispatchers. Author biographical information. Abstract. 2 tables. 3 figures. 41 references.

1.192 Kirschman, Ellen Freeman. "Wounded Heroes: A Case Study and Systems Analysis of Job-Related Stress and Emotional Dysfunction in Three Police Officers." **Dissertation Abstracts International** 44: 1279B. Ph.D. dissertation, Wright Institute (Berkeley), 1983. Order No. DA8319021.

Interviews with police officers, their wives, supervisors, and administrators—and an examination of personnel records and workers' compensation files—formed the basis of the case histories in this study.

1.193 Kling, Elizabeth Ann. "Factors Related to the Appraisal of Stress in Firefighters." **Dissertation Abstracts International** 49: 4008B. Ph.D. dissertation, Purdue University, 1988. Order No. DA8825547.

The author learned that firefighters experience more stress when helping an injured firefighter than when helping an injured stranger, and that it is perhaps more stressful for firefighters to help an innocent victim than one who is responsible.

1.194 Krebs, Dennis R. "Medical Emergency Defense and Incident Control—A Training Program." **Fire Engineering**

137 (June 1984): 37-38.

Describes a Medical Emergency Defense and Incident Control (MEDIC) training program. The eight-hour program was developed by the author and Trooper Mark Gabriele, Maryland State Police. Topics covered in the program include: proper positioning of the medic unit when responding to highway incidents, techniques showing the safe approach to that vehicle, and defensive maneuvers if the victim is armed or becomes violent. Author biographical information. 3 photographs.

1.195 Kroes, William H. "Job Stress in Policewomen: An Empirical Study." **Police Stress** 5 (Winter 1982): 10-11.

Thirty-four female police officers—average age 34.4 years—were the subjects. Police experience was, on the average, 9.7 years. Most of the subjects were from the Los Angeles, California area. The authors learned that the stress experienced by female police officers was essentially the same as that experienced by male officers. However, female officers experienced the additional stress of being female, and at times, being resented for this fact by male officers. Author biographical information. 1 illustration. 3 tables. 2 references.

1.196 Kroes, William H. and Sam Gould. "Job Stress in Policemen: An Empirical Study." **Police Stress** 1 (Spring 1979): 9-10, 44 and 46.

Male police officers from the Wilshire Crest Medical Group in Los Angeles, California participated in this research. Most of the officers were from the Los Angeles Police Department (LAPD), and the Los Angeles County Sheriff's Department. The average age of the officers was 36.1 years; the average police experience was 11.7 years. Lack of administrative support was found to be a very strong stressor. 2 photographs. 3 tables. Author biographical information. 4 references.

1.197 Kroes, William H., Bruce L. Margolis and Joseph J. Hurrell, Jr. "Job Stress in Policemen." **Journal of Police Science and Administration** 2 (1974): 145-155.

One hundred police officers in Cincinnati, Ohio were studied. The officers, ranging in age from twenty-one to fifty-three years, were interviewed during the summer of 1972. Four major sources of stress were identified during the interviews: the courts, administration, equipment, and community relations. Author biographical information. 7 tables. 4 footnotes.

1.198 Krooglik, George. "Mental Illness Within the Police Force: A Problem That Won't Go Away." **Police Stress** 8 (Winter 1987): 17-18.

An Australian perspective regarding mental illness and New South Wales police. Author biographical information. 1 illustration.

1.199 Lane, Gary. "Memories of a Close Call." **Fire Command** 51 (June 1984): 34-35.

The rescue in a burning building, on Christmas day, of firefighter Gary Lane by Jeff Sloan, another firefighter. Lane, an Indianapolis, Indiana firefighter had fallen through the floor of an old house. Author biographical information. 1 photograph. Includes the text of a letter by Lane to fellow firefighters.

1.200 Lawrence, Anne-Marie. "Firefighter Burnout." **Canadian Emergency Services News** 5 (July/August 1982): 96-98.

Firefighter burnout in Vancouver, B.C. Includes comments by firefighters Terry Zweng, Jim Burchill, and Dave Galpin. Also includes comments by Captain Colin Wade, North Vancouver Fire Department and Chief Robin Tadd, Training Officer, North Vancouver Fire Department. 2 illustrations.

1.201 Lawrence, Christina Louise. "Female Police Officers: Relationship Between Social Support, Occupational Stress and Strain." **Dissertation Abstracts International** 47: 2171B-2172B. Ph.D. dissertation, California School of Professional Psychology, Los Angeles, 1986. Order No. DA8616487.

Buffering theory and the additive model of social support were studied in relation to ninety-seven female police officers, ranging in age from twenty to forty-five years. The Work Relationships Index, Police Stress Survey, Burn-Out Inventory, and the Physiological Symptoms Questionnaire were used. The author did not find any buffering interactions.

1.202 Lawrence, Richard A. "Police Stress and Personality Factors: A Conceptual Model." **Journal of Criminal Justice** 12 (1984): 247-263.

Consists of the following sections: defining stress, theoretical issues in stress research, ipsative versus normative measures, a conceptual model of individual stress response, applying the model to stress measurement, the sample, research instruments, the Police Stress Inventory (PSI), results, and conclusion. Author biographical information. Abstract. 3 figures. 4 tables. 11 notes. 50 references.

1.203 Lawrence, Richard Allen. "The Measurement and Prediction of Police Job Stress." **Dissertation Abstracts International** 40: 2281A. Ph.D. dissertation, Sam Houston State University, 1978. Order No. DA7923326.

Police officers from three, Texas police departments were the study sample. The researcher used a Police Stress Inventory and the Sixteen Personality Factor Questionnaire. This study revealed four job stressors, two of them being court appearances and community relations.

1.204 Lehtinen, Marlene W. "Sexism in Police Departments." **Trial Magazine** 12 (September 1976): 52-55.

Patrol duties have traditionally been denied to female police officers because of the commonly held belief that most female officers are too emotional and physically weak for patrol work. Research in England—particularly in Liverpool in 1969—has been used to dispute these claims. It has also been argued that female officers can often defuse potentially violent situations better than can their male counterparts, the reason being that since women are perceived as being less threatening than men, there is less of a need for potentially violent men to respond violently to them. New York and Washington, DC are cities which extensively utilize female officers on patrol. Author biographical information. 4 references.

1.205 Leonard, John A. and G. Patrick Tully. "Occupational Stress and Compensation in Law Enforcement." **FBI Law Enforcement Bulletin** 49 (July 1980): 22-26.

Different types of police work produce different levels of stress, undercover narcotics work being very stressful, relative to other types of police work. Complicating attempts to clearly define police stress are different stress tolerance levels in different officers. Early retirement is one way of compensating police officers who, because of occupational stress, can no longer adequately carry out their duties. A psychologist employed fulltime and inhouse is highly recommended to deal with police officer stress. Author biographical information. 11 footnotes.

1.206 Lester, David. "Cynicism of Police and Job Satisfaction." **Psychological Reports** 54 (1984): 558.

Viewing Arthur Niederhoffer's cynicism scale as five subscales did not appear to improve its usefulness in predicting attitudes, such as work satisfaction. The researcher concluded this in a study of 141 police officers. Author biographical information. 3 references.

1.207 Lester, David. "Job Satisfaction, Cynicism, Education and Belief in an Internal Locus of Control in Police." **Psychological Reports** 50 (1982): 1214.

This research examined claims made in 1978 by G. Griffin, R. Dunbar, and M. McGill. Author biographical information. 4 references.

1.208 Lester, David. "Perceived Stress in Police Officers and Belief in Locus of Control." **Journal of General Psychology** 107 (1982): 157-158.

A study of seventy-three police officers revealed that officers who believed in an external locus of control reported higher levels of job-related stress. Author biographical information. 2 footnotes.

1.209 Lester, David. "Subjective Stress and Sources of Stress for Police Officers." **Psychological Reports** 50 (1982): 1094.

This investigation demonstrated that sources of stress were quite different for two groups of police officers. Normal police work and peer and family problems were stressful for municipal police officers. Lack of support from non-police persons was stressful for state police officers. Seventy-three officers participated in this study. Author biographical information. 1

reference.

1.210 Lester, David and Julie Gallagher. "Stress in Police Officers and Department Store Managers." **Psychological Reports** 46 (1980): 882.

In a study of sixteen police officers and fourteen department store managers, the authors learned that there is not more stress in police work than in other occupations. Author biographical information. 2 references.

1.211 Lester, David, Lewis A. Leitner and Israel Posner." "The Effects of a Stress Management Training Programme on Police Officers." **International Review of Applied Psychology** 33 (1984): 25-31.

Examines a stress management training program which consists of four phases. The first phase describes stress in terms of biological and psychological factors. The next three phases are about stress reduction techniques. The first phase, rational emotive training, is based on the work of A. Ellis (1973). The second phase, assertive action training, is based on research by A.J. Lang and P. Jakubowski (1976). The fourth phase of the program teaches relaxation skills. The time required to complete the program is four or five days. A follow-up session is held three to six months later. The program was administered to police administrators—fifty-five males, mean age of 42.3 years—in New Jersey. Author biographical information. 1 table. 12 references. French abstract.

1.212 Lester, David, Lewis A. Leitner and Israel Posner. "A Note on Locus of Control and Stress in Police Officers." **Journal of Community Psychology** 13 (1985): 77-79.

When a person's body reacts to a demand made upon it, that person's body is subjected to stress. If the demand is pleasureable, for example, sexual activity, the body's reaction is referred to as eustress. If the demand is not pleasureable, such as being in a car accident, the body's reaction is referred to as distress. Eustress is more likely to result if an event is predictable and a person has control over the event. In a study of forty-eight police officers in New Jersey, who were administered eight stress tests, the researchers concluded that less stress may be experienced if individuals feel less controlled by others. Life events, frustration level, work overload, boredom/loneliness, poor nutrition, lack of self-confidence, type A behavior, and anxious reactivity were studied. Author biographical information. 1 table. 11 references.

1.213 Lester, David and Stanley R. Mink. "Is Stress Higher in Police Officers? An Exploratory Study." **Psychological Reports** 45 (1979): 554.

Police officers in a small town and office workers were compared regarding stress. There were few differences in stress noted in the two groups, each group consisting of fifteen individuals. Author biographical information. 2 references.

1.214 Lester, David and Erich Tappert. "Subjective Stress and Internal-External Locus of Control." **Perceptual and Motor Skills** 53 (1981): 590.

Forty-two police officers were the subjects in this study. Author biographical information. 2 references.

1.215 Levin, Bernard H. and Walter E. Brown. "Susceptibility to Boredom of Jailers and Law Enforcement Officers." **Psychological Reports** 36 (1975): 190.

The Sensation-Seeking Scale and Boredom Susceptibility subscale were used in this research, in which the subjects were forty-two patrolmen and thirty-one jailers. The subjects were attending classes at the Central Shenandoah Criminal Justice Training Center. Author biographical information. 1 reference.

1.216 Levin, Warren. "The Medical View of Stress: An Update." **Police Stress** 1 (Spring 1980): 22-23 and 28.

The author talks about participants and topics concerning the Second International Symposium on the Management of Stress. The symposium was held in Monte Carlo, France. Individuals in attendance represented over twenty-five countries. Most of the attendees were from the medical profession. The opening remarks were by Dr. Hans Selye. Dr. Linus Pauling also spoke at the symposium. Author biographical information. 1 photograph.

1.217 Levitov, Justin E. and Bruce Thompson. "Stress and Counseling Needs of Police Officers." **Counselor Education and Supervision** 21 (1981): 163-168.

Approximately 57% of police officers provided usable returns, when they were surveyed regarding stress and counseling needs. The officers were surveyed with the aid of the Self-Report Form and a demographic survey. Fifty-nine percent of these officers indicated they would seek assistance if counseling was available. Author biographical information. Abstract. 1 table. 18 references.

1.218 Levy, Ruth J. "Predicting Police Failures." **Journal of Criminal Law, Criminology and Police Science** 58 (1967): 265-276.

The author studied personnel files of over 2100, former police officers, who had been designated as failures or nonfailures, during the time period 1952-1962. The officers had been employed by fourteen law enforcement agencies. Three groups of police officers—failures, nonfailures, and currents (employed)—were compared in terms of age and education. Environmental stresses are also discussed. This study was financially supported by the National Institute of Mental Health. Author biographical information. 3 tables. 24 references.

1.219 Lewis, Rodney W. "Toward an Understanding of Police Anomie." **Journal of Police Science and Administration** 1 (1973): 484-490.

The views of Arthur Niederhoffer and Emile Durkheim are discussed extensively. Suicide in the New York Police Department (NYPD) is examined. Cynicism is also covered. Author biographical information. 1 table. 14 footnotes.

1.220 Lieber, Arnold L. "Consultation With the Police: The Psychiatrist as Organizational Change Agent." **Comprehensive Psychiatry** 19 (1978): 57-64.

The City of Miami Police Department hired a part-time psychiatric consultant in April 1972, a position initially funded by the Law Enforcement Assistance Administration (LEAA). This was the continuation of a modernization program begun earlier, involving the Stanford Research Institute, University of Miami, and Florida International University. Major functions of the psychiatric consultant included: establishment of trust and rapport, human systems analysis and problem identification, field training instructor program, and senior staff management seminar. Seven guidelines for the psychiatrist or organizational consultant are included. Author biographical information. 4 references.

1.221 Linedecker, Clifford L. "The 'Ripper.'" Chapter in **Thrill Killers**, by Clifford L. Linedecker, 225-235. Toronto: Paperjacks Ltd., 1987.

New York firefighters responded to a hotel fire in Times Square in December 1979. One of the firefighters crawled across the floor of a smoke-filled room towards a figure on a bed. He realized, when he was about to perform mouth-to-mouth resuscitation, that the victim did not have a head. Another headless body was found in the same room. Both young women were killed by Richard Cottingham, a computer operator from Lodi, New Jersey.

1.222 Lipson, Glenn Scott. "San Ysidro Massacre: Post-Traumatic Stress Among the Police As Related to Life Stress and Coping Style." **Dissertation Abstracts International** 47: 2172B-2173B. Ph.D. dissertation, California School of Professional Psychology, San Diego, 1986. Order No. DA8618143.

This research was funded by the National Institute of Mental Health and the San Diego Police Department, San Diego, California. The purpose of the research was to study posttraumatic stress disorder (PTSD) related to police officers, who were at the McDonald's restaurant in San Ysidro, California on July 18, 1984, when twenty-one persons were murdered and nineteen others were wounded. The response rate for questionnaires sent to officers who were at the massacre, and to a contrast group, was 70%. The Health and Daily Living Form-B, the Reaction Index, and the Impact of Events Scale were three major research instruments used.

1.223 Lombardo, Lucien X. "Occupational Stress in Correction Officers: Sources, Coping Strategies, and Implications." Chapter in **Corrections At the Crossroads: Designing Policy**, edited by Sherwood E. Zimmerman and Harold D. Miller, 129-149. Beverly Hills, CA: Sage Publications, Inc., 1981.

Fifty corrections officers in the eastern U.S. were interviewed. Physical danger and mental strain were identified as stress-producing conditions related to officer contact with inmates. Inmate behavior toward officers and attempts by officers to maintain impartiality, in dealing with inmates, also contributed to officer stress. A feeling, on the part of officers, of powerlessness within the organization was another type of stress reported. Officers felt there was inadequate communication between them and prison administrators. 1 table. 7 notes.

1.224 "Lonely Recovery for Hero Cop." **Police Stress** 6 (Spring 1983): 14.

Dan Hampton, a member of the San Francisco Police Department (SFPD), killed an armed man in 1980, who was holding a woman hostage. Six months after this incident, Hampton was still having psychological problems because he had killed the hostage taker. Hampton wishes he had been approached for help because he feels it would not have been proper for him to seek assistance. Seeking help would have conflicted with his police image.

1.225 Loo, Robert. "Occupational Stress in the Law Enforcement Profession." **Canada's Mental Health** 32 (September 1984): 10-13.

Six major topics: occupational stress, police stressors, women in policing, stress reactions, stress in the police family, and psychological services for police forces. Abstract. Author biographical information. 1 table. 20 references.

1.226 Loo, Robert. "Post-Shooting Stress Reactions Among Police Officers." **Journal of Human Stress** 12 (Spring 1986): 27-31.

The primary research instrument was a questionnaire mailed to sixty-six members of the Royal Canadian Mounted Police (RCMP), who had been involved in shootings. The response rate was 85%. Anger over the incident, nightmares, loss of appetite, flashbacks, guilt feelings, and irritability were some of the more common stress reactions to the shootings. Five recommendations for the benefit of the police force were made. An earlier version of this paper was presented at the Annual Conference, Canadian Psychological Association, Ottawa, Ontario, June 1984. Author biographical information. Abstract. 3 tables. 1 note. 8 references.

1.227 Malloy, Thomas E. and G. Larry Mays. "The Police Stress Hypothesis: A Critical Evaluation." **Criminal Justice and Behavior** 11 (1984): 197-224.

The stress of police work (evidence related to the police stress hypothesis and analysis of the evidence); police stress and its concomitants: the available evidence (Is police work stressful? Is police work more stressful than other occupations? The stress-illness relationship); theoretical assumptions and methodological concerns in police-stress research; and an alternative theoretical paradigm (the proximity-control hypothesis and the stress-diasthesis model). Author biographical information. Abstract. Author's note. 2 figures. 93 references.

1.228 Mann, Philip A. "Stress Training." in **Psychological Consultation With a Police Department: A Demonstration of Cooperative Training in Mental Health,** by Philip A. Mann, 62-64. Springfield, IL: Charles C. Thomas, 1973.

Films as an aid in stress training.

1.229 Margalit, Baruch A. "The Effects of Stressors and Social Support on Aggressive Behavior in the Police Force." **Dissertation Abstracts International** 46: 3583B. Ph.D. dissertation, Georgia State University, College of Arts and Sciences, 1985. Order No. DA85-28645.

The Interpersonal Behavior Survey (IBS), the Social Support Questionnaire, and the State-Trait Personality Inventory (STPI) were administered to police recruits and officers in Atlanta, Georgia. Levels of aggressiveness and assertiveness, degree of available support, anxiety, expression of anger, and somatic complaints are discussed in relation to the recruits and officers.

1.230 Maris, Lou and Mariann Maris. "The Mechanics of Stress Release: The Transcendental Meditation Program and Occupational Stress." **Police Stress** 1 (Spring 1979): 29-35.

Blood pressure, sleep, anxiety, and brain waves are examined with regard to transcendental meditation (TM), as an easy-to-learn technique for reducing stress in police officers. Author biographical information. 1 photograph. 9 charts. 12 footnotes.

1.231 Martin, Carol Ann. "Altruism and Fortitude—Can a 'Lady' Trade Kitchen Table Tranquility for Police Car Stress?" **Police Stress** 2 (Fall 1979): 35-37.

The author, a professor in corrections and law enforcement, elaborates on her research into work values considered most important by women police, and changes in career expectations for these women. A desire to help and protect others was the most important work value which characterized the research sample. Security was the fifth most important value. Adventure was the eighth. The author spent three years on her research and surveyed nearly 300 police departments. Author biographical information. 1 photograph. 2 tables.

1.232 Mason, John Howard. "Stress in Paramedics." **Dissertation Abstracts International** 43: 1428A. Ph.D. dissertation, Ohio State University, 1982. Order No. DA82-22128.

Seventy-seven male paramedics in the Columbus Fire Department, Columbus, Ohio were the sample. The Environmental Stress Scale, Role Questionnaire, Internal/External Locus of Control Instrument, and the State-Trait Anxiety Scale were four of the research instruments used. Infant death, mass casualities, and child birth with complications were stressors identified by the author's research.

1.233 Massey, Charles E. "Police Stress—One Answer to the Problem." **Police Stress** 1 (Spring 1979): 27-28.

Role of the police chaplain in dealing with police stress. Author biographical information. 1 photograph.

1.234 Masztal, Jaci Jarrett. "Sources of Stress in Law Enforcement: Defined and Compared Across Department, Location, and Tenure." **Dissertation Abstracts International** 49: 1971A. Ph.D. dissertation, Illinois Institute of Technology, 1988. Order No. DA8817448.

Nearly 4000 police officers—state, county, city—were surveyed with the aid of a Sources of Stress (SOS) Inventory. The subjects represented fourteen law enforcement agencies. Eight stressor component categories were identified.

1.235 Mayhall, Pamela D. and David Patrick Geary. "Job Stress and Its Consequences." in **Community Relations and the Administration of Justice**, Second Edition, by Pamela D. Mayhall and David Patrick Geary, 54-57. New York, NY: John Wiley and Sons, 1979.

Harold E. Russell, Daniel Cruse, and Jessee Rubin are three researchers mentioned. 1 table.

1.236 Mayhall, Pamela D. and David Patrick Geary. "Reducing Stress." in **Community Relations and the Administration of Justice**, Second Edition, by Pamela D. Mayhall and David Patrick Geary, 57-59. New York, NY: John Wiley and Sons, 1979.

Describes three ways of reducing stress. 1 table.

1.237 McCaghy, Charles H. "Cops Talk Back." **Urban Affairs Quarterly** 4 (1968): 245-247, 249 and 251-255.

A review essay about three books on police work: **The Police on the Urban Frontier: A Guide to Community Understanding** (by George Edwards, 1968); **The Police: Damned If They Do, Damned If They Don't** (by Herbert T. Klein, 1968); and **Walking the Beat: A New York Policeman Tells What It's Like on His Side of the Law** (by Gene Radano, 1968). 2 notes.

1.238 McGuire, Robert J. "The Human Dimension in Urban Policing: Dealing With Stress in the 1980s." **Police Chief** 46 (November 1979): 26-27.

Four main categories of police stressors and a few examples: external stress (entering unfamiliar alleys); operational stress (encountering drug addicts and family violence); organizational stress (paramilitary character of the police department); and personal stress (conflict of personal values with peer group pressures). This stress is revealed by: high rates of heart disease; stomach disorders; divorce; and suicide. The New York Police Department (NYPD) deals with stress by means of: alcoholism counseling; the psychological services unit; and a violence-prone officer identification system. Author biographical information. 1 photograph.

1.239 McMurray, Harvey Lee. "Police Postassault Reactions and the Buffering Effects of Social Support." **Dissertation Abstracts International** 49: 1971A. Ph.D.

dissertation, Rutgers The State University of New Jersey-Newark, 1988. Order No. DA8816710.

Police officers from Washington, DC and Newark, New Jersey—who had been assaulted during a six-month period in 1986—were the subjects in this study.

1.240 Meadows, Robert J. "Arresting Police Officer Stress." **Training and Development Journal** 38 (September 1984): 12 and 14.

After a look at four levels of stress, this article outlines a helping process model, which consists of seven elements: empathy, respect, concreteness, genuineness, self-disclosure, confrontation, and immediacy. 1 figure. 6 references.

1.241 Meichenbaum, Donald and Ray Novaco. "Stress Inoculation: A Preventative Approach." **Issues in Mental Health Nursing** 7 (1985): 419-435.

Cognitive-behavioral-skills treatments have arisen from the application of behavior therapy to stress reactions. Stress-inoculation training is one such treatment. This treatment has been used therapeutically with clinical populations. In this article, however, stress inoculation procedure is used in a preventative context with a nonclinical population of law enforcement officers. The procedure involved cognitive preparation; skill acquisition and rehearsal; and application and practice. Author biographical information. 46 references.

1.242 "The Men Who Bear the Bad Tidings." **Canadian Emergency Services News** 4 (March/April 1981): 56-58.

The stress on police officers when they inform citizens of a death in the family. 1 illustration.

1.243 Meyers, Linda Irene. "A Methodological Approach to Programming for Stress Reduction in a Suburban Police Department." **Dissertation Abstracts International** 43: 878B. PSY.D. dissertation, Rutgers University, 1982. Order No. DA8219037.

The author, a clinical psychologist, conducted a needs assessment in a suburban police department, and talks about five areas of need. One area of need is discussed in relation to a program module.

1.244 Miale, Frank J. "Fire Fighters and the Fear Syndrome." **Fire Service Today** 50 (November 1983): 10-11.

A lieutenant in the New York Fire Department attempts, eleven years after a fire, to account for his actions during that fire. Author biographical information.

1.245 Mills, Robert B. "Simulated Stress in Police Recruit Selection." **Journal of Police Science and Administration** 4 (1976): 179-186.

Describes the Cincinnati Simulated Stress Group Method, a method of evaluating the personality of a police recruit candidate. The evaluation is conducted by a team of psychologists. Candidates carry out verbal and behavioral tasks. Role playing by pairs of candidates is used to gauge the suitability of candidates for police work. The Cincinnati Simulated Stress Group Method is directly job-related and its acceptance by candidates is high. It is, furthermore, a better indicator of how candidates would likely behave in actual police work situations than could be predicted by paper-and-pencil or interview methods. Author biographical information. 2 tables. 11 footnotes.

1.246 Miskiman, Donald. "Stress and the Rural Emergency Responder." **Canadian Emergency News** 12 (January/February 1989): 26-32 and 34-35.

Elaborates on a critical incident stress debriefing (CISD) program used successfully by the author in rural Alberta. Author biographical information. 12 references.

1.247 Missbach, Joseph Collner. "An Exploratory Study of the Relationship Between Occupational Stress, Strain, and Coping and Job Satisfaction in a County Sheriff's Department." **Dissertation Abstracts International** 46: 1325B. Ph.D. dissertation, Ohio State University, 1984. Order No. DA8504058.

Age, sex, shift, and length of time with department were a few of the variables studied in this research, which had a sample of 284 county sheriff's deputies.

1.248 Mitchell, Jeffrey T. "Development and Functions of a Critical Incident Stress Debriefing Team." **JEMS** 13 (December 1988): 42-46.

Looks at critical incident stress debriefing (CISD) teams, general functions of a CISD team, formal critical incident stress debriefing, follow-up service, and other CISD team considerations. 1 illustration. Author biographical information. 12 references.

1.249 Mitchell, Jeffrey T. "The Psychological Impact of the Air Florida 90 Disaster on Fire-Rescue, Paramedic and Police Officer Personnel." in **Proceedings of the First International Assembly on Emergency Medical Services**, Baltimore, Maryland, June 13-17, 1982, edited by R. Adams Cowley, 239-244. Washington, DC: U.S. Government Printing Office, 1982. Technical Report No. DOT HS 806 302.

Air Florida Flight 90 crashed in Washington, DC on January 13, 1982. Seventy-eight people died; five survived. Two months later, the author presented a stress management seminar for rescue personnel involved in rescue operations at the Air Florida crash scene. Anxiety, frustration, anger, and irritability were the immediate reactions. Some personnel later experienced delayed stress reactions, consisting of depression, guilt, flashbacks, nightmares, headaches. Psychological debriefings and physical activity were recommended as stress alleviation strategies. 20 references.

1.250 Mitchell, Jeffrey T. "Recovery From Rescue." **Canadian Emergency Services News** 5 (November/December 1982): 34-36.

The Kansas City Hyatt Regency Hotel disaster in July 1981 in Kansas City, Kansas, and the Pacific Southwest Airlines (PSA) crash in 1978 in San Diego, California, precipitated stress in rescue workers. Trauma surgeons, paramedics, and psychiatrists report stress in themselves at, and after, these and other disasters. Six strategies for reducing stress in rescue workers are discussed. Author biographical information. 2 photographs. 16 references.

1.251 Mitchell, Jeffrey Thomas. "Effects of Stress Management Training on Paramedic Coping Styles and Perceived Stress Levels." **Dissertation Abstracts International** 45: 1617B-1618B. Ph.D. dissertation, University of

Maryland, 1983. Order No. DA8412031.

A two-day, stress management workshop proved to be a better vehicle for dealing with paramedic stress than was a videotaped stress information program. This conclusion was reached in a study of seventy-seven, Baltimore City and suburban Maryland county paramedics. Thirty-seven paramedics took part in the workshop; forty paramedics viewed the videotape.

1.252 Monahan, Lynn Hunt and Richard E. Farmer. "Change." Chapter in **Stress and the Police: A Manual for Prevention**, by Lynn Hunt Monahan and Richard E. Farmer, 112-131. Pacific Palisades, CA: Palisades Publishers, 1980.

Draws the reader's attention to assessing change possibilities (with the aid of a change identification worksheet) and issues affecting change.

1.253 Monahan, Lynn Hunt and Richard E. Farmer. "Definition of Stress." Chapter in **Stress and the Police: A Manual for Prevention**, by Lynn Hunt Monahan and Richard E. Farmer, 1-17. Pacific Palisades, CA: Palisades Publishers, 1980.

Environmental demands and inner emotional conflicts can produce stress, when an individual's adaptive resources are taxed or exceeded. Both mild and extreme forms of physical illnesses are related to stress. A few of the mild forms are: headaches, stomach gas, hives, and high blood pressure. Some of the extreme forms are: migraine, ulcers, exema, and stroke. Overeating, overdrinking, smoking, sleeping, and suicide are common ways of attempting to reduce anxiety and depression. Family, peers, and other people are often subjected to hostile behavior by individuals affected by stress. 2 figures. 1 footnote.

1.254 Monahan, Lynn Hunt and Richard E. Farmer. "Identifying Stress in Your Life." Chapter in **Stress and the Police: A Manual for Prevention**, by Lynn Hunt Monahan and Richard E. Farmer, 41-63. Pacific Palisades, CA: Palisades Publishers, 1980.

Self-identification of stress can be accomplished with the aid of the following: personal stress source inventory, police job-related stress source inventory, stress effects inventory, personal behavior analysis, and police job-related stress behavior analysis.

Information on how to score each of these is provided.

1.255 Monahan, Lynn Hunt and Richard E. Farmer. "Reducing Stress: Individual Techniques." Chapter in **Stress and the Police: A Manual for Prevention,** by Lynn Hunt Monahan and Richard E. Farmer, 64-82. Pacific Palisades, CA: Palisades Publishers, 1980.

Stress can be reduced through both intervention (counseling) and prevention (systematic relaxation) approaches. The following aspects of counseling are discussed: reasons for counseling, goals of counseling, the counseling process, why does counseling help, how to find a good counselor, and counseling the police. 1 figure.

1.256 Monahan, Lynn Hunt and Richard E. Farmer. "Reducing Stress: Interpersonal Techniques." Chapter in **Stress and the Police: A Manual for Prevention,** by Lynn Hunt Monahan and Richard E. Farmer, 83-111. Pacific Palisades, CA: Palisades Publishers, 1980.

Peer support systems and family communication are examples of interpersonal techniques for stress reduction. Time regarding family communication can be divided into four types: private, couples, family, and social. Over-involvement with peers and being a "twenty-four-hour-a-day police officer" can discourage family communication.

1.257 Monahan, Lynn Hunt and Richard E. Farmer. "The Stress-Behavior Model." Chapter in **Stress and the Police: A Manual for Prevention,** by Lynn Hunt Monahan and Richard E. Farmer, 18-40. Pacific Palisades, CA: Palisades Publishers, 1980.

The authoritarian personality, type A behavior, cultural myths, anger, sex roles, and television are factors in stress. Expectations and stress-producing styles in intimate relationships and marriage are other factors in stress, as is the nature of police work. 2 figures. 1 footnote.

1.258 Moore, Eileen. "Stress and the Emergency Responder." **Canadian Emergency Services News** 11 (January/February 1988): 6.

More stress management programs are required in Canada to help police officers, firefighters, and paramedics. These personnel witness traumatic incidents daily. The trauma is even greater when one of their own is seriously injured or killed. Members of these professions sometimes turn to alcohol or suicide to cope with stress. Both the Canadian Association of Fire Chiefs and the Ontario Association of Chiefs of Police support counseling programs. 1 photograph.

1.259 Moore, Larry and John T. Donohue. "The Patrol Officer: Special Problems/Special Cures." **Police Chief** 45 (November 1978): 41-43.

A focus on five types of stressors patrol officers encounter: capability, functional, department, community, and criminal justice system stressors. Some officers exhibit stress by using excessive force in dealing with suspects. Other officers become depressed. Running and jogging are recommended as ways of dealing with stress, especially depression. Author biographical information. 2 photographs.

1.260 "More Danger Than Ever in Being a Fireman Now." **U.S. News and World Report** 63 (September 11, 1967): 15.

Looks at the relationship between race riots and hostility against firefighters in Bridgeport, Connecticut; Newark, New Jersey; and Cincinnati, Ohio. Mentions specific ways in which buildings are booby-trapped, so firefighters, who enter the buildings, are injured or killed. Gives the number of firefighters killed and injured in eleven U.S. cities in which there were race riots.

1.261 Morecock, Robert Clifton. "The Effect of Progressive Muscle Relaxation and Stress Management Interventions on Anxiety, Stress, and Locus of Control of Paramedics." **Dissertation Abstracts International** 49: 2906B. Ph.D. dissertation, University of Houston, 1988. Order No. DA8819502.

This research consisted, in part, of fifty-four paramedics, four experimental conditions, progressive muscle relaxation (PMR), and the Medical Personnel Stress Scale.

1.262 Morris, Hoyt. "Psychological Services: Clinical

Service or Management Tool." **Police Chief** 47 (February 1980): 32-33.

A look at the police department psychological services unit (PSU), and the conflicts associated with it, in terms of police management and rank and file concerns. Author biographical information. 1 photograph.

1.263 "Mother/Daughter Cops." **Ebony** 43 (September 1988): 90, 92 and 96.

A profile of two Detroit, Michigan police officers—Marilyn Jenkins and Simone Martin, her daughter. They are that city's only mother-and-daughter police officers. Officer Martin who, with her partner, works the streets on foot, claims that much of her work is public relations, and that she is never really afraid. 7 photographs.

1.264 Moyer, Imogene L. "An Exploratory Study of Role Distance as a Police Response to Stress." **Journal of Criminal Justice** 14 (1986): 363-373.

E. Goffman's concept of role distance was used in this research, concerning field observations of police-citizen encounters, and police coping strategies regarding stress. Verbal denial of danger and playful pranks among officers were also used to deal with stress. Officers usually exhibited this behavior when they dealt with drunks, were in dangerous situations, had disagreements with other officers, and engaged in trivial interactions with citizens. Author biographical information. Abstract. Acknowledgements. 1 note. 26 references.

1.265 Murphy, Marilynn Pack. "Effects of In-House Psychological Services on Police Officer Empathy and Cynicism." **Dissertation Abstracts International** 43: 880B. Ph.D. dissertation, United States International University, 1982. Order No. DA8216927.

Two methods were used in this study: objective questionnaires and observation of officers on patrol. Two hundred and eighty police officers, representing six departments in California, were the subjects. The idea of in-house psychological services appealed to 78% of officers without such services.

1.266 Navarre, Raymond Joseph. "Stress and Firefighters."

**Dissertation Abstracts International** 44: 3969B. Ph.D. dissertation, University of Toledo, 1983. Order No. DA8406612.

A two-part questionnaire was designed with the aid of twelve Toledo, Ohio firefighters, who were excluded from further participation in this research. The questionnaire was developed to focus on two aspects of stress: causes of job-related stress and behavioral effects of job-related stress. One hundred and fifty-three firefighters were administered the questionnaire.

1.267 Ndetei, D.M. "The Association and Implications of Anxiety and Depression in University Medical and Paramedical Students in Kenya." **East African Medical Journal** 64 (March 1987): 214-226.

Three hundred and four students were the subjects for this investigation. Forty-three percent of the students felt they should seek help regarding their anxiety and depression. Depression was more severe in the female subjects than in the male subjects. Author biographical information. Abstract. 5 tables. 1 appendix. Acknowledgements. 36 references.

1.268 "New York Cop Sues City for $25 M." **Police Stress** 5 (Winter 1982): 12.

The $25 million lawsuit of Louis Marchini, a New York police officer, who is suing the city. Marchini contends that police officials harrassed and intimidated him to the extent that he had a mental breakdown. Marchini had been receiving psychotherapy for depression. The seventeen-year veteran is a highly decorated police officer.

1.269 Niederhoffer, Arthur. "Anomie and Cynicism." Chapter in **Behind the Shield: The Police in Urban Society**, by Arthur Niederhoffer, 90-102. Garden City, NY: Doubleday and Co., Inc., 1967.

This chapter first defines anomie then relates anomie to cynicism. The views of Emile Durkheim and Robert K. Merton are discussed. William Parker, a former chief of the Los Angeles Police Department (LAPD), is quoted regarding the future of society. Suicide by police officers in the New York Police Department (NYPD) is mentioned. Eleven hypotheses about police cynicism are stated. 1 table. 19 footnotes.

1.270 Niederhoffer, Arthur. "The Study of Police Cynicism." Appendix in **Behind the Shield: The Police in Urban Society,** by Arthur Niederhoffer, 187-242. Garden City, NY: Doubleday and Co., Inc., 1967.

The appendix consists of: the hypotheses, the questionnaire, the cynicism questionnaire, the sample, results of the study, analysis of the results, the evidence for the hypotheses, and a summary. 1 figure.

1.271 Niederhoffer, Arthur and Elaine Niederhoffer. "Power, Status, and the Family: The Policeman and the Physician." Chapter in **The Police Family: From Station House to Ranch House,** by Arthur Niederhoffer and Elaine Niederhoffer, 41-57. Lexington, MA: D.C. Heath and Co., 1978.

A comparative look at police officers and physicians in terms of different variables, including: duties actually performed versus stereotypes, status, marital problems, children, divorce, and suicide. 2 tables. 41 footnotes.

1.272 "NIJ Urges Police Agencies to Help Officers Deal With Stress." **Criminal Justice Newsletter** 17 (November 3, 1986): 7.

Provides basic information about a National Institute of Justice (NIJ) study of police stress. The study is based on stress management programs in eight police departments. The study, which has forty recommendations, is available from the U.S. Government Printing Office.

1.273 Nixon, Robert G. "Burnout Revisited." **Emergency Medical Services** 16 (January/February 1987): 44-45 and 48-53.

Addresses the issue of burnout in emergency medical services (EMS) personnel by making reference to life scripts, belief systems, and motivations for being in EMS work. 1 figure. 2 tables. Author biographical information.

1.274 Norton, John M. "Avoidable Stress." **Police Stress** 6 (Spring 1983): 15.

A police officer who, in the line of duty, justifiably

killed a man was demoted to a desk job because of political reasons. The man broke the officer's left arm with a lead pipe, as the officer protected children the man had abducted. Later, the man's family threatened to sue the city. 1 illustration.

1.275 Novaco, Raymond W. "A Stress Inoculation Approach to Anger Management in the Training of Law Enforcement Officers." **American Journal of Community Psychology** 5 (1977): 327-346.

Consists of three main topics: the disposition for anger among police, anger-management training, and implications for officer selection and research. D. Meichenbaum advocated use of stress inoculation for dealing with anxiety and pain. Author biographical information. Abstract. 2 footnotes. 4 tables. 66 references.

1.276 O'Neill, John. "'Tough Guy's' Letter Touches Cops." **Police Stress** 1 (Fall 1978): 10.

Words of encouragement to fellow police officers from Detective Arnold James who, along with his partner, Detective John McManus, was wounded in a shootout in Mattapan, Massachusetts. James—who lost the sight of his left eye—was more seriously wounded than his partner. Nevertheless, James did not want fellow officers to feel discouraged about their own careers.

1.277 O'Neill, Michael W., Wayne B. Hanewicz, Lynn M. Fransway and Christine Cassidy-Riske. "Stress Innoculation Training and Job Performance." **Journal of Police Science and Administration** 10 (1982): 388-397.

Some of the major topics discussed in this study, which tested three hypotheses, were: human stress in general, police stress in particular, and four modes of stress prevention. The experimental subjects were members of the Washtenaw County Sheriff's Department. Accidents, injuries, sick leave, separations, citizens' complaints, internal complaints, disciplinary actions, and use of firearms were studied in relation to job performance. Author biographical information. 1 figure. 1 table. Acknowledgement. 19 references.

1.278 Palmer, C. Eddie. "A Note About Paramedics' Strategies for Dealing With Death and Dying." **Journal of Occupational Psychology** 56 (1983): 83-86.

Six ways paramedics cope with death and dying: educational desensitization processes; use of humor; language alternation; scientific fragmentation and escape into work; and rationalization. Data for this paper was obtained by: participant observation; direct observation; informal interviews; conversations; monitoring of paramedic radio; and document inspection. Author biographical information. Abstract. 4 references.

1.279 Palmer, C. Eddie. "'Trauma Junkies' and Street Work: Occupational Behavior of Paramedics and Emergency Medical Technicians." **Urban Life** 12 (1983): 162-183.

Talks about data collection, emergency medical services (EMS) activity, types of calls responded to, becoming a trauma junkie, street work, and the roles of paramedics. Four of the main roles are: medical authority figure, lifesaver, information specialist, and partner. Six methods of gathering data were used in this research. Author biographical information. 2 tables. 3 notes. 18 references. 1 appendix. (41 EMS Radio Signals).

1.280 "Paramedic Conference Looks At Stress, Burnout." **Canadian Emergency Services News** 3 (September/October 1980): 59.

Announcement of a conference on Stress and Paramedic Burnout scheduled for Estes Park, Colorado, September 28-30, 1980. A few of the scheduled faculty: Robert V. Casanova, Dr. Norman Dinerman, Chestra Johnston, and Dr. Ron Crowell.

1.281 Parise, Laurence. "The Policewoman." Chapter in **Handbook for Law Enforcement Wives**, edited by Barbara E. Webber, 103-108. Chicago, IL: L.E. Publishers, Inc., 1974.

A policewoman, who attained the rank of sergeant, not only coped with resentment—for different reasons—from male and female officers, but also endured the stress associated with raising a family.

1.282 Pendergrass, Virginia E. and Nancy M. Ostrove. "A Survey of Stress in Women in Policing." **Journal of Police Science and Administration** 12 (1984): 303-309.

Questionnaires, assuring anonymity for respondents, were used in a study of police employees in Montgomery County, Maryland. The Police Stress Survey and Pearson Product Moment Correlations were also used. Male and female subjects were divided into three groups: sworn police officers, police technicians, and civilian employees. Research results report on: sex and employee status of the sample compared to the departmental population, diagnosed stress related diseases by sex and employee status, mean psychological/behavioral consequences as a function of employee status and sex, correlations between job stress index and stress consequences, and other factors. Author biographical information. 8 tables. 14 references.

1.283 Pendleton, Michael Roy. "Police Stress: Value Disparity, Self-Esteem and Occupational Strain." **Dissertation Abstracts International** 44: 2277B-2278B. Ph.D. dissertation, University of Washington, 1983. Order No. DA8319441.

Value disparities, self-esteem, and occupational strain were studied in 253 police officers paid to participate in this research project. Three of the questionnaires administered to the officers were: the Rokeach Value Survey, Spielburger Anxiety Measure, and the Cornell Medical Index. Multiple regression was used to analyze the data.

1.284 Perr, Irwin N. "A Unique Review of Rejected Police Candidates: Psychiatric and Psychologic Aspects." **Bulletin of the American Academy of Psychiatry and the Law** 11 (1983): 371-378.

The New Jersey Civil Service Commission established, in 1973, a Medical Review Board, which advises the commission regarding police candidates for public positions. At least 67% of police officers in New Jersey are in public positions governed by civil service law. Between June 1973 and March 1982, 539 police candidates were rejected and appealed. The Medical Review Board consists of a psychiatrist, psychologist, and one other member. Author biographical information. 5 tables. 10 references.

1.285 Perroni, Carolyn. "Managing Stress." **Fire Command** 54 (November 1987): 47.

The views of Dr. Jeffrey T. Mitchell on stress and its management in firefighters. Mitchell is Assistant

Professor, Emergency Health Service Department, University of Maryland, Baltimore County. Stress is discussed in relation to volunteer and career firefighters. Critical incidents and posttraumatic stress disorder (PTSD) are covered. Nightmares, flashbacks, and anxiety are a few of the symptoms of the latter. The image of firefighters as strong, fearless, and cool is a major obstacle to firefighters dealing with stress. Debriefings, special relaxation techniques, and change of duty are some of the ways firefighters can deal with stress. 1 photograph.

1.286 Phelps, Lourn. "Police Tasks and Related Stress Factors From an Organizational Perspective." in **Proceedings of Symposium, Job Stress and the Police Officer: Identifying Stress Reduction Techniques**, Cincinnati, Ohio, May 8-9, 1975, edited by William H. Kroes and Joseph J. Hurrell, Jr., 146-156. Washington, DC: U.S. Government Printing Office, 1975.

Police stress is attributed to three major factors: environmental (work related, personal, and public); interpersonal (personality diversity, physical-emotional, personality costs); and administrative (work climate, communication, organizational design). Twelve strategies for reducing police stress are outlined. Author biographical information. 5 footnotes. 1 appendix.

1.287 Phillips, Jenny Eva Decker. "A Sociological Analysis of Occupational Stress and Job Satisfaction of Police in Selected Rural and Urban Parishes in Louisiana." **Dissertation Abstracts International** 37: 7331A. Ph.D. dissertation, Louisiana State University and Agricultural and Mechanical College, 1976. Order No. DA77-10393.

One urban and two rural parishes in Louisiana were locales for this investigation. Education and age were two variables associated with police stress. Higher amounts of stress were found in sheriff deputies than in city police officers.

1.288 Poole, Eric D. and Robert M. Regoli. "Alienation in Prison: An Examination of the Work Relations of Prison Guards." **Criminology** 19 (1981): 251-270.

This study examined prison guards and their relations with inmates, superiors, and fellow officers. Five types of alienation were investigated: powerlessness, normlessness, meaninglessness, social isolation, and self-estrangement. Anonymous and confidential questionnaire responses and formal interviews were used. The guards feel the prison is disordered and adrift, that they are working alone, and that they have little job satisfaction. Author biographical information. Abstract. 1 figure. 1 table. 3 notes. 23 references.

1.289 Poole, Eric D. and Robert M. Regoli. "An Examination of the Effects of Professionalism on Cynicism Among Police." **Social Science Journal** 16 (October 1979): 59-66.

Data for this research was obtained via questionnaire from police officers in three law enforcement agencies in the U.S. Responses were anonymous and the combined response rate was 76%. The authors contend police cynicism can be reduced by commitment to a professional ideology. Author biographical information. 6 tables. 29 notes.

1.290 Poole, Eric D., Robert M. Regoli and Roy Lotz. "Linkages Between Professionalism, Work Alienation and Cynicism in Large and Small Police Departments." **Social Science Quarterly** 59 (1978): 525-534.

A questionnaire, consisting of 103 items, was administered to police officers in the U.S. Pacific Northwest. The response rate was over 70%. Five dimensions of professionalism were analyzed in relation to cynicism and work alienation. The study found that the latter may be reduced by professionalism. Author biographical information. 1 table. 5 footnotes. 28 references.

1.291 Posner, Israel, Lewis A. Leitner and David Lester. "Stress, Mood and Job Satisfaction in Police Administrators." **Stress** 1 (Autumn 1980): 5-7.

The Profile of Mood States and the Job Descriptive Index were two research instruments used in this study, in which fifty-six police administrators and supervisors were the subjects. The subjects took part in stress reduction training, which lasted fifteen hours. Police administrators, relative to the average person, had lower job satisfaction, but not higher levels of stress. Author biographical information. 5 references. 2 tables.

1.292 Price, John "Jack." "What's a Chaplain?" **Police Stress** 1 (Fall 1978): 11.

Contemporary police chaplains do not fit stereotype images of clergymen portrayed in the mass media or elsewhere. Author biographical information. 1 photograph.

1.293 Quintanilla, Guadalupe and Harry D. Caldwell. "The Houston Police Department's Hispanic Culture/Language Program." **Police Chief** 46 (September 1979): 56-57.

Because the population of Houston, Texas is growing by approximately 6000 people each month, and about 19% of the newcomers are Hispanic, this increases the stress of those police officers who cannot speak Spanish. To decrease stress and facilitate communication between police officers and Hispanics is the objective of the Houston Police Department's Hispanic culture/language program. Author biographical information. 2 photographs.

1.294 Rafky, David M. "Police Cynicism Reconsidered: An Application of Smallest Space Analysis." **Criminology** 13 (1975): 168-192.

According to this research, cynicism—contrary to A. Niederhoffer's expectations—was found not to be prevalent among police officers outside New York City. Niederhoffer's sample and this sample each contained approximately 200 subjects. The Scale of Police Cynicism was used in both studies. Abstract. Author biographical information. 3 tables. 3 figures. 16 references.

1.295 Reese, James T. "Life in the High-Speed Lane: Managing Police Burnout." **Police Chief** 49 (June 1982): 49-53.

Covers five topics regarding burnout: definition, causes, symptoms, coping strategies, and steps in counseling. Burnout is an inappropriate response to stress, frequently associated with individuals who are excessively committed to their work and, because of this, develop a lack of commitment. The three major categories of symptoms of burnout, and examples of symptoms, are: emotional (apathy, irritability, overcompensation), behavioral (withdrawal), and physical (headaches, insomnia, indigestion). Adequate sleep, proper diet, and learning how to accept things that cannot be changed are three ways of dealing with burnout. Author biographical information. 1 photograph. 17 footnotes.

1.296 Reeves, Joy B. "Exploring Differential Occupational Stress and the Male Sex Role." **Free Inquiry in Creative Sociology** 13 (May 1985): 5-9.

Compares stress in executives and police officers, and considers amount of stress experienced, causes of stress, and a sex role perspective. The author's research indicates that executives experience less stress than police officers. Author biographical information. 44 references.

1.297 Reeves, Joy B. "Police Stress: A Sex Role Perspective." **Police Stress** 5 (Winter 1982): 6-9.

Examines, from the viewpoint of D. David and R. Brannon, the male sex role, and relates it to police stress. The David and Brannon model consists of four themes: "No Sissy Stuff," "The Big Wheel," "Sturdy Oak," and "Give 'Em Hell.'" A solution to police stress is proposed. Author biographical information. 2 illustrations. 32 references.

1.298 Regoli, Robert M. "An Empirical Assessment of Niederhoffer's Police Cynicism Scale." **Journal of Criminal Justice** 4 (1976): 231-241.

Reveals that Arthur Niederhoffer's police cynicism scale has an extremely low reliability and validity, and that it measures five dimensions of cynicism. The five dimensions concern: relations with the public; organizational functions; police dedication to duty; police social solidarity; and training and education. Nine police agencies—324 police officers—in Washington and Idaho were surveyed for this study. Author biographical information. Abstract. 3 tables. 2 appendices. Acknowledgement. 10 references.

1.299 Regoli, Robert M. and Eric D. Poole. "Measurement of Police Cynicism: A Factor Scaling Approach." **Journal of Criminal Justice** 7 (1979): 37-51.

Demonstrates several shortcomings of Arthur Niederhoffer's police cynicism scale. For example, the authors contend the scale is neither logically nor empirically valid. The scale does not represent a unidimensional construct. There are various types of police cynicism associated with specific individual or organizational characteristics. Author biographical information. Abstract. 5 tables. 2 appendices. 10 notes. 25 references.

1.300 Regoli, Robert M., George Rivera, Jr. and John P. Crank. "Police Cynicism in the United States and Transkei." **Sociology and Social Research** 72 (1988): 118-120.

When cynicism in police officers in Transkei, Africa was compared to cynicism in police officers in New York, it was learned that cynicism was less severe among the Transkeian officers. Economic conditions in Transkei were perceived to act as a bulwark against police cynicism. It appeared that poverty in Transkei made steady employment as a police officer attractive. Author biographical information. 1 note. 7 references. 1 table.

1.301 Reiser, Martin. "A Psychologist's View of the Badge." **Police Chief** 37 (September 1970): 24-26.

The author's perceptions of police work have changed, since—as psychologist with the Los Angeles Police Department (LAPD), Los Angeles, California—he has gone on patrol once a month, and has experienced firsthand what officers experience. This article was presented at the California State Psychological Association Convention, Monterey, California, January 17, 1970. Author biographical information. 8 footnotes.

1.302 Reiser, Martin. "Some Organizational Stresses on Policemen." **Journal of Police Science and Administration** 2 (1974): 156-159.

Loss of group identification, the internal discipline structure within a police department, and peer group influence are three major stressors encountered by police officers. This article is based on a paper presented at the American Psychological Association Convention, Montreal, Quebec, August 27, 1973. Author biographical information. 17 footnotes.

1.303 Reiser, Martin. "Stress, Distress, and Adaptation in Police Work." **Police Chief** 43 (January 1976): 24 and 26-27.

Talks about stress from the viewpoints of Hans Selye, George B. Whatmore, and Walter Cannon. States that stress in police work is often role related. The police officer is an authority symbol and omnipresent mental health agent, who works in a dangerous and threatening environment. Role playing, exercise, proper nutritional balance, and biofeedback techniques are recommended for stress management. Author biographical information. 1 photograph. 37 footnotes.

1.304 Reiser, Martin, Robert J. Sokol and Susan J. Saxe. "An Early Warning Mental Health Program for Police Sergeants." Chapter in **Stress and Police Personnel,** by Leonard Territo and Harold J. Vetter, 212-215. Boston, MA: Allyn and Bacon, Inc., 1981.

Police sergeants and psychiatrists participated in a mental health pilot project—between April 1970 and April 1971—in the Los Angeles Police Department (LAPD). Problems encountered with the project and evaluations of the project are discussed. 2 end notes.

1.305 Rianoshek, Richard Jay. "A Study Exploring the Psychosocial Antecedents of Police Stress." **Dissertation Abstracts International** 47: 2232B. Ph.D. dissertation, Kansas State University, 1986. Order No. DA86-17129.

In an attempt to more fully understand the police personality, the author was interested in the relationship between the early childhood experiences of police officers, and the more recent social-emotional issues of officers. The research sample were twenty police officers. One of the author's findings was that siblings were occasionally law breakers. Another finding was that police, sometimes, were important role models.

1.306 Richey, Larry D. "The Question of Stress Training." **Police Chief** 41 (May 1974): 63-67.

A critique of nonstress training in the Los Angeles County Sheriff's Department. The nonstress training policy was advocated by Assistant Sheriff, Howard Earle. The critique claims the study by Earle is misleading and the results based on a poorly controlled methodology. Author biographical information. 1 photograph.

1.307 Rios, Bob, Darrel Parisher and Robert R. Reilley. "Need for Psychological Services As Perceived by Urban Police Departments." **Psychological Reports** 43 (1978): 126.

One hundred and seventy-four urban police departments were randomly selected in this national survey. The following were some of the psychological services requested by the police departments: personal and family counseling for officers, screening of job applicants, workshops in alcohol and drug abuse, workshops in cultural awareness, and workshops in abnormal behavior. Author biographical information. 1 reference.

1.308 Roache, M. Shannon, G.A. Shouksmith, K.E. Voges and N.R. Long. **The Perception of Stress By Prison Officers and Their Wives: An Occupational Study.** [Palmerston North:] Massey University Department of Psychology, 1982.

Results of a study done in New Zealand, by researchers from the Massey University Department of Psychology, who spent a year and a half gathering data. Prison officers (575) and their wives (301) were surveyed at seventeen institutions. The researchers used questionnaires, interviews, and group discussions. The study consists of ten main parts: (1) Research Problem; (2) Research Aims and Design; (3) Review of Relevant Literature; (4) Prison Officers and Their Job; (5) Personal and Health Factors of Prison Officers; (6) Job Survey; (7) Relationships Among Variables; (8) Effects of Occupational Stress on Families: Questionnaire for Wives; (9) Nature of Occupational Stress in Prison Officers: A Theoretical Model; and (10) Conclusions and Recommendations. 30 tables. 2 figures. 4 appendices. 169 references.

1.309 Roberts, Scott W. and Keith J. Karren. "Job Satisfaction Among Paramedics." **JEMS** 12 (March 1987): 48-49.

Approximately 200 paramedics in Utah took part in this study. Over 95% of the subjects were male. The mean age was 31.8 years. The State-Trait Anxiety Inventory, Myers-Briggs Type Indicator, Internal-External Locus of Control Scale, and Minnesota Satisfaction Questionnaire were the research tools used. Extroverts were more satisfied with their jobs than were introverts. Author biographical information. 3 tables. 10 references.

1.310 Ronan, Richard. "Delta 88." **Police Stress** 1 (Spring 1979): 23 and 26.

The crash at Logan International Airport in Boston, Massachusetts of a Delta Airlines plane in July 1973. Reactions of police, family, and medical personnel regarding the victims. Author biographical information.

1.311 Rosburg, Marjorie Ott. "A Comparison of the Anxiety Levels of College Students: Nurses, Police, and Firefighters vs. General College Students." **Dissertation Abstracts International** 49: 2082A. Ph.D. dissertation, University of California, Riverside, 1988. Order No. DA8822061.

Age, marital status, number supported by income, and ethnicity were some of the demographic variables studied. The State-Trait Anxiety Inventory (STAI) was used to measure anxiety. Nurses experienced the highest degree of anxiety—higher than that of police and firefighter students.

1.312 Ruddock, Robert L. "Recruit Training: Stress v. Nonstress." **Police Chief** 41 (November 1974): 47-50.

On December 15, 1972, the forty-eighth police recruit class graduated from the Columbus Division of Police, Columbus, Ohio. Unlike previous classes, the forty-eighth was trained using the guidance method. This article reports on the forty-eighth class, and includes reactions of recruits to the guidance method. Abstract. Author biographical information. 1 photograph.

1.313 Russo, Philip A., Jr., Alan S. Engel and Steven H. Hatting. "Police and Occupational Stress: An Empirical Investigation." Chapter in **Police At Work: Policy Issues and Analysis**, edited by Richard R. Bennett, 89-106. Beverly Hills, CA: Sage Publications, Inc., 1983.

The subjects in this research were police officers from three communities in Ohio—Fairfield, Hamilton, and Middletown—and one community in Indiana—Richmond. Ninety-eight percent of the officers were male, 55% had a high school education, and 58% were under the age of thirty-five. Moodiness was the stress symptom found most often in these subjects; heart trouble was found least often. Domestic violence, child abuse, and drownings were also very stressful to officers dealing with such incidents. Author biographical information. 12 tables. 6 notes. 27 references.

1.314 Sandy, Joan Phillips and Donald A. Devine. "Four Stress Factors Unique to Rural Patrol." **Police Chief** 45 (September 1978): 42-44.

Four rural stress factors: security (absence of readily available back-up), social factors (relative absence of anonymity), working conditions (limited training), and inactivity (boredom and job dissatisfaction). Author biographical information. 2 photographs. 6 references.

1.315 Sarason, Irwin G., James H. Johnson, John P. Berberich and Judith M. Siegel. "Helping Police Officers to Cope With Stress: A Cognitive-Behavioral Approach." **American Journal of Community Psychology** 7 (1979): 593-603.

Eighteen police academy trainees—ten males and eight females—were the subjects. The subjects—ranging in age from twenty-two to thirty-four years—were enrolled in the Seattle Police Academy, Seattle, Washington. They were assigned to either a stress management program or to a control condition. Self-report and physiological measures were taken. The authors learned that stress management may be most effective when the program is about situations likely to be encountered by trainees. Author biographical information. Abstract. 2 footnotes. 2 reference notes. 15 references.

1.316 Sawangnetr, Somchart. "Stress Among Assistant Police Inspectors in Bangkok, Thailand." **Dissertation Abstracts International** 49: 1584A. Ph.D. dissertation, Florida State University, 1988. Order No. DA8814431.

A theoretical model of police stress was tested with the aid of 403 questionnaire responses and a four-step procedure, including reliability assessment and exploratory factor analysis.

1.317 Schilling, Charles G. "Taking the Mystery Out of Stress Management." **Police Stress** 1 (Spring 1980): 13-14.

A police officer gives an intelligent, concise, common sense explanation of police stress. Author biographical information. 1 photograph.

1.318 Schlossberg, Harvey and Lucy Freeman. **Psychologist With a Gun.** New York, NY: Coward, McCann and Geoghegan, Inc., 1974.

Harvey Schlossberg is a detective with the New York Police Department (NYPD) and has a doctorate degree in psychology. This book is an account of his life as a police officer and his work as psychologist with the NYPD.

1.319 Schreiber, Francis Barry. "Design, Implementation and Evaluation of a 24 Hour Crisis Intervention Training Program for Police." **Dissertation Abstracts International** 38: 3094A. Ph.D. dissertation, University of Colorado, Boulder, 1977. Order No. DA7724287.

Discusses a crisis intervention training program for police officers in Boulder, Colorado. The program is about the proper and effective handling of the domestic disturbance call. The program is based on programs in New York and Louisville, Kentucky. Officer safety, legal issues, techniques for calming upset persons, mediation, and referral are some of the areas covered. Lectures, guest speakers, and simulated disturbances are also part of the program.

1.320 Schwartz, Jeffrey A. and Cynthia B. Schwartz. "The Personal Problems of the Police Officer: A Plea for Action." in **Proceedings of Symposium, Job Stress and the Police Officer: Identifying Stress Reduction Techniques**, Cincinnati, Ohio, May 8-9, 1975, edited by William H. Kroes and Joseph J. Hurrell, Jr., 130-141. Washington, DC: U.S. Government Printing Office, 1975.

Some personal problem areas of police officers: workaholism, burnout, divorce, alcoholism, heart disease, back trouble, hypertension, retirement problems, and suicide. A few of the potential remedies: career development alternatives, psychological services, police officers' spouses, and phased retirement programs. Author biographical information.

1.321 Schweiger, Karol. "Firefighter! A Photographic Salute." **Atlantic Advocate** 69 (April 1979): 36-39.

Peter Ormandy, a freelance photographer and a research technician at the University of New Brunswick in Fredericton, exhibited 130 photographs of firefighters, and their work, at the Fredericton National Exhibition Centre. 2 photographs.

1.322 Scott, Charles Walter. "The Burn-Out Syndrome in

Ambulance Paramedics." **Dissertation Abstracts International** 41: 1149B. Ph.D. dissertation, United States International University, 1980. Order No. DA80-19055.

Fifty-three paramedics in Riverside and San Bernardino Counties were studied in 1974 and 1979. Major research tools used were the Sixteen Personality Factor Questionnaire, Maslach Burn-Out Inventory, Life Experiences Survey, and the State-Trait Anxiety Inventory. Research focussed on two types of variables: situational and personality. Emotional exhaustion, depersonalization, personal accomplishment, income, and opportunities for promotion were studied. Ten main conclusions were made on the basis of this investigation.

1.323 Selye, Hans. "The Stress of Police Work." **Police Stress** 1 (Fall 1978): 7-8.

Contends that police work is more stressful than the air traffic control profession. Shift work, prejudice, and hostility are a few of the stressors associated with police work. Stress reduction, as practiced by the Boston Police, is recommended to other police officers. Author biographical information. 1 photograph.

1.324 Sepe, John and Louis Telano. **Cop Team.** New York, NY: Pinnacle Books, 1975.

Undercover police officers, John Sepe and Louis Telano, known throughout the New York underworld as the "Lone Ranger and Tonto," are the subject of this book.

1.325 Sewell, James D. "The Development of a Critical Life Events Scale for Law Enforcement." **Journal of Police Science and Administration** 11 (1983): 109-116.

Inventories of stressful life events; development of the survey instrument; final survey instrument and sample selection; respondent profile; analysis of the professional life events scale; and implications. Includes a Law Enforcement Critical Life Events Scale, which consists of 144 items. Author biographical information. 21 references.

1.326 Sewell, James D. "Stress in University Law Enforcement." **Journal of Higher Education** 55 (1984): 515-523.

University law enforcement officers have unique problems. On the one hand, their stress is similar to stress experienced by other urban as well as by rural law enforcement officers. On the other hand, their stressors are relatively unique to the university setting. This article examines thirteen stressors and how to deal with them: role conflict, overtraining, negative public image, "macho" self-image, boredom, false sense of security, university administrative demands, low priority support, use of the agency for training, media coverage, community impact, people pain, and potential for abuse of authority. Author biographical information. 3 footnotes. 18 references.

1.327 Shaver, Phillip, Robert Schurtman and Thomas O. Blank. "Conflict Between Firemen and Ghetto Dwellers: Environmental and Attitudinal Factors." **Journal of Applied Social Psychology** 5 (1975): 240-261.

Bedford-Stuyvesant, Brownsville, and Ocean Hill are three sections of Brooklyn, New York in which this research took place. The authors believe false alarms in these areas should be viewed as expressions of protest by certain residents. The authors learned that young nonwhites exhibited most hostility to firefighters. Firefighters are seen as being biased against nonwhites and as doing unnecessary damage. Author biographical information. Abstract. 5 tables. 1 figure. 8 footnotes. 31 references.

1.328 Shay, Patrick S. "Dispatcher's Job Is Strenuous." **Canadian Emergency Services News** 8 (November/December 1985): 35.

Simulated dispatching by student emergency medical technicians (EMTs), at the Lebanon County Emergency Management Agency, Lebanon County, Pennsylvania. The students learned about emotional and physical stress, and about communication and teamwork. 1 photograph. Author biographical information.

1.329 Sheppard, Harold L. "A Note on the Application of Stress Research Findings to Problems of Police Job Stress." in **Proceedings of Symposium, Job Sress and the Police Officer: Identifying Stress Reduction Techniques**, Cincinnati, Ohio, May 8-9, 1975, edited by William H. Kroes and Joseph J. Hurrell, Jr., 142-145. Washington, DC: U.S. Government Printing Office, 1975.

The priority of preventing police stress should be given more attention than preparing to rehabilitate officers afflicted with stress disorders. Author biographical information.

1.330 Sherman, Lewis J. "A Psychological View of Women in Policing." **Journal of Police Science and Administration** 1 (1973): 383-394.

Women in policing in Indianapolis, Indiana; Miami, Florida; Peoria, Illinois; and Washington, DC. Also discusses women in policing in England, Israel, and Sweden. Lists six reasons why women should be hired for policing. Author biographical information. 18 footnotes.

1.331 Shev, Edward E. and Jeremy Joan Hewes. "Cops and Their Families." Chapter in **Good Cops/Bad Cops: Memoirs of a Police Psychiatrist,** by Edward E. Shev and Jeremy Joan Hewes, 129-140. San Francisco, CA: San Francisco Book Co., Inc., 1977.

Describes the average police officer on the basis of data obtained in San Francisco, California. Looks at situations in which police officers experience hostility on account of the people with whom they deal. Gives reasons for police isolation relative to the rest of the community. Alcohol, opportunities for heterosexual intercourse, and bribery are three common temptations faced by police officers. Shift work and worry that his children may rebel to the point of breaking the law further complicate the police officer's life.

1.332 Silbert, Mimi H. "Job Stress and Burnout of New Police Officers." **Police Chief** 49 (June 1982): 46-48.

Reports on a study of 267 police officers in the San Francisco Police Department (SFPD), San Francisco, California. The study was undertaken in October 1980 by the department's training consultant. Eighty-one percent of the officers were male, 19% were female, and the mean age was twenty-eight years. Five of the highest symptoms of stress for officers on duty were: headaches, being tense, backaches, stomach aches, and loss of appetite. Poor pay was the highest stressor. Black officers reported the lowest stress. Asian officers reported physical exhaustion most often. Author biographical information. 1 photograph. 4 footnotes.

1.333 Silverstein, Joan M. "The Psychologist As Panel Member." **Social Action and the Law** 11 (1985): 72-74.

The value of having a psychologist assist with police personnel selection procedures is discussed, with reference to the selection procedure used by the Montclair Police Department. 2 footnotes.

1.334 Singleton, Gary W. and John Teahan. "Effects of Job-Related Stress on the Physical and Psychological Adjustment of Police Officers." **Journal of Police Science and Administration** 6 (1978): 355-361.

Ninety male police officers were the subjects and were divided into groups of thirty officers each: a low physical stress group; a moderate physical stress group; and a high stress or lethal behavior group. The mean age of the subjects was twenty-nine years. The Taylor Manifest Anxiety Scale (MAS), Situation Anxiety Scale (SAS), and Social Desirability Scale (SD) were a few of the research instruments used. Depression, anxiety, hostility, and paranoia were some of the variables measured. The greater the physical stress at work, the greater the likelihood the officer would have family problems at home. Author biographical information. 2 tables. 19 footnotes.

1.335 Sisson, P. Joe, Gary L. Arthur and George M. Gazda. "Stress and Emotions in Behavior." Chapter in **Human Relations for Criminal Justice Personnel**, by P. Joe Sisson, Gary L. Arthur and George M. Gazda, 25-47. Boston, MA: Allyn and Bacon, Inc., 1981.

Covered are the following: sociological, psychological, and physiological models of stress. Also covered are: family relationship and stress; environmental stressors; work role and stress; personality and stress; anger, fear, guilt, and frustration. 84 references.

1.336 "Slain Doctor's Heirs Sue Town." **Police Stress** 7 (Autumn 1984): 24.

A lawsuit regarding the shooting death of Dr. Alan Shields, a psychiatrist, by James Palmer, a former police officer.

1.337 Slater, Stephen L. and Ed Lovette. "Firearms Stress Training: Lessons Learned." **Police Chief** 45 (July

1978): 51.

Elaborates on the decision-making firearms course at the New Mexico Department of Criminal Justice Training and Education Bureau. Author biographical information. 2 photographs.

1.338 Sokol, Robert J. and Martin Reiser. "Training Police Sergeants in Early Warning Signs of Emotional Upset." **Mental Hygiene** 55 (1971): 303-307.

Outlines a program administered by the Los Angeles Police Department (LAPD), and the Los Angeles County Department of Mental Health. The program was implemented in April 1970 in the West Valley and Northeast Divisions. Harbor Division was a control. The length of training for each sergeant was approximately twelve hours. Author biographical information. Abstract. 4 references.

1.339 Somodevilla, S.A. "The Psychologist's Role in the Police Department." **Police Chief** 45 (April 1978): 21-23.

A police psychologist can fulfill a number of roles, including: diagnostician, counselor, researcher, teacher, and consultant. His remarks are based on his experiences with the Dallas Police Department, Dallas, Texas. He also talks about the problems and pitfalls of being a police psychologist, and the preferred qualifications. Author biographical information. 1 photograph.

1.340 Somodevilla, S.A., Charles F. Baker, Wayne R. Hill and Noel H. Thomas. "Stress Management in the Dallas Police Department." Chapter in **Stress and Police Personnel,** by Leonard Territo and Harold J. Vetter, 287-294. Boston, MA: Allyn and Bacon, Inc, 1981.

Police officers and their dependents can enter the Dallas Police Department counseling program in three ways: via internal affairs, through supervisory referral, and by self-referral. Biofeedback training is widely used in the Dallas Police Department. The Psychological Services Unit is discussed in terms of purpose, staffing, and accountability.

1.341 "Spotting the Problem Policeman." **Science Digest** 73

(April 1973): 29-30.

Dr. Robert B. Mills states that aptitude tests, role playing, and peer interaction can be used to spot the problem police officer. Four findings about police recruits are included. Dr. Mills has a decade of experience screening would-be police officers.

1.342 Stotland, E. "Stress and Police Mental and Physical Health." **Government Reports Announcements and Index** 84 (May 25, 1984): 46. NTIS PB84-166412.

Stress, value systems, recreational experiences, and blood pressure were some of the variables studied in this research. Fire department and other municipal employees were compared to the police officers studied. The investigation took place in a western U.S. city.

1.343 Stotland, Ezra. "Self-Esteem and Stress in Police Work." in **Proceedings of Symposium, Job Stress and the Police Officer: Identifying Stress Reduction Techniques**, Cincinnati, Ohio, May 8-9, 1975, edited by William H. Kroes and Joseph J. Hurrell, Jr., 3-16. Washington, DC: U.S. Government Printing Office, 1975.

Contends that high self-esteem can make certain individuals relatively immune to certain stress. When this is not possible, high self-esteem can enable certain people to cope better with stress than might otherwise be the case. Specific examples, which show how to maintain or increase the self-esteem of police officers, are given. 4 references. Author biographical information.

1.344 Stratton, John G. "The Big Ones—Traumatic Incidents." Chapter in **Police Passages**, by John G. Stratton, 225-247. Manhattan Beach, CA: Glennon Publishing Co., 1984.

Examples of traumatic incidents—usually involving shootings—and the effect of these incidents on police officers. Flashbacks, reexamining the meaning of life, and guilt are frequently associated with traumatic incidents. 1 figure. 9 references.

1.345 Stratton, John G. "Keeping It Together—Managing Stress." Chapter in **Police Passages**, by John G.

Stratton, 287-318. Manhattan Beach, CA: Glennon Publishing Co., 1984.

Eighteen warning signs indicating likelihood of excessive stress. Thirty-item check list of signs of stress. Twenty-item "hurry sickness" check list. Forty-three item Life Stress Chart. RISKO Chart. Longevity Game. Model plan to reduce stress. 18 references.

1.346 Stratton, John G. "Letting Go—Retirement." Chapter in **Police Passages**, by John G. Stratton, 277-286. Manhattan Beach, CA: Glennon Publishing Co., 1984.

Preparation for retirement—at least five years prior to leaving work—can help minimize the trauma many people experience upon retiring. 10 references.

1.347 Stratton, John G. "Police Stress: An Overview." Chapter in **Stress and Police Personnel**, by Leonard Territo and Harold J. Vetter, 73-82. Boston, MA: Allyn and Bacon, Inc., 1981.

Covers law enforcement stressors, effects of stress on the police officer, and common emotional problems of police. Associated with the latter are the police officer as workaholic, exhaustion, alcoholism, traumatic experiences, and marital relations. 20 references.

1.348 Stratton, John G. "Police Stress and the Criminal Investigator." **Police Chief** 46 (February 1979): 22-26.

Many things contribute to stress experienced by criminal investigators. One is having to investigate several cases concurrently and, therefore, having to manage time very efficiently. Another is a lenient court system which demonstrates sympathy for criminals, rather than for stressed detectives, who apprehend the criminals. A third is the isolation of feelings by detectives because of their encounter with death, injury, and traumatized victims. The lack of cooperation from citizens in the investigation of crime also contributes to stress experienced by criminal investigators, as does a court system whose hours of operation are usually during the day, not taking police shift work into account. Fatigue, a sixth stressor, results from the preceding stressors. Author biographical information. 1 photograph. 18 references.

1.349 Stratton, John G. "Police Stress: Part II,

Considerations and Suggestions." Chapter in **Stress and Police Personnel**, by Leonard Territo and Harold J. Vetter, 203-211. Boston, MA: Allyn and Bacon, Inc., 1981.

Four main areas are dealt with: warning signals of police stress, common management methods of dealing with this stress, officer stress reduction methods, and organizational approaches to stress reduction. Traditionally, police departments dealt with officer stress in one or more of the following ways: ignoring the officer, hiding or transferring the officer, firing the officer, giving the officer disability retirement, rehabilitating the officer. Physical exercises, diet, and relaxation techniques are vehicles to officer stress reduction. 8 references.

1.350 Stratton, John G. "Psychological Services for Police." **Journal of Police Science and Administration** 8 (1980): 31-39.

Nine main topics: professional psychology joins law enforcement, selection of psychologists, psychological screening, psychological counseling, job evaluation, selection for special assignments, management consultations, special programs, and training. Author biographical information. 11 footnotes.

1.351 Stratton, John G. "Throughout One's Career—Stress." Chapter in **Police Passages**, by John G. Stratton, 101-148. Manhattan Beach, CA: Glennon Publishing Co., 1984.

Examines five major types of stress—external, internal, police work itself, personal, and criminal investigator—and gives examples of each. 2 figures. 25 references.

1.352 Stratton, John G. "Traumatic Incidents and the Police." **Police Stress** 6 (Spring 1983): 4-7.

Main topics analyzed: officer involved shootings, typical procedures for officer involved shootings, differences between killing someone in a war and in a police officer context, the traumatic incident as crisis, and suggestions for dealing with traumatic incidents. Author biographical information. Acknowledgement. 3 illustrations.

1.353 Stratton, John G., David A. Parker and John R. Snibbe. "Post-Traumatic Stress: Study of Police Officers

Involved in Shootings." **Psychological Reports** 55 (1984): 127-131.

This research was about deputy sheriffs in the Los Angeles area, who had been involved in shooting incidents. Sixty out of 114 deputies returned completed, anonymous questionnaires to the researchers. The questionnaires were about the reactions of the officers to the shooting incidents. Flashbacks, sleep problems, nightmares, loss of appetite, fear of legal problems, and depression were common reactions. Author biographical information. Abstract. 4 tables. 8 references.

1.354 "Stress Management, Police Psychology a Growing Field." **Criminal Justice Newsletter** 15 (December 17, 1984): 1-3.

Highlights the remarks of three individuals involved in providing stress management courses for police officers. The individuals are: Thomas Granahan, East Orange Police Department, East Orange, New Jersey; Dr. Michael R. Mantell, San Diego Police Department, San Diego, California; and Dr. Harvey Goldstein, Prince George's County Police Department, Prince George's County, Maryland.

1.355 Stroud, Carsten. **The Blue Wall: Street Cops in Canada.** Toronto: Seal Books, 1984.

The author, who spent a year with Canadian police officers, writes about police work in cities such as Vancouver, B.C.; Winnipeg, Manitoba; Toronto, Ontario; and Montreal, Quebec.

1.356 Sultan, Steven, Susan Saxe and Martin Reiser. "Some Stress Factors in an Airborne Law Enforcement Unit." **Journal of Police Science and Administration** 8 (1980): 61-65.

The Los Angeles Police Department (LAPD) put its first helicopter into service in 1956. The Behavioral Science Services Section of the LAPD distributed seventy questionnaires to airborne personnel. The purpose of the questionnaires was to identify stressors affecting these personnel. Pilots, observers, sergeant/supervisors, lieutenants, and civilian personnel were surveyed. Author biographical information. 2 tables. 3 footnotes.

1.357 Swanson, Charles R. and Leonard Territo. "Stress and Police Personnel." Chapter in **Police Administration: Structures, Processes, and Behavior,** by Charles R.

Swanson and Leonard Territo, 233-260. New York, NY: Macmillan Publishing Co., Inc., 1983.

A comprehensive chapter comprised of ten major sections: what is stress?; stress in law enforcement; job stress in police officers; alcoholism and police officers; suicide and police officers; stress and the police administrator; midlife crisis and the middle-aged manager; stress and the police family; marital problems as an administrative concern; and organizational and individual programs for coping with stress. 2 tables. 64 footnotes.

1.358 Sweeney, Earl M. "Stress and Its Toll on the Public and the Officer." Chapter in **The Public and the Police: A Partnership in Protection,** by Earl M. Sweeney, 50-60. Springfield, IL: Charles C. Thomas, 1982.

Examples of police stressors: frequent changes in mealtimes, family social schedules, unreasonable and demanding citizens, walking a foot beat alone, lenient sentencing by the courts, high-speed vehicle pursuits, verbal abuse from demonstrators, and harassing phone calls at home or work. There are four ways to handle stress: eliminate the stressor, adapt to the stress, solidify family relationships, and seek outside help.

1.359 Symonds, Martin. "Emotional Hazards of Police Work." **American Journal of Psychoanalysis** 30 (1970): 155-160.

A paper presented to the American Psychiatric Association, May 8, 1969. The author—prior to becoming Consultant Psychiatrist to the New York Police Department (NYPD)—was a NYPD police officer from 1940 to 1947. 10 references.

1.360 Szyrynski, Victor. **Understanding of Stress.** Ottawa: Royal Canadian Mounted Police, 1976.

A twenty-four-page publication which explains stress. There are seven major areas discussed: nature of stress; symptoms of stress; stress in different periods of life; special stress areas and life problems facing members of police; prevention of harmful effects of stress and of "stress diseases;" the AKS (attitude, knowledge, skill) principle; management of stress and crisis; and breakdown and rehabilitation. 1 figure. 1 appendix. 15 references.

1.361 Tatar, Mark Alan. "The Police Personality and Desirable Qualities of Hostage Negotiators: An Investigation of Psychological Dimensions and Approaches to the Assessment of State Policemen Who Volunteer for Training As Hostage Negotiators." **Dissertation Abstracts International** 43: 2396B. Ph.D. dissertation, Syracuse University, 1982. Order No. DA8229021.

After personality and motivation measures were used to study police officers interested in becoming hostage negotiators, a factor analysis of the measures indicated the officers were characterized by emotional stability, extraversion, instinctual gratification, and liberal orientation.

1.362 Tenszen, Michael. "Police Who Kill—and Live With It." **Police Stress** 6 (Spring 1983): 34-35.

An account of a police officer in Toronto, Ontario who, with another officer, was confronted by an armed man in a boarding house. The officer who shot the armed man—the man had a knife and history of violence—never fully overcame the stress associated with the July 11, 1977 incident. Dr. Frank Evans, Director of Medical and Health Services, Metropolitan Toronto Police, counsels officers involved in shootings. In Boston, Massachusetts Ed Donovan, President, International Law Enforcement Stress Association, is head of stress counseling at the Boston Police Department. 1 illustration.

1.363 Territo, Leonard and Harold J. Vetter. "Organizational and Individual Programs for Coping With Stress." in **Stress and Police Personnel,** by Leonard Territo and Harold J. Vetter, 271-278. Boston, MA: Allyn and Bacon, Inc., 1981.

Six organizational and individual programs for coping with stress: enhancement of awareness and self-esteem; physical fitness: exercise and diet; biofeedback and relxation training; peer counseling; alcoholic counseling programs; and psychological services. 8 references.

1.364 Terry, W. Clinton, III. "Police Stress As a Professional Self-Image." **Journal of Criminal Justice** 13 (1985): 501-512.

Consists of four main parts: the professionalization of police stress, the study of police stress, police stress as an integrating ideology, and public perception of police stress as a professionalizing ideology. Police departments have traditionally had little or no control over factors which would largely contribute to police work being viewed by the public as a profession. For example, police departments have had virtually no control over judicial decisions. Also, police departments have had very little influence regarding local political decisions. Although the public accepts the fact of stress in police work, the public does not view police work as a profession, in the way it accepts law and medicine as stressful professions. Author biographical information. Abstract. 8 notes. 90 references.

1.365 Teten, Howard D. and John W. Minderman. "Police Personal Problems—Practical Considerations for Administrators." **FBI Law Enforcement Bulletin** 46 (January 1977): 8-15

Goes into detail regarding nine potential remedies for dealing with police stress. Four of the remedies: allow little or no beat rotation; discourage constant rotation of supervisors; require complete retraining after five years; and devise a debriefing system. Author biographical information. 53 footnotes. 38 references.

1.366 "Therapy Group Provides Range of Services for NY Police." **Criminal Justice Newsletter** 13 (November 8, 1982): 1-3.

Sal Conti is a police officer and psychotherapist in New York, where he is affiliated with Diagnositc and Counseling Services, a treatment agency for police officers and their families. Conti, who has a master's degree, patrols subways and trains, as a member of the transit police. The seventeen-year police veteran and several associates provide confidential counseling.

1.367 Thibault, Edward A. and Norman L. Weiner. "The Anomic Cop." **Humboldt Journal of Social Relations** 1 (1973): 36-41.

When police officers were compared to police science students, it was learned that anomia among police can—to a certain extent—be reduced by higher education. This paper was originally presented at the Sixty-Eighth Annual Meeting, American Sociological Association, August 27-30, 1973. 4 tables. 2 notes. 23 references.

1.368 Thomas, Cynthia. "Stress and the Weaker Sex." **Police**

**Stress** 1 (Spring 1980): 29-30.

A black, female police officer in Detroit, Michigan discusses her frustration, in trying to gain acceptance by male officers. Even after she saved her white partner's life by shooting a black man—who later died—she still was not accepted by some officers as a fellow officer. Author biographical information. 1 photograph.

1.369 Toch, Hans. "Alienation As a Vehicle of Change." **Journal of Community Psychology** 7 (1979): 3-11.

Attempts to describe the alienated police officer, and how his alienation can be overcome. Author biographical information. 7 footnotes. 1 reference note. 32 references.

1.370 Toch, Hans. "Police Morale: Living With Discontent." **Journal of Police Science and Administration** 6 (1978): 249-252.

A look at morale and organizational goals in police organizations. Author biographical information. 11 footnotes.

1.371 Tompkins, C.L. "Organization As a Stressor: A Police Perspective." **Government Reports Announcements and Index** 84 (June 22, 1984): 37. NTIS AD-A139 462/6.

A master's thesis in which the physical hazards of police work are acknowledged, and the organizational aspects of police work are viewed as also being stressful. Stress models and police cynicism are also covered.

1.372 "Trauma Team Helps Vancouver Police." **Canadian Emergency Services News** 10 (January/February/March 1987): 41.

Sergeant Larry Young, head of the Vancouver Police Department (VPD) Emergency Response Team (ERT) in Vancouver, B.C., was killed in a shootout on February 2, 1987. A post-critical incident trauma team, consisting of five police officers, provided counseling to the other members of the ERT.

1.373 Urbanowicz, Gary R. "Hardened by Death Heartened by

Hope." **JEMS** 12 (July 1987): 11.

Reactions of an emergency medical technician (EMT) to the death of friends in a car accident. Author biographical information. 1 photograph.

1.374 Vincent, Claude Louis. "The Policeman: Factors in the Construction of the Police Personality." **Dissertation Abstracts International** 36: 7671A. Ph.D. dissertation, Wayne State University, 1975. Order No. DA7611018.

The author, through participant observation, was interested in attitudes, values, perceptions, and other variables associated with the police occupational personality. This personality, although functional in a job context, was somewhat dysfunctional in civilian life.

1.375 Violanti, John M. and James R. Marshall. "The Police Stress Process." **Journal of Police Science and Administration** 11 (1983): 389-394.

Examines police occupational stressors, experienced individual stress, and police coping responses. Five hundred police officers were surveyed via questionnaire. Depersonalization and authoritarianism were measured as examples of stressors. Cynicism and deviance were police coping responses. They failed to lessen stress. Author biographical information. 3 tables. 2 figures. Acknowledgement. 25 references.

1.376 Violanti, John Mario. "Police Stress and Coping: An Organizational Analysis." **Dissertation Abstracts International** 42: 401A-402A. Ph.D. dissertation, State University of New York at Buffalo, 1981. Order No. DA-8114727.

The researcher, a member of the New York State Police, studied twenty-one local police departments in the western part of that state. He found a strong relationship between stress and alcohol use, and that senior officers experienced less stress and coped more effectively than did junior officers. The researcher, to determine this, examined two types of police coping.

1.377 Vulcano, Brent A., Gordon E. Barnes and Lawrence J. Breen. "The Prevalence of Psychosomatic Disorders Among a Sample of Police Officers." **Social Psychiatry** 19 (1984): 181-186.

This study by Canadian researchers had a sample of 571 police officers. Headaches, constipation, nervous stomach, and diarrhea were some of the psychosomatic disorders studied. High blood pressure, asthma, and colitis were also noted. When the psychosomatic symptoms and conditions of the police officers were compared to other population samples, the researchers found that the occupational stress of police work could account for higher rates of psychosomatic symptoms and conditions in police officers relative to other samples. Author biographical information. Abstract. 2 tables. 2 footnotes. 19 references.

1.378 Wagner, Marcia. "Action and Reaction: The Establishment of a Counseling Service in the Chicago Police Department." Chapter in **Stress and Police Personnel,** by Leonard Territo and Harold J. Vetter, 295-303. Boston, MA: Allyn and Bacon, Inc., 1981.

The Chicago Police Department Counseling Unit was established on January 7, 1975. The Psychiatric Advisory Board, however, handled counseling issues as early as the early 1960s. The Counseling Unit became a more flexible body, dealing with police officer problems before the problems became too serious. Six case examples are given. 1 end note.

1.379 Wagner, Marcia. "Airline Disaster: A Stress Debrief Program for Police." **Police Stress** 1 (Spring 1980): 16-20.

Over 500 Chicago, Illinois police officers were associated with work relating to the crash of American Airlines flight 191, which crashed at O'Hare Field on May 25, 1979. A stress debrief program was held for these officers on June 14. Nineteen professional people—psychiatrists, psychologists, social workers, and others—worked with groups of officers. Only 20% of the officers attended the program. The aim of the program was to prevent stress symptoms and, if this was not possible, to at least minimize their effect. Author biographical information. 4 photographs.

1.380 Wallace, LeAnn. "Stress and Its Impact on the Law Enforcement Officer." **Campus Law Enforcement Journal** 8 (July-August 1978): 36-40.

Draws the readers attention to: stress, law enforcement stressors, the effects of stress upon the officer, police work stress compared to other occupations, and methods to reduce the effects of stress. Author biographical information. 35 references.

1.381 Wallace, Paul A., Roy R. Roberg and Harry E. Allen. "Job Burnout Among Narcotics Investigators: An Exploratory Study." **Journal of Criminal Justice** 13 (1985): 549-559.

The sample for this research were 115 police officers from the San Francisco Bay area in San Francisco, California. The officers were from Fremont, Hayward, Newark, San Leandro, and Alameda County. The officers were divided into three groups: narcotics investigators, ex-narcotics investigators, and patrol officers. All were administered the Maslach Burnout Inventory (MBI). Emotional exhaustion, depersonalization, and lack of personal accomplishment were three key variables measured. Narcotics investigators had higher burnout scores, regarding most aspects of burnout, than did the two comparison groups. Five policy recommendations are discussed. Author biographical information. Abstract. 5 tables. Acknowledgement. 3 notes. 15 references.

1.382 Ward, Gary E. "Physiological, Psychological and Social Issues Specifically Related to the Police Profession." **Law and Order** 27 (January 1979): 12, 16-18 and 20.

Main areas covered: shift work, divorce, police suicide, and marital relations and family life. Other areas covered include: courts, administration, equipment, community relations, relations with supervisors, isolation/boredom, and pay. Author biographical information. 1 reference.

1.383 Washington, Brenda. "Stress Reduction Techniques for the Female Officer." in **Proceedings of Symposium, Job Stress and the Police Officer: Identifying Stress Reduction Techniques,** Cincinnati, Ohio, May 8-9, 1975, edited by William H. Kroes and Joseph J. Hurrell, Jr., 35-49. Washington, DC: U.S. Government Printing Office, 1975.

The focus is on physical ability, self-confidence, and emotional stability in female police officers. Specific psychological stress reduction techniques are highlighted. A table indicates the physical differences between males and females as related to physical agility tests. 13 footnotes. 18 references. Author biographical information.

1.384 Weaver, William C., Jr. "Stress and the EMS Dispatcher." **Emergency Medical Services** 16 (August 1987): 18, 20, 23 and 25-26.

Five effects of stress and examples of each: subjective (apathy), behavioral (restlessness), cognitive (frequent forgetfulness), physiological (difficulty in breathing), and organizational (job dissatisfaction). Altering reward systems, changing work flows, and instituting stress-training exercises can help reduce stress. Eight ways to personally minimize stress are also included. 2 figures. 1 photograph. Author biographical information.

1.385 Webb, Stephen D. **Causes, Manifestations, and the Resolution of Stress Among Police.** Victoria: University of Victoria Department of Sociology, 1979.

This report is comprised of six chapters: (1) General Nature of Stress; (2) Level of Stress and Strain in Police Work; (3) Sources of Stress; (4) Consequences of Stress; (5) Stress Prevention and Alleviation Strategies; and (6) Future Orientations to Police Stress: Action or Research. 181 references. 1 figure. 1 appendix.

1.386 Webb, Stephen D. and David L. Smith. "Police Stress: A Conceptual Overview." **Journal of Criminal Justice** 8 (1980): 251-257.

Presents a conceptual overview of police stress by examining: the environmental sources of stress, individual differences, the stress response, strain—the consequences of stress, and stress and the police. Author biographical information. Abstract. 1 figure. Acknowledgement. 44 references.

1.387 Welch, I. David, Donald C. Medeiros and George A. Tate. "Police Officers." Chapter in **Beyond Burnout: How to Enjoy Your Job Again When You've Just About Had Enough,** by I. David Welch, Donald C. Medeiros and George A. Tate, 93-109. Englewood Cliffs, NJ: Prentice-Hall, Inc., 1982.

The first part of this chapter is about twelve problems concerning police officer stress. The problems are: self-esteem, police work itself, the criminal justice system, public appreciation, public support services, people interactions, emotional insulation, emotional isolation, time demands, satisfying personal life, physical role conflicts, and status. The second part of the chapter looks at five symptoms of police burnout. They are: physical, intellectual, emotional, social, and spiritual. The third and last part of the chapter discusses four cures for police burnout. They are: physical, emotional, social and spiritual.

1.388 Wellman, Robert Jonathan. "Accident Proneness in Police Officers: Personality Factors and Problem Drinking As Predictors of Injury Claims of State Troopers." **Dissertation Abstracts International** 43: 538B. Ph.D. dissertation, University of Connecticut, 1982.

The sample population for this investigation were 240 male police officers in a police department in New England. The officers were divided into four groups of injury claimants, representing claims made between 1971 and 1981. The Guilford-Zimmerman Temperament Survey and the Mortimer-Filkins Questionnaire were two of the research tools used. This research identified an "accident prone" police officer personality.

1.389 Wenz, Friedrich V. "Death Anxiety Among Law Enforcement Officers." **Journal of Police Science and Administration** 7 (1979): 230-235.

In this study, in which the sample consisted of 120 male police officers, death anxiety was an ever-present concern for rookies and married officers with children. The author believes that police education has neglected death education. Author biographical information. 23 footnotes.

1.390 Wexler, Judie Gaffin and Deana Dorman Logan. "Sources of Stress Among Women Police Officers." **Journal of Police Science and Administration** 11 (1983): 46-53.

Twenty-five female police officers, in a police department in California, were the subjects. They were interviewed over a nine-month period, beginning in November 1980. The results of the interviews are reported in terms of the following: negative attitudes of male officers; training; rumors; exposure to tragedy and trouble; group blame; responses of other men (men who are not police officers); and danger. The most stressful thing about being a female police officer was the fact that being female was simply biologically different from being male. Author biographical information. 3 tables. 2 footnotes. Acknowledgement. 25 references.

1.391 Whisenand, Paul M. "Controlling the Stress of Management." Chapter in **The Effective Police Manager,** by Paul M. Whisenand, 259-300. Englewood Cliffs, NJ: Prentice-Hall, Inc., 1981.

A chapter dealing with many topics, including: the stressee and the stressor; the wear and tear of stress; disease; homeostasis; what happens under stress; hyperstress; hypostress; problem personalities; emotions; values; power; stress and longevity; what can be done about stress; and reading, recreation, and relaxation. 3 figures. 1 table. 46 notes.

1.392 Whisenand, Paul M. and R. Fred Ferguson. "Psychological Stress." in **The Managing of Police Organizations,** Second Edition, by Paul M. Whisenand and R. Fred Ferguson, 399-401. Englewood Cliffs, NJ: Prentice-Hall, Inc., 1978.

Long before scientific studies of stress in police work, television and movies portrayed police work as stressful. Scientific studies later confirmed what the media had contended earlier. One study was of police officers in Cincinnati, Ohio.

1.393 White, Jacquelyn W., P. Scott Lawrence, Carolyn Biggerstaff and Terry D. Grubb. "Factors of Stress Among Police Officers." **Criminal Justice and Behavior** 12 (1985): 111-128.

Subjects were members of the Greensboro City Police Department, Greensboro, North Carolina. The average age of the subjects was 35.8 years. A major research instrument used was the modified Police Stress Inventory. A demographic questionnaire, burnout scale, and a coping strategies survey were also used. Factor analysis identified three main areas of stress in police officers: physical/psychological threat; evaluation systems, and lack of support. Author biographical information. Abstract. 1 appendix. 2 notes. 20 references.

1.394 White, John Hubert, Jr. "Evolution, Incidence and Components of U.S. Police Agency Mental Health Services." **Dissertation Abstracts International** 48: 567A-568A. Ph.D. dissertation, North Texas State University, 1987. Order No. DA8713991.

This study used questionnaires mailed during the fall of 1986. The questionnaires were sent to 366 police agencies, and the useable response rate was 76.8%. Approximately 65% of the respondents had police mental health services. These services were also available to police family members. One-third of the 300 individuals with mental health degrees had doctoral degrees in psychology.

1.395 White, Steve. "The Holiday Blues." **Police Stress** 8 (Winter 1987): 6-7.

Reasons for loneliness, guilt, and other psychological conditions, in the context of the time period between Thanksgiving and New Year's Day. Dr. Lester Grinspoon and Dr. Jerry M. Weiner comment. Tips on dealing with the conditions are given. 2 illustrations.

1.396 White, Sydney W. "The Management of Stress." Chapter in **The Environment of the First-Line Police Supervisor**, by Robert C. Trojanowicz, 203-244. Englewood Cliffs, NJ: Prentice-Hall, Inc., 1980.

The main topics examined: causes of stress, stress in organizations, stressors in police and other occupations, effects of stress, managing stress, and the supervisor's role. More specifically, the following are discussed: shift work, anxiety, depression, job dissatisfaction, blood pressure, heart rate, cholesterol levels, smoking, workload, role conflict, role ambiguity, self-image, meditation, and biofeedback. 1 figure. 90 footnotes.

1.397 Whited, Charles. **Chiodo: Undercover Cop.** Chicago, IL: Playboy Press, 1973.

Three years in the life of Dan Chiodo, an undercover police officer with the New York Police Department (NYPD).

1.398 Whittemore, L.H. **Cop! A Closeup of Violence and Tragedy.** New York, NY: Holt, Rinehart and Winston, 1969.

Police work in three large cities during the 1960s: Harlem, New York; South Side, Chicago; and Haight-Ashbury, San Francisco.

1.399 Wiechman, Dennis Jay. "Police Cynicism Toward the Judicial Process." **Journal of Police Science and Administration** 7 (1979): 340-345.

The author used data pertaining to the Evansville Police Department, Evansville, Indiana. He learned that police officer cynicism decreases with length of service and rank. Furthermore, the police are a heterogeneous group, who should not be thought of as being in a homogeneous state. Author biographical information. 18 footnotes. 2 tables. 1 appendix.

1.400 Willwerth, James. **Badge of Madness: The True Story of a Psychotic Cop.** New York, NY: Fawcett Crest, 1977.

The madness of Pete Bon Viso, a police officer with the New York Police Department (NYPD).

1.401 Wilson, O.W. and Roy Clinton McLaren. "Stress Units." in **Police Administration,** Fourth Edition, by O.W. Wilson and Roy Clinton McLaren, 283. New York, NY: McGraw-Hill Book Co., 1977.

Stress counseling in the Boston Police Department, Boston, Massachusetts.

1.402 Wilt, G. Marie and James D. Bannon. "Cynicism or Realism: A Critique of Niederhoffer's Research Into Police Attitudes." **Journal of Police Science and Administration** 4 (1976): 38-45.

Cynicism in police officers in New York and Detroit, Michigan is compared, and the conclusion reached that Arthur Niederhoffer's cynicism scale does not really measure cynicism. Author biographical information. 6 tables. 12 footnotes.

1.403 Wood, Chris, Derek Wolff, John Howse, Lisa Van Dusen, Leigh Ogsten and Glen Allen. "Police Under Fire." **Maclean's** 102 (January 9, 1989): 30-33.

The shooting death by police of a black, seventeen-year-old youth, who was in a stolen car. The youth, Michael Wade Lawson, was killed by a bullet fired by plainclothes Peel Regional Police. Accusations of racist violence by police resulted from the incident. This incident and others contribute to low morale, divorce, alcohol abuse, and depression among Canadian police officers. 7 photographs.

1.404 Workman, Michael Eugene. "Police Officer Stress Events and Their Relationship to Symptoms and Illnesses: A Rating Scale." **Dissertation Abstracts International** 43: 271B. ED.D. dissertation, University of Northern Colorado, 1982. Order No. DA8213278.

Three groups of police officers were researched, and nine null hypotheses tested, in the author's attempt to predict health problems in police officers confronted with high stress.

1.405 Zausmer, Fred Joseph. "Factors of Stress in the Oklahoma City Police Department: A Consideration Thereof." **Dissertation Abstracts International** 37: 1189B-1190B. Ph.D. dissertation, University of Oklahoma Health Sciences Center, 1976. Order No. DA7619404.

The volunteer participants in this investigation were 310 members of the Oklahoma City Police Department. The author carried out his research between January 1975 and October 1975. He was especially interested in the following: blood pressure, resting pulse, indices of Machiavellianism and risk taking, and the results of a personal data questionnaire. Six conclusions and five recommendations are given.

# 2

# Physiological Factors

2.001 Almand, Lloyd B. "Fitness—At Last." **Fire Command** 51 (April 1984): 38-41.

The Foothill Fire Protection District, Rancho Cucamonga, California implemented a physical fitness program, after it realized how much money was being spent on vehicle maintenance and on the medical cost of on-the-job injuries. The program is a combination of aerobicise and weight-training, which includes a preprogram fitness appraisal. Author biographical information. 5 cartoon illustrations. 1 photograph. Profile of the Foothill Fire Protection District.

2.002 Anderson, Harvey T. "Blood Pressure Screening in the Fire Department." **JEMS** 5 (June 1980): 27-28.

Thirty-five million Americans have high blood pressure and 600,000 die annually of heart attacks. Fire departments in a number of cities endorse blood pressure screening, including departments in Homewood, Illinois; Chicago, Illinois; and Loma Linda, California. Author biographical information. 1 photograph.

2.003 Anderson, James Henry. "The Effect of EMG Biofeedback and Relaxation Training on Police Personnel Responses to Occupational Stress." **Dissertation Abstracts International** 36: 3665B. Ph.D. dissertation, California School of Professional Psychology, San Francisco, 1975. Order No. DA76711.

Twenty-four police personnel, who volunteered to take part in this study, were randomly assigned to one of four relaxation training groups. All groups completed thirty-two sessions, during a four-month period, and two hypotheses were tested and supported.

2.004 Anderson, K.E. and J.M. Melius. "Health Hazard Evaluation Report HETA 85-375-1861, International

Association of Fire Fighters (IAFF), Los Angeles, California." **Government Reports Announcements and Index** 88 (October 15, 1988): 147. NTIS PB88-224159/GAR.

After having responded to a chemical warehouse fire in Sun Valley, California, firefighters, paramedics, and police officers were affected, physiologically and psychologically, because of exposure to the fire and chemicals. Forgetfulness, rashes, and headaches were three of the problems noted in these individuals. Some symptoms lasted over a year.

2.005 Arters, Linda B. "Physical Fitness for EMS Providers: A Case History of the Hobbs, N.M. Mandatory Program." **JEMS** 13 (January 1988): 50-55.

The beginnings of physical fitness for members of the Hobbs Fire Department—Hobbs, New Mexico—go back to 1982, and to Bob Gallagher, then Director of Fire and Emergency Medical Services for Hobbs, and Michael Ross of New Mexico Junior College (NMJC). A department-wide, mandatory fitness program began in 1984. Benefits of the program became evident three years later and included, for example, savings in sick-time wages. A similar program was instituted in 1985 for the Hobbs Police Department. Author biographical information. 4 photographs. 1 table.

2.006 Axelberd, Mark and Jose Valle. "Stress Control Program for Police Officers of the City of Miami Police Department." Chapter in **Stress and Police Personnel**, by Leonard Territo and Harold J. Vetter, 279-286. Boston, MA: Allyn and Bacon, Inc., 1981.

The stress control program for police officers of the Miami Police Department, Miami, Florida has three major components: psychological, physiological, and nutritional. There are ten training sessions, each session lasts forty hours, and fifteen officers attend each session. Deep muscle relaxation, breathing exercises, jogging, and a food questionnaire are discussed.

2.007 Axford, A.T., C.B. McKerrow, A. Parry Jones and Pamela Le Quesne. "Accidental Exposure to Isocyanate Fumes in a Group of Firemen." **British Journal of Industrial Medicine** 33 (1976): 65-71.

Reports on a factory fire, which took place in November 1967, and the effects of chemical fumes on the thirty-five firefighters at the scene. Most of the firefighters experienced symptoms which were gastrointestinal, respiratory or neurological in nature. Almost four years after the fire, in which storage tanks containing chemicals were damaged, twenty firefighters had respiratory symptoms. Author biographical information. Abstract. 10 tables. 2 figures. 11 references.

2.008 Bahrke, Michael S. "Voluntary and Mandatory Fitness Programs for Fire Fighters." **Physician and SportsMedicine** 10 (August 1982): 126-130 and 132.

Fifty male firefighters in Lawrence, Kansas were studied regarding physical fitness. The firefighters took part in voluntary and mandatory programs. The author learned that a mandatory program could more effectively improve fitness than could a voluntary program. Author biographical information. Abstract. 2 photographs. 2 tables. 13 references.

2.009 Barnard, R.J. and H.W. Duncan. "Heart Rate Responses During Fire Fighting." **Medicine and Science in Sports** 6 (1974): 71.

Firefighters in Los Angeles, California took part in this research. They were connected to Avionics ECG (electrocardiogram) recorders. Emotional factors, physical work, and severe heat were listed as causes of very high heart rates. Firefighters should participate in a physical fitness program on a regular basis. Abstract of a paper presented at the Twenty-First Annual Meeting, American College of Sports Medicine, Knoxville, Tennessee, May 9-11, 1974. Author biographical information.

2.010 Barnard, R. James and Donald F. Anthony. "Effect of Health Maintenance Programs on Los Angeles City Firefighters." **Journal of Occupational Medicine** 22 (1980): 667-669.

In 1971, the Los Angeles City Fire Department began a mandatory physical fitness program for all its members. There were more than 3200 members at that time. The objective of the program was to reduce cardiovascular disease and on-duty injuries. Exercise and the Kasch Step Test were focal points of the program. Cholesterol measurements were introduced in 1972. Research results cover: Kasch Fitness Scores, blood pressure, cholesterol, and body weight. Author biographical information. 5 figures. 19 references.

2.011 Barnard, R. James and Henry W. Duncan. "Heart Rate and ECG Responses of Fire Fighters." **Journal of Occupational Medicine** 17 (1975): 247-250.

Electrocardiographic and heart rate responses were monitored in thirty-five firefighters in the Los Angeles, California area, during a twenty-four hour work day. The age of the firefighters was between twenty-three and forty-two years. The authors concluded that an ischemic condition in the heart may be related to high anxiety and inhaled pollutants in firefighters. Author biographical information. 3 tables. 6 figures. 17 references.

2.012 Barnard, R. James, Gerald W. Gardner, Nicholas V. Diaco and Albert A. Kattus. "Near-Maximal ECG Stress Testing and Coronary Artery Disease Risk Factor Analysis in Los Angeles City Fire Fighters." **Journal of Occupational Medicine** 17 (1975): 693-695.

A history questionnaire, blood pressure, skinfold fat measurements, and treadmill test were associated with this investigation, which involved firefighters from Los Angeles, California. The firefighters—ninety men with a mean age of forty-six years—were compared to insurance executives in terms of variables such as cholesterol values and smoking habits. This research suggests that ischemic heart disease in firefighters may be job associated. Author biographical information. 2 tables. 10 references.

2.013 Barnard, R. James and Joe S. Weber. "Carbon Monoxide: A Hazard to Fire Fighters." **Archives of Environmental Health** 34 (1979): 255-257.

Research which involved the measurement of carbon monoxide (CO), in twenty-five fires in Los Angeles, California, attempted to relate the findings to heart disease in firefighters. Author biographical information. Abstract. 1 table. 17 references.

2.014 Bartsch, Werner. "The Firefighters: Saving Everybody But Themselves." **Maclean's** 92 (February 12, 1979): 16d.

Points out that many more firefighters than police officers die on the job annually. Stress, associated with sudden demands, resulting in heart disease, is the number one killer of firefighters. Death from collapsing debris or from burns is relatively infrequent compared to heart disease. The Toronto Fire Department, Toronto,

Ontario has a program for its firefighters in which diet, exercise, and psychological problems are discussed. 1 photograph.

2.015 Bendix, Gilbert G. "Asbestos Exposure of Firefighters." **Journal of Occupational Medicine** 23 (1981): 305.

Abstract of a paper presented at the Sixty-Sixth Annual Meeting, American Occupational Medical Association, Atlanta, Georgia, April 27-May 1, 1981.

2.016 Bendix, Selina. "Firefighter Exposure to Environmental Carcinogens." **Journal of Combustion Toxicology** 6 (May 1979): 127-135.

Topics discussed: excess cancer incidence in firefighters; benzene and leukemia; benzene exposure of firefighters; firefighter exposure to other carcinogens (including asbestos, chlorinated hydrocarbons, acrylonitrile, and benzidine); carcinogens from wood and fossil fuels; pesticides; plastics; and multiple exposures. This article is based on a paper presented at the Third International Conference on Fire Safety, San Francisco, California, January 16-20, 1978. Author biographical information. Abstract. 1 figure. 44 references.

2.017 Bendix, Selina. "Firefighter Exposure to Organic Carcinogens." **Journal of Occupational Medicine** 23 (1981): 305.

Abstract of a paper presented at the Sixty-Sixth Annual Meeting, American Occupational Medical Association, Atlanta, Georgia, April 27-May 1, 1981.

2.018 Bergen, George T. and Curt R. Bartol. "Stress in Rural Law Enforcement." **Perceptual and Motor Skills** 56 (1983): 957-958.

A study of police officers and stress in nine, rural police departments in Vermont. Questionnaires and Spielberger's State-Trait Anxiety Inventory were administered to the officers. The questionnaire response rate was 62%. High blood pressure and indigestion were reported by the subjects. This study produced little evidence that rural and urban law enforcement have relatively the same amount of stress. Author biographical information. Abstract. 4 references.

2.019 Blankenship, Ann and R. Donald Hagan. "Taste-Testing Demonstrations for Firefighters." **Journal of Nutrition Education Supplement** 18, No. 1 (1986): S71-S72.

Concern for public safety, emotional stress, intense activity, monotonous duties, and sedentary living are associated with firefighting. Firefighters typically consume large amounts of foods having saturated fat, cholesterol, and sodium. Fire alarms interrupt one-third of fire station meals. The taste-testing project indicated that saturated fat, cholesterol, sodium, and calories can be reduced in meals eaten by firefighters, without the food losing its taste. Among the data used by the authors was data from the Institute for Human Fitness, Texas College of Osteopathic Medicine. Author biographical information. 1 figure. 2 references.

2.020 Boyd, Gerald W. "Fatigue." in **The Will to Live: Five Steps to Officer Survival**, by Gerald W. Boyd, 19-20. Springfield, IL: Charles C. Thomas, 1980.

Long hours of overtime, high case loads, time spent in court, and a second job are common causes of fatigue in police officers.

2.021 Boyd, Gerald W. "Step Two—Physical Fitness and Defensive Tactics." Chapter in **The Will to Live—Five Steps to Officer Survival**, by Gerald W. Boyd, 24-36. Springfield, IL: Charles C. Thomas, 1980.

Emphasizes the importance to police officers of aerobic exercise. Jogging, bicycling, and swimming are three examples. Aerobic exercise can be done on an individual basis or—if boredom becomes a problem—as a team effort. Two hours per week is needed to remain fit. Officer survival is really the responsibility of individual officers. 3 figures.

2.022 Brown, A., J.E. Cotes, I.L. Mortimore and J.W. Reed. "An Exercise Training Programme for Firemen." **Ergonomics** 25 (1982): 793-800.

The subjects in this study were thirty English firefighters who volunteered to participate. They were compared, regarding exercise, to mine rescue workers, factory workers, and U.S. firefighter recruits. Age, height, body mass, body fat, and oxygen uptake were some of the variables investigated. Different types of running constituted the exercise. Author biographical information. English abstract. French abstract. German abstract. 5 tables. Acknowledgements. 13

references.

2.023 Burgess, William A. "A Program to Design Better Respiratory Equipment for the Fire Fighter." in **Proceedings of a Symposium on Occupational Health and Hazards of the Fire Service**, South Bend, Indiana, January 11-13, 1971, 31-34. [Washington, DC: International Association of Fire Fighters], 1971.

Gives an overview of a program to design better respiratory equipment for firefighters. The program is a cooperative venture of three organizations. They are: the Massachusetts Institute of Technology Charles S. Draper Laboratory (MIT CSDL), the Harvard School of Public Health (HSPH), and the Boston Fire Department. Author biographical information. 1 photograph. 1 table. 2 references.

2.024 Burgess, Wm. A., Reinhard Sidor, John J. Lynch, Paul Buchanan and Edward Clougherty. "Minimum Protection Factors for Respiratory Protective Devices for Firefighters." **American Industrial Hygiene Association Journal** 38 (1977): 18-23.

A study by the Harvard School of Public Health (HSPH) and the Boston Fire Department, Boston, Massachusetts. Firefighters involved in fighting seventy-two structural fires had with them air sampling devices, which measured carbon monoxide and oxygen concentrations. Total sampling time was 1329 minutes. One hundred was proposed as a minimum protection factor for breathing apparatus for fighting structural fires. Author biographical information. Abstract. 9 figures. 1 table. Acknowledgements. 4 references.

2.025 Burkell, Charles J. "Don't Turn a Deaf Ear to Hearing Losses." **Fire Engineering** 137 (February 1984): 55-57.

Reports on noise exposure in firefighters in Newburg, N.Y. The National Institute of Occupational Safety and Health (NIOSH) wanted to study hearing loss in the Newburg firefighters. A summary of the report was released by the NIOSH in February 1982. Fire departments in Tucson, Arizona; Anaheim, California; Jacksonville, Florida; and Los Angeles, California have taken steps to reduce noise levels that firefighters encounter. Author biographical information. 1 illustration. 2 tables.

2.026 Cady, Lee D., Jr. "Program for Increasing Health and Fitness of Firefighters." **Journal of Occupational Medicine** 26 (1984): 300.

Abstract of a paper presented at the Sixty-ninth Annual Meeting, American Occupational Medical Association, Los Angeles, California, April 29-May 4, 1984.

2.027 Cady, Lee D., Jr., Phillip C. Thomas and Robert J. Karwasky. "Program for Increasing Health and Physical Fitness of Fire Fighters." **Journal of Occupational Medicine** 27 (1985): 110-114.

Looks at the value of a program for increasing health and physical fitness of firefighters in Los Angeles, California. The program was established in 1970 by the Los Angeles County Occupational Health Service. One indication of the program's success: physical work capacity (PWC) increased 16% by 1982. Another indication: the number of habitual smokers decreased by nearly half. Author biographical information. Abstract. 8 tables. Acknowledgement. 5 references.

2.028 Carlson, Gene. "The Medical Profile." **Fire Engineering** 141 (December 1988): 8.

States why firefighters should have a medical profile, which is updated annually. Indicates what type of information should be in the profile. Relates the profile to pension and medical insurance claims, and to employee morale. Author biographical information.

2.029 Carlson, Gene. "Shape Up for Safety's Sake." **Fire Engineering** 138 (June 1985): 8.

Most fatal injuries among firefighters are caused by stress. Heat, noise, and fire gases affect the firefighter's cardiovascular system. Volunteer and career firefighters can benefit from a physical fitness program. There are such programs at fire departments in Greensburg, Pennsylvania and Emmaus, Pennsylvania. 1 photograph.

2.030 Collingwood, Thomas R. "Police Stress and Physical Activity." **Police Chief** 47 (February 1980): 25-27.

Four categories of major stressors for police officers. Stress and inactivity. Stress prevention and reduction strategy. Physical program development (rest, hygiene, diet, exercise). Author biographical information. 1 photograph. 26 references.

2.031 Croisant, P. and C. Kanetzke. "Physiological Profiles of Successful and Unsuccessful Female Candidates for Firefighter." **Medicine and Science in Sports and Exercise** 17 (1985): 196.

Fifty-four female applicants for firefighter were assessed in a number of ways, including physique, aerobic capacity, and muscular strength. Abstract of a paper presented at the Annual Meeting, American College of Sports Medicine, Nashville, Tennessee, May 26-29, 1985. Author biographical information.

2.032 Curtis, Arthur V., Charles O. Dotson and Paul O. Davis. "A Simplified Technique for the Determination of Percent Body Fat in Male Public Safety Personnel." **Medicine and Science in Sports and Exercise** 14 (1982): 160.

Abstract of a paper presented at the Annual Meeting, American College of Sports Medicine, Minneapolis, Minnesota, May 26-29, 1982.

2.033 Dahlbäck, Gunnar O. and Ulf I. Balldin. "Physiological Effects of Pressure Demand Masks During Heavy Exercise." **American Industrial Hygiene Association Journal** 45 (1984): 177-181.

Five individuals, three of whom were divers, were the subjects in this research. The mean age of the five subjects was thirty-seven years. The purpose of the research was to investigate different types of respiratory protective masks and work performance. This study is relevant to firefighter health and safety. Author biographical information. Abstract. 6 figures. 17 references.

2.034 Davidson, Marilyn J. "The Coronary-Prone Type A Behavior Pattern and the Policeman: A Crosscultural Comparison." **Police Stress** 1 (Spring 1980): 39-41.

A study of seventy-five police officers in Australia's Northern Territories (NT). All the officers were male and had a mean approximate age of thirty-six years. The randomly-selected subjects were surveyed via questionnaires. The return rate was about 65%. Data obtained was compared to data for U.S. police officers. Author biographical information. 1 photograph. 3 tables.

2.035 Davis, James A. and Jack H. Wilmore. "Validation of a Bench Stepping Test for Cardiorespiratory Fitness Classification of Emergency Service Personnel." **Journal of Occupational Medicine** 21 (1979): 671-673.

The aim of this research was to validate the modified Kasch Pulse Recovery Step Test (KPRST), using a sample of 114 male members of the California Highway Patrol, who ranged in age from twenty-four to fifty-six years. Author biographical information. Abstract. 3 tables. Acknowledgements. 21 references.

2.036 Davis, Paul O., Robert J. Biersner, R. James Barnard and James Schamadan. "Medical Evaluation of Fire Fighters: How Fit Are They for Duty?" **Postgraduate Medicine** 72 (August 1982): 241-245 and 248.

Firefighters are subjected to numerous stressors. Wind chill, heat, high noise levels, and deadly gases (for example, hydrogen cyanide and phosgene) are a few of the stressors. Furthermore, protective clothes and equipment used by firefighters reduce work efficiency. Auditory, orthopedic, respiratory, and cardiovascular status should be noted in medical examinations of firefighters. Author biographical information. Abstract. 1 photograph. 52 references.

2.037 Davis, Paul O. and Charles O. Dotson. "Physiological Aspects of Fire Fighting." **Fire Technology** 23 (1987): 280-291.

A focus on firefighter environmental stressors (temperature, noise, breathing atmosphere, respiratory mask considerations, physical requirements), and medical evaluation (cardiovascular system, orthopedic status, aging and job performance). Author biographical information. Abstract. 1 figure. 54 references.

2.038 Davis, Paul O., Charles O. Dotson and D. Laine Santa Maria. "Relationship Between Simulated Fire Fighting Tasks and Physical Performance Measures." **Medicine and Science in Sports and Exercise** 14 (1982): 65-71.

The results of this investigation, which had a sample of one hundred firefighters, were reported in terms of the following: relationships between criteria measures of fire fighting ability and physical measures; prediction of criteria measures; regression equations for predicting fire fighting physical performance; and physical performance examination. Author biographical information. Abstract. 6 tables. 13 references.

2.039 Davolos, Dominick D. "Heart Problems and the Fire Fighter." in **Proceedings of a Symposium on Occupational Health and Hazards of the Fire Service**, South Bend, Indiana, January 11-13, 1971, 63-68. [Washington, DC: International Association of Fire Fighters], 1971.

Alarm reactions, threat to life, and the demand to preserve life and property are stressful to firefighters. Extreme heat, extreme humidity, extreme cold, and carbon monoxide are other stressors to which firefighters are subjected. James Kaufman discusses a computerized health program, which monitors the health of firefighters. Author biographical information. 2 photographs.

2.040 Day, Hughes W. "Be Kind to Your Heart and Live Longer!" **International Fire Fighter** 33 (February 1950): 2-5.

The remarks by a Kansas City, Kansas physician at the Fire Department Instructors' Conference, Memphis, Tennessee, January 10, 1949.

2.041 Devlin, Frank. "Fire Fighter Fitness—An Often Overlooked Area of Maintenance." **Fire Engineering** 137 (January 1984): 32-33.

Firefighter fitness can be achieved through either a scheduled maintenance program or a voluntary program. Weight lifting, jogging, hockey, and boxing can be a part of these programs. Most firefighters who die while on duty die of a heart attack. Author biographical information. 2 photographs. 1 graph.

2.042 Donnan, S. "Mortality in British Firemen: A Cohort Study With a 'Healthy Worker' Standard." **Journal of Epidemiology and Community Health** 37 (1983): 163-164.

Abstract of a paper presented at the Society for Social Medicine, Aberdeen, Scotland, September 1982.

2.043 Donovan, Dan. "'Police on the Run.'" **Police Stress** 1 (Spring 1979): 11-12.

An account of the Massachusetts State Police (MSP) Striders, a road running club, whose members run for exercise and enjoyment. Author biographical information. 1 drawing. 3 photographs.

2.044 Douglas, D.B., R.B. Douglas, D. Oakes and G. Scott. "Pulmonary Function of London Firemen." **British Journal of Industrial Medicine** 42 (1985): 55-58.

In 1976, 1006 firefighters in London were interviewed and examined; 895 were studied one year later. Forced expiratory volume (FEV) and forced vital capacity (FVC) were measured for both groups of firefighters. Respiratory symptoms were more prevalent in firefighters who were smokers than in those who were nonsmokers. Author biographical information. Abstract. 2 tables. 13 references.

2.045 DuBois, Paul E. "Promoting Physical Fitness in the Fire Service: 'A State-Wide Effort." **Fire Journal** 78 (May 1984): 51-53 and 55.

Promotion of physical fitness in firefighters in Massachusetts by means of a pilot project at Bridgewater State College, Bridgewater, Massachusetts. The Massachusetts Resource Center for Firefighter Fitness was established at the college. The center offers four services: technical assistance, "Adopt a Fire Department," clearinghouse information, and a training program. Author biographical information. 1 illustration. 2 photographs. 16 footnotes. 1 table.

2.046 Dugan, James and Ray Navarre. "How to Implement a Successful Physical Fitness Program." **Fire Command** 53 (February 1986): 40-41.

Twelve guidelines for establishing a fire department physical fitness program and five program components. Author biographical information. 2 photographs. 2 cartoon illustrations.

2.047 Duncan, Henry W., Gerald W. Gardner and R. James Barnard. "Physiological Responses of Men Working in Fire Fighting Equipment in the Heat." **Ergonomics** 22 (1979): 521-527.

Heart rate, oxygen uptake, thermal responses, plasma volume, weight change, and breathing rate were studied in eleven firefighters in Los Angeles, California. Author biographical information. English abstract. 3 figures. 15 references. French abstract. German abstract.

2.048 Elliott, S.K. and A.R. Zeiner. "Effects of Physical Fitness Training on Resting and Reactive Blood Pressures of Normotensive and Hypertensive Firemen." **Psychophysiology** 16 (1979): 200.

Abstract of a paper presented at the Eighteenth Annual Meeting, Society for Psychophysiological Research, Madison, Wisconsin, September 15-18, 1978.

2.049 Ely, Daniel L. and Richard A. Mostardi. "The Effect of Recent Life Events Stress, Life Assets, and Temperament Pattern on Cardiovascular Risk Factors for Akron City Police Officers." **Journal of Human Stress** 12 (1986): 77-91.

Three hundred and thirty-one male police officers from the Akron City Police Department, Akron, Ohio were the sample. The controls were forty-eight male volunteers employed by the city. The Holmes-Rahe Schedule of Recent Life Changes (SRLC), Taylor-Johnson Temperament Analysis (TJTA) inventory, and the Life Assets Inventory (LAI) comprised a psychosocial questionnaire administered to the participants. A blood profile, blood pressure readings, and EKG (electrocardiogram) were other variables in this study. Diastolic blood pressure (DBP), norepinephrine (NE) levels, and recent life change unit (LCU) scores were higher in the police officers than in the control group. A fixed shift system was recommended in lieu of rotating shifts. Author biographical information. Abstract. 5 tables. 2 figures. 3 notes. 64 references.

2.050 "EMT/Paramedic Fitness." **Emergency Medical Services** 18 (March 1989): 14, 16 and 18.

Five emergency medical services (EMS) personnel talk about fitness: Laryl Vanden Berg (Carroll, Iowa); Jim Segerstrom (Sonora, California); Dean Alexander (Norwood, Pennsylvania); Michael J. Jakubczyk (Hammond, Indiana); and Walter C. Kennedy, Jr. (Quincy, Massachusetts). 1 photograph.

2.051 Engler, Luther Joseph. "**Rotating vs. Permanent Shift Schedules.**" Master's thesis, Rutgers University, 1980.

Circadian rhythms and rotating versus permanent shift schedules in police officers in Newark, New Jersey. The officers were surveyed via questionnaire and only 5% of the officers preferred the rotating schedule. Eating habits and sleep disorders were also investigated.

2.052 Escobar, Martha Cecilia. "Psychosocial Predictors of Physical Indices of Coronary Heart Disease in Male Police Officers." **Dissertation Abstracts International** 46: 4057B. Ph.D. dissertation, California School of Professional Psychology, Los Angeles, 1985. Order No. DA8522848.

The subject population for this investigation was randomly selected and consisted of 426 male police officers. Three types of variables were studied: personal, environmental, and mediator. Ethnicity, marital status, and smoking are three examples of personal variables. Assignment and shift work are two examples of environmental variables. Job satisfaction and overtime are two mediator variables. The best predictors of cardiovascular risk are variables such as push-ups, sit-ups, alcohol, and smoking habits.

2.053 Faling, L.J. and E.B. Weiss. "Comparison of Acute Smoke Inhalation in Non-Firemen and in Firemen." **American Review of Respiratory Disease Annual Meeting Supplement** 119 (April 1979): 111.

Abstract of a paper presented at the Annual Meeting, American Thoracic Society/American Lung Association, Las Vegas, Nevada, May 13-16, 1979.

2.054 Fell, Ronald D., Wayne C. Richard and William L. Wallace. "Psychological Job Stress and the Police Officer." **Journal of Police Science and Administration** 8 (1980): 139-144.

Data for this study was obtained in Tennessee from death certificates, mental health centers, and general hospitals. One hundred and thirty occupations were compared, regarding stress-related diseases. Police officers had significantly high, premature death from circulatory system diseases. Police officers had the third highest suicide rate—after laborers and painters. Also, police officers had a high rate of hospitalization because of digestive system ailments. Author biographical information. 8 footnotes. 5 tables.

2.055 "Firemen's Safety Tags Sound SOS." **Science Digest** 92 (May 1984): 87.

PASS (personal alert safety system) will emit a very loud noise, when a firefighter who wears the device is immobile for more than thirty seconds. If a firefighter loses consciousness, PASS will be activated, and the location of the firefighter will be relatively easy to determine. 1 photograph.

2.056 Firenze, Robert J. "Problems Involving Hazardous Materials." in **Proceedings of a Symposium on Occupational Health and Hazards of the Fire Service,** South Bend, Indiana, January 11-13, 1971, 69-74. [Washington, DC: International Association of Fire Fighters], 1971.

Eight types and examples of hazardous materials: flammable (gasoline), detonable (dynamite), toxic (chlorine), corrosive (sulfuric acid), oxidizers (nitrates), radioactive (radium), highly reactive (calcium carbide), and etiological agents (carcinogenic). The identification of materials by hazard signal arrangement is discussed with the aid of illustrations. Also discussed is a train derailment at Glendora, Mississippi, September 11, 1969. The train was transporting vinyl chloride. Author biographical information. 1 photograph. 2 figures. 5 references.

2.057 "The Four Fives." **Newsweek** 68 (October 31, 1966): 44.

How twelve firefighters died fighting a fire in a Manhattan drugstore. 2 photographs.

2.058 Friel, James K., Anthony Gabriel and Michael Stones. "Nutritional Status of Firefighters." **Canadian Journal of Public Health** 79 (1988): 275-276.

Firefighters are often subjected to strenuous physical activity, and the hazards of chemicals and temperature extremes. The cardiovascular system is stressed during firefighting. This study, which focused on the nutritional status of firefighters, involved thirty-five firefighters from St. John's, Newfoundland. When mean energy and nutrient intakes of firefighters were determined, it was learned that more fat, cholesterol, protein, sodium, and potassium were consumed than is recommended. This study found the average firefighter to be overweight or obese. Author biographical information. 3 tables. 10 references.

2.059 Froines, John R., William C. Hinds, Richard M. Duffy, Edward J. Lafuente and Wen-Chen V. Liu. "Exposure of Firefighters to Diesel Emissions in Fire Stations." **American Industrial Hygiene Association Journal** 48 (1987): 202-207.

Experiments have shown that diesel engine emissions can produce tumors in animals. Firefighters have frequent exposure to these emissions. This research was done at the request of the International Association of Fire Fighters and the Los Angeles, Boston, and New York fire departments. Personal sampling techniques were used and it was learned that almost a quarter of diesel particulates were methylene chloride extracts. Author biographical information. Abstract. 2 figures. 1 table. Acknowledgements. 14 references.

2.060 Frost, Sidney W. and William W. Durfor. "Confidential Fitness Reports." **Fire Command** 53 (November 1986): 36-37, 42 and 44.

Bill Roberts, Fire Chief of the Austin Fire Department in Austin, Texas, established a physical fitness program for firefighters in 1984. Since 1986, a microcomputer has provided automated physical fitness reports. Heart attack and stroke risk are two of the variables covered by the reports. Author biographical information. 8 figures. 2 photographs. Profile of the Austin Fire Department. One of the figures is a six-item heart attack and stroke risk test. The test covers: cigarette smoking, body weight, salt intake, saturated fat/cholesterol, physical activity, and stress and tension.

2.061 Gardner, G.W., R.J. Barnard, N.V. Diaco and A.A. Kattus. "Near-Maximal ECG Stress Testing and CHD Risk Factor Analysis in Los Angeles City Firemen." **Medicine and Science in Sports** 6 (1974): 71.

Subjects were ninety Los Angeles (LA), California firefighters. They ranged in age from forty to fifty-nine years. This investigation did not determine why an unexpected high incidence of heart disease exists in LA firefighters. Heart disease is the primary reason these firefighters receive disability pensions. By way of comparison, a group of LA insurance executives had a higher incidence of risk factors, yet had a lower incidence of heart disease. Abstract of a paper presented at the Twenty-first Annual Meeting, American College of Sports Medicine, Knoxville, Tennessee, May 9-11, 1974. Author biographical information.

2.062 Genovesi, Michael G., Donald P. Tashkin, Sawtantra Chopra, Marshall Morgan and Charles McElroy. "Transient Hypoxemia in Firemen Following Inhalation of Smoke." **Chest** 71 (1977): 441-444.

The firefighters in this article responded to a fire at a high-rise office building in Los Angeles, California on November 12, 1974. Large quantities of polyvinylchloride materials were burned. Hypoxemia was evident in nineteen firefighters. The firefighters were examined at the emergency room, University of California, Los Angeles. Author biographical information. Abstract. 2 tables. Acknowledgement. 12 references.

2.063 Gettman, Larry R. "Aerobics and Police Fitness." **Police Stress** 1 (Fall 1978): 22-24.

A report on a study conducted by the Institute for Aerobics Research, Dallas, Texas and the International Association of Chiefs of Police. The purpose of the study, funded by the Law Enforcement Assistance Administration, was to examine the effects of physical conditioning programs on police officers. Heart rate, blood chemistry profiles, and assessment of percent body fat were some of the variables examined by the author. Author biographical information. 5 photographs. 4 references.

2.064 Gharabegian, Areg, Kevin M. Cosgrove, John R. Pehrson and Trung D. Trinh. "Forest Fire Fighters Noise Exposure." **Noise Control Engineering Journal** 25 (November/December 1985): 96-111 and 114-115.

Employees of the U.S. Department of Agriculture (USDA) Forest Service, who fight forest fires, were studied in relation to their equipment, in order to quantify noise exposures to which the employees were subjected. Measured and published data was used. Chain saws, air compressors, bulldozers, and helicopters were examples of equipment studied. Noise levels were compared to that allowable by the Occupational Safety and Health Administration (OSHA). Author biographical information. Abstract. 7 photographs. 11 figures. 7 tables. Acknowledgements. 17 references.

2.065 Gold, Avram, Wm. A. Burgess and Edward V. Clougherty. "Exposure of Firefighters to Toxic Air Contaminants." **American Industrial Hygiene Association Journal** 39 (1978): 534-539.

Members of the Boston Fire Department, Boston, Massachusetts were the subjects. The members were exposed, during ninety sample runs, to six gases: nitrogen dioxide, hydrogen chloride, hydrogen cyanide, carbon monoxide, oxygen, and carbon dioxide. Levels of carbon dioxide and nitrogen dioxide, and oxygen depression, did not appear to represent major hazards. The most important potential hazard was due to carbon monoxide. Hydrogen cyanide presented the second most important potential hazard. Abstract. Author biographical information. 5 figures. 1 table. Acknowledgements. 20 references.

2.066 Gonzalez, Frank. "Save Your Back." **Fire Command** 55 (June 1988): 38-39.

Sixty percent of injuries sustained by firefighters are back injuries. Superior techniques for general back care have been developed in Sweden. San Antonio, Texas has a Back Wellness Program for firefighters and paramedics. Author biographical information. 4 photographs.

2.067 Greene, Carroll Hartley, III. "The Effectiveness of Diaphragmatic Breathing As a Strategy for Management of Situational Anxiety in Police Officers." **Dissertation Abstracts International** 45: 1901B. Ph.D. dissertation, Virginia Commonwealth University, 1984. Order No. DA8416799.

Three anxiety reduction strategies were used with three treatment groups of police officers. The officers were pretested and posttested, and were monitored for skin conductance response (SCR) and self-report measures of anxiety level.

2.068 Griggs, Thomas R. "The Role of Exertion As a Determinant of Carboxyhemoglobin Accumulation in Firefighters." **Journal of Occupational Medicine** 19 (1977): 759-761.

The setting for this research was in a smoke-filled building, where twenty firefighters, attending the 1976 North Carolina State Fire College and Pump School, participated in a search-and-rescue drill. Author biographical information. Abstract. 2 figures. 12

references. Acknowledgement.

2.069 Gruber, Charles A. "The Relationship of Stress to the Practice of Police Work." **Police Chief** 47 (February 1980): 16-19 and 68-69.

Poor supervision; absence or lack of career development opportunities; an inadequate reward or reinforcement system; offensive policies; and excessive paperwork are examples of intraorganizational police stress. A detailed outline provides information on how to alleviate the preceding five problems. Relaxation and meditation; biofeedback; exercise; diet; and enforced vacations; leaves of absence; and disability retirement are examples of ways to reduce stress. Author biographical information. 1 photograph. 2 tables. 53 references.

2.070 Hageman, Mary J.C. "Responses of Police Rookie Officers to Stress." **Journal of Police Science and Administration** 10 (1982): 235-243.

Stress in police rookie officers was studied by monitoring vitamin c, zinc, and urinary pyrrole levels. Hugh Riordan, Director, Center for the Improvement of Human Functioning, Wichita, Kansas and Richard LaMunyon, Police Chief, Wichita Police Department, were instrumental in this investigation. An earlier version of this paper was presented at the Annual Meeting, Academy of Criminal Justice Sciences, Oklahoma City, Oklahoma, March 1980. Author biographical information. 15 figures. Acknowledgement. 30 references.

2.071 Hageman, Mary Jan, Robert B. Kennedy and Norman Price. "Coping With Stress." **Police Chief** (February 1979): 27-28 and 70.

Diet is one important way in which stress can be reduced in police officers. White refined sugar and flour products should be avoided. Coffee, tea, and cola should also be avoided. Natural foods—rather than foods which contain factory chemicals—should be eaten. Fruits, vegetables, and nuts are healthier than ice cream products. Author biographical information. 1 photograph. 9 references.

2.072 Haynes, William D. "Physical Factors: Constant Possibilities of Death or Injury." Chapter in **Stress Related Disorders in Policemen**, by William D. Haynes,

46-52. San Francisco, CA: R. and E. Research Associates, Inc., 1978.

Eating and sleeping habits, as affected by shift work, are related to the police officer's diurnal pattern. Air pollution, exhaust fumes, rain, hail, sleet, snow, hot temperatures, and cold temperatures affect many police officers, perhaps more frequently than many other people, since police work "must go on," regardless of the weather.

2.073 Haynes, William D. "Recommendations for Alleviation of Stress-Related Disorders." Chapter in **Stress Related Disorders in Policemen**, by William D. Haynes, 70-74. San Francisco, CA: R. and E. Research Associates, Inc., 1978.

Periodic physical examinations and stress reduction programs.

2.074 Haynes, William D. "Stress-Related Disorders in Police Officers." Chapter in **Stress Related Disorders in Policemen**, by William D. Haynes, 53-60. San Francisco, CA: R. and E. Research Associates, Inc., 1978.

Cardiovascular diseases; digestive dysfunctions (colitis, ulcers); hypertension/high blood pressure; hemorrhoids; headaches; psychological disorders (functional paranoia, emotional repression, insomnia, excessive sleeping, alcoholism, suicide); arthritis; and premature death exclusive of homicide.

2.075 "Hearing Loss in EMS Providers." **JEMS** 10 (September 1985): 22.

The relationship between siren noise and hearing loss was studied in members of the Houston Fire Department, Houston, Texas. Approximately 200 firefighters, ranging in age from twenty-one to fifty-nine years, took part in the research.

2.076 Hildebrand, Joanne Fish. "Stress Research: Part 2." **Fire Command** 51 (June 1984): 55-58.

Five main topics: stress adaptation, environmental stressors, psychological stressors, the stress response, and stress outcomes. High blood pressure is an example of stress adaptation. A high level of noise is an example of an environmental stressor. Pediatric death exemplifies a powerful psychological stressor. Sweaty hands, vomiting, muscle tremors, headaches, skin rashes, and insomnia illustrate the stress response. Heart disease among firefighters is a common result of stress. Author biographical information. 3 photographs. 1 figure. 2 references.

2.077 Hines, Kenneth. "Hearing Protection." **Fire Command** 53 (June 1986): 40-41.

Firefighters are routinely exposed to engine noise, sirens, and air horns. Disposable earplugs, earmuffs, and premolded earplugs can help prevent hearing loss. Author biographical information. 1 table. 4 photographs. Profile of the Chesterfield Fire Protection District, St. Louis, Missouri.

2.078 Honig, Audrey and Martin Reiser. "Stress Disability Pension Experience in the Los Angeles Police Department: A Historical Study." **Journal of Police Science and Administration** 11 (1983): 385-388.

Hypertension, anxiety, low back pain, and gastrointestinal disorders were reasons given by police officers, who were granted disability pensions by the Los Angeles Police Department (LAPD), Los Angeles, California. The number of such pensions granted between 1972 and 1981 rose dramatically. Author biographical information. 1 table. 7 references.

2.079 House, Jerry L. "Training and Physical Fitness for Police Personnel: Is There a Problem?" **Police Stress** 6 (Spring 1983): 16-21.

Reports on responses from police departments which were sent questions regarding training and physical fitness. Representative departments: California Highway Patrol, Sacramento, California; Delaware State Police, Dover, Delaware; Kansas Highway Patrol, Topeka, Kansas; Kentucky State Police, Frankfort, Kentucky; Nebraska State Patrol, Lincoln, Nebraska; North Dakota State Highway Patrol, Bismarck, North Dakota; and Ohio State Highway Patrol, Columbus, Ohio. Author biographical information. 5 illustrations.

2.080 Hutchinson, Jay. "Swirls of Hot Air Pose Risk to Firefighters." **New Scientist** 112 (November 6, 1986): 34.

Donald Haines, U.S. Forest Service, and Mahlon Smith,

Michigan State University, conducted wind tunnel experiments in order to better understand crown fires and longitudinal vortices. 1 photograph.

2.081 "Hyperbaric Chamber Aids Fire Fighter." **Fire Command** 54 (August 1987): 14.

Treatment for smoke inhalation of Captain Ralph Break, St. Louis Fire Department. After being treated at the scene of a fire, and later at the St. Louis University Medical Center, he was flown to St. Luke's Hospital, Chesterfield, Missouri, where he was treated in the hospital's hyperbaric chamber.

2.082 Jacobs, Donald T. "Alarm Stress." **Fire Command** 54 (August 1987): 18.

Recurring alarm sounds cause stress in firefighters because the alarms cue the body for action. Firefighters experience an unnecessary adrenaline rush even when an emergency response is not required. A computer assisted dispatch system (CADS) can alert only the fire units which will respond to a particular call and bypass all other units, thus preventing, at a particular time, most firefighters from experiencing alarm stress. Author biographical information. 1 illustration.

2.083 Johnson, David W., Robert J. Hammond and Robert E. Sherman. "Hearing in an Ambulance Paramedic Population." **Annals of Emergency Medicine** 9 (1980): 557-561.

The following were investigated: the amount of noise present in ambulances, the hearing status of emergency ambulance personnel relative to the normal population, and hearing loss and experience (number of years) in the ambulance service. Author biographical information. Abstract. 6 tables. 13 references.

2.084 Kirmeyer, Sandra L. and Alice Diamond. "Coping by Police Officers: A Study of Role Stress and Type A and Type B Behavior Patterns." **Journal of Occupational Behaviour** 6 (1985): 183-195.

Thirty-one police officers—twenty-nine males and two females—were the subjects. The mean age of the subjects was thirty-five years. Two behavior patterns in the officers were studied—type A and type B. Hostility-aggression, impatience, and competitive achievement-striving characterize the type A individual. Type B is non-aggressive, patient, and non-competitive. Three hypotheses were tested. Author biographical information. Abstract. 2 tables. 25 references.

2.085 Ko, N.W.M. "Responses of Firemen to Aircraft and Traffic Noise." **Journal of Sound and Vibration** 40 (1975): 287-292.

This research, done in Hong Kong, involved sixty-eight firefighters in two fire stations. The firefighters were surveyed via questionnaire, based on a study in London in 1971. The title of the British study was: **Second Survey of Aircraft Noise Annoyance Around London (Heathrow) Airport.** Among the results reported, regarding the Hong Kong firefighters, were the percentage of firefighters whose activities were disturbed by aircraft and traffic noises, and the percentage of firefighters with self-rating on acclimatization to aircraft and traffic noise. 1 figure. 5 tables. Author biographical information. 13 references.

2.086 Koyal, S., J.G. Mohler, R.C. Jung, J. Joseph and C.R. Collier. "Chronic Smoke Exposure and Work Intolerance in Firefighters." **Federation Proceedings** 38 (1979): 943.

Abstract of a paper presented at the Sixty-third Annual Meeting, Federation of American Societies for Experimental Biology, Dallas, Texas, April 1-10, 1979.

2.087 Kreitner, Robert, Margaret A. Sova, Steven D. Wood, Glenn M. Friedman and William E. Reif. "A Search for the U-Shaped Relationship Between Occupational Stressors and the Risk of Coronary Heart Disease." **Journal of Police Science and Administration** 13 (1985): 122-131.

California Highway Patrol (CHP) officers were the research population in this study. In addition to the use of questionnaires, the authors used measurements pertaining to height, blood pressure, lung function, and other variables. Three hypotheses were tested and four major conclusions were reached. Author biographical information. 3 figures. 1 appendix. 27 references.

2.088 Krohn, Lawrence H. "High Resolution Electrocardiography." in **Proceedings of a Symposium on Occupational Health and Hazards of the Fire Service,** South Bend, Indiana, January 11-13, 1971, 49-50 and 54. [Washington, DC: International Association of Fire Fighters], 1971.

Reports on a four-year study to prevent heart attacks, using high resolution electrocardiography (HRE). The study was very successful and its subjects were firefighters in Detroit, Michigan. The final version of the study was published in the **Detroit Fire Fighter,** October 1970. The author claims the report may have saved the lives of approximately eighteen men. Author biographical information. 1 photograph.

2.089 Kuorinka, Ilkka and Olli Korhonen. "Firefighters' Reaction to Alarm, an ECG and Heart Rate Study." **Journal of Occupational Medicine** 23 (1981): 762-766.

This investigation, which took place in Helsinki, Finland, had twenty-two firefighters as subjects. The mean age of the subjects was 34.2 years; the age range was between 21.8 and 49.8 years. Results of the research are reported in terms of: firefighter fitness, pulse rate reaction to alarm, pulse rate reaction to alert alarms without call out, and ECG (electrocardiogram) changes after alarm. Author biographical information. Abstract. 4 figures. 2 tables. 20 references.

2.090 Lemon, P.W.R. and R.T. Hermiston. "The Human Energy Cost of Fire Fighting." **Journal of Occupational Medicine** 19 (1977): 558-562.

Firefighters employed by the Windsor Fire Department, Windsor, Ontario were the subjects. There were twenty subjects and they ranged in age from twenty-three to forty-three years. They were examined regarding: percent body fat, muscular strength, aerobic capacity, and anaerobic capacity. They then performed four tasks: aerial ladder climb, rescue of a "victim," hose drag, and ladder raise. The tasks were very demanding, even though they were not associated with stressors present at actual fires—for example, heat, humidity, and decreased oxygen. Author biographical information. Abstract. 3 photographs. 2 figures. 4 tables. Acknowledgements. 27 references.

2.091 Lester, David. "Occupational Injuries, Illnesses and

Fatalities in Police Officers." **Police Chief** 48 (October 1981): 43 and 63.

Provides statistical data for Connecticut, California, Hawaii, Oregon, Colorado, and Wyoming, regarding occupational injuries, illnesses, and fatalities in police officers. Author biographical information. 1 photograph. 4 references.

2.092 Lester, David. "Type A Personality in Police Officers." **Psychological Reports** 52 (1983): 730.

Forty-three municipal and twenty-four state police officers were studied, regarding type A personality (high risk for heart attacks). Questionnaires, one of which was a thrill-seeking questionnaire, were administered to the officers. Age, military history, height, and weight were some of the variables examined. Author biographical information. 2 references.

2.093 Lester, David and Anthony Solis. "Type A Personality, Stress, and Job Satisfaction in Police Officers." **Perceptual and Motor Skills** 51 (1980): 890.

The Job Descriptive Index was one of several research instruments used in this study of thirty-six police officers. The study found little evidence regarding type A behaviors—high risk of heart attack—and job satisfaction. Author biographical information. 4 references.

2.094 Lettvin, Maggie. "Eating to Combat Stress." **Police Stress** 7 (Autumn 1984): 14-18.

One can combat stress by eating foods which contain magnesium, calcium, and potassium. Examples are as follows: magnesium (bran, molasses, almonds, and peanuts); calcium (spinach, salmon, and shrimp); and potassium (cauliflower, celery, cucumber, and mushrooms). Author biographical information. 4 illustrations. 1 photograph.

2.095 Levine, M.S., B.H. Cohen and C.G. Graves. "Restrictive Pulmonary Defects in Baltimore Firefighters." **American Review of Respiratory Disease Annual Meeting Supplement** 119 (April 1979): 227.

Abstract of a paper presented at the Annual Meeting, American Thoracic Society/American Lung Association,

Las Vegas, Nevada, May 13-16, 1979.

2.096 Levine, Marshal S. and Bertha Hohman. "Do Face Masks Provide Protection? Yes, According to This Study." **Fire Journal** 72 (September 1978): 52-55.

Reviews a series of studies conducted by the Johns Hopkins University School of Hygiene and Public Health, and the Baltimore City Fire Department, Baltimore, Maryland. The studies were on the benefits of face mask use by firefighters. The researchers were interested in measuring firefighter exposure to levels of carbon monoxide and cyanide. The National Bureau of Standards (NBS) helped finance the studies. Author biographical information. 3 photographs. 4 figures. 7 footnotes.

2.097 Levine, Marshal S. and Edward P. Radford. "Occupational Exposures to Cyanide in Baltimore Fire Fighters." **Journal of Occupational Medicine** 20 (January 1978): 53-56.

Occupational exposures to cyanide in 479 firefighters in Baltimore, Maryland were monitored during the six-month period, October 1, 1973 to March 31, 1974. Blood samples were taken from firefighters, as they were about to leave the scene of fires. The samples were analyzed at the Johns Hopkins University School of Hygiene and Public Health. Thiocyanate levels were studied. The Baltimore Fire Department and the International Association of Fire Fighters cooperated in this study. Author biographical information. Abstract. 7 figures. Acknowledgements. 11 references.

2.098 Lindell, James W. "Year-Round Police Fitness Training." **Police Chief** 42 (September 1975): 38 and 64.

Joseph D. McNamara, Chief of Police, Kansas City Police Department, Kansas City, Missouri, implemented a year-round, police fitness training program. The program is based on the aerobics work of Dr. Kenneth H. Cooper. Author biographical information. 1 photograph. 1 footnote.

2.099 Liou, Saou-Hsing. "Biological Monitoring of Carcinogen Exposure Effects Among Firefighters." **Dissertation Abstracts International** 49: 3706B. Ph.D. dissertation, Johns Hopkins University, 1988. Order No. DA8819084.

Two indices—one of which was the sister chromatid exchange (SCE)—were used in this research, involving forty-three firefighters and a control group. SCE frequency in firefighters was considerably lower than in the control group.

2.100 Los Angeles County Sheriff's Department. **The Physiological Fitness of Deputies Assigned to the Patrol Function and Its Relationship to the Formulation of Entrance Standards for Law Enforcement Officers, Final Report.** Los Angeles, CA: Los Angeles County Sheriff's Department, 1973.

Three main topics: medical and physical fitness characteristics of patrolmen; psychological tests as predictors of performance of patrolmen; and psychophysiological reactions of officers to experimentally induced stress. The study was done between September 1970 and the end of July 1973, and involved 500 subjects. Spinal mobility, pulmonary function, cardiovascular efficiency, and oxygen consumption were studied. The Personal History Index (PHI), Job Satisfaction Questionnaire (JSQ), and Sixteen Personality Factor Questionnaire (16PF) were three tests used. 123 tables. 60 figures. List of abbreviations. 79 references. 14 appendices.

2.101 Mann, Charles. "The New Fire Fighters." **Science Digest** 92 (April 1984): 70-74 and 99.

The International Association of Fire Chiefs, the Marriott Corp., and the San Francisco Fire Department sponsored—in San Francisco, California in October 1983—three days of firefighting demonstrations. The focus of the demonstrations were fires in sixteen mock hotel rooms. Eighty percent of fire deaths in the U.S. are attributed to smoke inhalation and firefighters have to deal with the increasing toxicity of fires. Haz-Mat squads deal with hazardous materials. The National Fire Academy in Emmitsburg, Maryland has a Haz-Mat program. 6 photographs. An inset section is entitled "Suited for Trouble." It deals with fire-suit technology.

2.102 Manning, Bill. "Hearing Ability Essential in Firefighting." **Fire Engineering** 137 (June 1984): 12.

Six points are made in this letter to the editor about the vital importance of hearing ability in firefighting.

2.103 Manning, James E. and Thomas R. Griggs. "Heart Rates in Fire Fighters Using Light and Heavy Breathing Equipment: Similar Near-Maximal Exertion in Response to Multiple Work Load Conditions." **Journal of Occupational Medicine** 25 (1983): 215-218.

Firefighters from the Rocky Mount Fire Department in Rocky Mount, North Carolina were the subjects. The subjects—all were men—ranged in age from twenty-one to thirty-one years. They participated in a fire-fighting exercise, which involved crews of two men each. Exertion levels did not vary significantly for any of the subjects: those with no self-contained breathing apparatus (SCBA), light SCBA, and heavy SCBA. Author biographical information. Abstract. 2 tables. 1 figure. Acknowledgement. 5 references.

2.104 Mastromatteo, E. "Mortality in City Firemen. I. A Review." **Archives of Industrial Health** 20 (1959): 1-7.

A review of literature concerning mortality in city firefighters examines: accidents and violence, respiratory diseases, pulmonary tuberculosis, gastrointestinal diseases, cancer, and cardiovascular-renal diseases. Author biographical information. 20 references.

2.105 Mastromatteo, E. "Mortality in City Firemen. II. A Study of Mortality in Firemen of a City Fire Department." **Archives of Industrial Health** 20 (1959): 227-233.

Canadian research in which mortality in active and pensioned firefighters—for the years 1921-1953—was studied, and compared to mortality in other men in Ontario. Among the 271 firefighters who died, the author learned there was a very high rate of cardiovascular-renal deaths. Author biographical information. 4 tables. 9 references.

2.106 McNulty, S., D. Jefferys, G. Singer and L. Singer. "Use of Hormone Analysis in the Assessment of the Efficacy of Stress Management Training in Police Recruits." **Journal of Police Science and Administration** 12 (1984): 130-132.

Forty-four male and female police recruits—mean age of 22.2 years—were the subjects in this research. The subjects were divided into an experimental group and a control group. Urine samples were used to study noradrenaline and adrenaline. Differences in mean increases in noradrenaline and adrenaline for the two groups are discussed. Author biographical information. 1 figure. 8 references.

2.107 Mealey, Michael. "New Fitness for Police and Fire Fighters." **Physician and SportsMedicine** 7 (July 1979): 96-100.

Fitness for police officers and firefighters in: the Los Angeles Fire Department (LAFD), Los Angeles, California; the Dallas Police Department (DPD), Dallas, Texas; and the Alexandria Fire Department (AFD), Alexandria, Virginia. Lower cholesterol levels, lower blood pressure, and a reduction in injuries are associated with these programs. Among the key personnel involved with the programs are: Dr. R. James Barnard (Los Angeles), Dr. Ladislav P. Novak (Dallas), and Dr. Paul O. Davis (Alexandria). 4 photographs. Author biographical information.

2.108 Moeller, Bruce J. "Medical Effects of Wearing Self-Contained Breathing Apparatus." **Fire Engineering** 138 (October 1985): 43, 45, 49 and 51.

The capabilities and limitations of self-contained breathing apparatus (SCBA) are discussed. Toxic gases—especially carbon monoxide—are the primary cause of smoke-related deaths. SCBA can prevent thermal injury to the lungs. Author biographical information. 2 photographs. 3 figures. 10 references.

2.109 Moulson, M.C., P.E. Litchfield and P.S. Freedson. "Consequences of a Sixteen Week Aerobic and Weight Training Regimen on Firefighter Fitness." **Medicine and Science in Sports and Exercise** 17 (1985): 196.

The main conclusion regarding this research was that physical performance and body composition of firefighters improved significantly, as a result of a sixteen week aerobic and weight-training regimen. The experimental group consisted of fifteen firefighters; the control group consisted of nine. The research was supported financially, in part, by the Massachusetts Department of Public Health. Abstract of a paper presented at the Annual Meeting, American College of Sports Medicine, Nashville, Tennessee, May 26-29, 1985. Author biographical information.

2.110 Musk, A.W., R.R. Monson, J.M. Peters and R.K. Peters.

"Mortality Among Boston Firefighters, 1915-1975." **British Journal of Industrial Medicine** 35 (1978): 104-108.

Among the findings in this study of 5655 Boston firefighters were the following: low death rate from suicide, increased risk of accidental death, and high rate of chronic nonspecific respiratory disease. Author biographical information. Abstract. 4 tables. 29 references.

2.111 Musk, A.W., J.M. Peters and C. Rubin. "Acute Changes in One Second Forced Expiratory Volume in Firefighters and Their Possible Relationship to Chronic Changes." **American Review of Respiratory Disease Annual Meeting Supplement** 117 (April 1978): 251.

Abstract of a paper presented at the Annual Meeting, American Thoracic Society/American Lung Association, Boston, Massachusetts, May 14-17, 1978.

2.112 Musk, A. William, John M. Peters and David H. Wegman. "Lung Function in Fire Fighters, I: A Three Year Follow-up of Active Subjects." **American Journal of Public Health** 67 (1977): 626-629.

In 1970, 1768 Boston, Massachusetts firefighters were examined. In 1974, and a mean time of 3.4 years between examinations, 1146 of the original firefighters were administered pulmonary function tests. Forced vital capacity (FVC) and forced expiratory volume (FEV) were measured. This study compares the 1970 and 1974 research results. Author biographical information. Abstract. 7 tables. 14 references. Acknowledgements.

2.113 Musk, A. William, John M. Peters and David H. Wegman. "Lung Function in Fire Fighters, II: A Five Year Follow-up of Retirees." **American Journal of Public Health** 67 (1977): 630-633.

A questionnaire and ventilatory function tests were used in this study of firefighters in the Boston Fire Department, Boston, Massachusetts. A group comprised of 1768 individuals were studied between August 1970 and January 1971. By February 1975, 211 of the original subjects had retired. The 1970/1971 studies were repeated on 109 of the retirees, who could be located. The National Institute of Occupational Safety and Health helped support this research. Author biographical information. Abstract. 5 tables. 15 references.

Acknowledgements.

2.114 Myhre, L.G., R.D. Holden, F.W. Baumgardner and D. Tucker. **Physiological Limits of Firefighters: Final Report October 1977-January 1979.** [Washington, DC: U.S. Government Printing Office], June 1979. Report ESL-TR-79-06.

Research by the United States Air Force (USAF) School of Aerospace Medicine into respiratory stresses and work capacity changes in firefighters, wearing a self-contained breathing apparatus (SCBA). The subjects were volunteers who ranged in age from twenty-five to forty-nine years, and who included both smokers and nonsmokers. Metabolic, ventilatory, cardiovascular, and hematological variables were some of the variables studied. 10 tables. 18 figures. 10 references. 4 appendices.

2.115 Myhre, L.G., D.M. Tucker and D.A. Clark. "Fitness and CHD Risk Factor Assessment of U.S.A.F. Groundcrew (Firefighters)." **Aviation, Space and Environmental Medicine** 57 (1986): 504.

Firefighters from four United States Air Force (USAF) bases were the subjects. Body fat, cholesterol (CHOL), high density lipoproteins (HDL), and triglycerides (TRI) were studied. The subjects were not very fit for firefighting, one indicator being that they were above average in body fat content. Abstract of a paper presented at the Annual Scientific Meeting, Aerospace Medical Association, Nashville, Tennessee, April 20-24, 1986. Author biographical information.

2.116 "New Hampshire Benefits Law Links Cancer Among Firefighters With the Job." **Fire Engineering** 140 (October 1987): 18.

New Hampshire is the sixth state to adopt a presumptive cancer benefits plan regarding firefighters and cancer. A firefighter's cancer is viewed by the law as resulting from the firefighter's job. The other states with this type of law are: California, Rhode Island, Illinois, North Dakota, and Maryland.

2.117 Newkirk, William L. and Richard P. Linden. "EMS Management: How to Handle Stress, Part 1." **Emergency Medical Services** 15 (July 1986): 35-40 and 84.

Stress, a specific group of physical and emotional responses, results from positive and negative, and from mental and physical demands. The Yerkes-Dodson curve is used to show the relationship between stress and performance. The curve was formulated in 1908 by Robert M. Yerkes and John D. Dodson. Stress and personality is discussed in relation to type A and type B personality. Meditation is recommended as a method of controlling stress. 3 tables. 2 figures. Author biographical information.

2.118 Newkirk, William L. and Richard P. Linden. "EMS Management: How to Handle Stress, Part 2." **Emergency Medical Services** 15 (August 1986): 34-37.

Determining cardiac risk, designing an exercise program, and controlling worrying are major topics covered. Also gives six characteristics of organizations which cause stress. 12 references. Author biographical information.

2.119 "NIOSH Warns Against Zinc Chloride in Training Smoke, Especially Indoors." **Fire Engineering** 140 (October 1987): 18.

At the request of the International Association of Fire Fighters (IAFF), the National Institute for Occupational Health and Safety (NIOSH) investigated smoke-generating devices that produce zinc chloride atmospheres. If used indoors, the devices produce smoke containing carcinogenic chemicals. Some of the NIOSH findings were scheduled for discussion at the Ninth Symposium, Occupational Health and Hazards of the Fire Service, Anaheim, California, October 18-22, 1987.

2.120 Ochoa, Ruby. "How Safe Is Your Breathing Air?" **Fire Service Today** 50 (May 1983): 38-39.

Compressed air quality standards are discussed in relation to a number of agencies. The standards are related to the self-contained breathing apparatus (SCBA) used by firefighters. The agencies include the: Compressed Gas Association (CGA), Occupational Safety and Health Administration (OSHA), U.S. Navy, Professional Association of Diving Instructors (PADI), National Oceanic and Atmospheric Administration (NOAA), and the Texas Research Institute (TRI). The intake air itself, carbon monoxide (CO), and oil vapors are sources of contamination. Air sampling kits can help determine quality of input air. Author biographical information. 1 table. 1 photograph.

2.121 Orvos, David R. "Biohazard." **Fire Engineering** 141 (April 1988): 49-50.

Biological hazards—pathogenic bacteria, fungi, and viruses—are often found in hospitals, university laboratories, and private research labs. Firefighters should be extremely cautious when dealing with a fire or related situation involving biohazards. Firefighters must take full protective measures, wear full turnout gear, and use disposable, chemical-resistant clothing, unless they have been told otherwise by a biohazard authority. Biohazardous material should never be touched, even when firefighters wear special gloves. Author biographical information. 2 photographs.

2.122 Page, Jim. "The Call Didn't Come." **JEMS** 5 (May 1980): 46.

Points out deficiencies in the emergency medical services (EMS) system in New York. The deficiencies contributed to the death, by heart attack, of Bob Schreiber, a paramedic in New York. 1 photograph.

2.123 Palmer, Stuart. "The Police Officer." in **Role Stress: How to Handle Everyday Tension,** by Stuart Palmer, 71-75. Englewood Cliffs, NJ: Prentice-Hall, Inc., 1981.

Sources of police stress and its physical and psychological indicators: heart disease, back trouble, diabetes mellitus, depression, and alcoholism. The high probability of being a homicide victim, collusion in theft, bribe-taking, and marital problems are other sources of police stress.

2.124 Peabody, Homer D. "Pulmonary Function and the Fire Fighters." **Journal of Combustion Toxicology** 4 (February 1977): 8-15.

This study found that pulmonary function varies according to an individual's race, smoking habits, age, and height. It also found that, over a ten-year period, the decrease in pulmonary function of San Diego, California firefighters was considerably greater than that of the general public. The forced expiratory volume at one second (FEV) was measured. Author biographical information. 2 figures. 6 tables. 13 references.

2.125 Peacock, Brian, Richard Glube, Marilyn Miller and

Patti Clune. "Police Officers' Responses to 8 and 12 Hour Shift Schedules." **Ergonomics** 26 (1983): 479-493.

Seventy-five police officers, who were members of the Dartmouth City Police Force in Dartmouth, Nova Scotia, were the subjects in this investigation. They were studied regarding six major variables: cardiorespiratory fitness, urinary catecholamines, critical flicker fusion frequency, grammatical reasoning, sleep patterns, and subjective indication of alertness. As a result of this research, the police force changed its shift schedules permanently from an eight-hour twelve-day cycle to a twelve-hour eight-day system. Author biographical information. 6 figures. Acknowledgements. English abstract. French abstract. German Abstract. Japanese abstract. 18 references.

2.126 Pepe, Paul E., James Jerger, Robert H. Miller, and Susan Jerger. "Accelerated Hearing Loss in Urban Emergency Medical Services Firefighters." **Annals of Emergency Medicine** 14 (1985): 438-442.

Approximately 200 firefighters from the Houston Fire Department in Houston, Texas were selected randomly for this study. After the subjects were administered hearing tests, it was learned there was a correlation between hearing loss and duration of siren noise exposure. Hearing loss could not be attributed to nonjob sources. These subjects, and other emergency medical services (EMS) firefighters, are in a profession in which age alone is not the only risk for hearing loss. This paper was presented at the Annual Meeting, University Association for Emergency Medicine, Louisville, Kentucky, May 1984. Author biographical information. Abstract. 4 figures. Acknowledgements. 7 references.

2.127 Peters, John M., Gilles P. Theriault, Lawrence J. Fine and David H. Wegman. "Chronic Effect of Fire Fighting on Pulmonary Function." **New England Journal of Medicine** 291 (1974): 1320-1322.

This study—based on data pertaining to 1430 Boston, Massachusetts firefighters—concluded that occupational exposures contribute to chronic impairment of pulmonary function. Forced vital capacity (FVC) and forced expiratory volume (FEV) were measured. The measurements were done during 1970-1972. Author biographical information. Abstract. 4 tables. 15 references.

2.128 Petratis, M.M., M.A. Williams, P.S. Fardy, T.R. Baechle, K.L. Ryschon, T.L. Fogland and L.A. Lindauer.

"Physical Work Capacity and Coronary Risk Factors in Police." **Medicine and Science in Sports and Exercise** 17 (1985): 196.

There were 186 male police officers in this study. The officers ranged in age from twenty-one to sixty years. Decreased levels of coronary risk factors (CRF) were associated with increased levels of physical work capacity (PWC). The PWC levels were estimated from maximal treadmill time (MIT). Abstract of a paper presented at the Annual Meeting, American College of Sports Medicine, Nashville, Tennessee, May 26-29, 1985. Author biographical information.

2.129 Phoon, W.O., C.N. Ong, S.C. Foo and W. Plueksawan. "An Epidemiologic Study of Lung Functions and Hearing Acuity Among Singapore Firemen." **Scandinavian Journal of Work, Environment and Health** 10 (1984): 126.

Over 500 firefighters—Chinese and Malays—were the subjects in this research, which included interviews, pulmonary function tests, and audiometry. Forced vital capacity (FVC), forced expiratory volume (FEV), and hearing threshold were examined. Abstract of a paper presented at the Third Conference, Epidemiology in Occupational Health, Singapore, Malaya, September 28-30, 1983. Author biographical information.

2.130 "Physical Fitness and Job Performance." **JEMS** 13 (January 1988): 54-55.

The American Ambulance Association, International Association of Fire Chiefs (IAFC), International Association of Firefighters, and the National Fire Protection Association have taken action regarding physical fitness. The Phoenix Fire Department, Phoenix, Arizona began a mandatory physical fitness program in 1977.

2.131 "Physical Fitness Training Programs." in **The Police Yearbook 1977**, 259-269. Gaithersburg, MD: International Association of Chiefs of Police, Inc., 1977.

Presented at the Eighty-third Annual Conference, International Association of Chiefs of Police, Miami Beach, Florida, September 25-30, 1976. The speakers were Thomas R. Collingwood and Michael L. Pollock.

2.132 Picher, Mark A. "Fire Fighter Heart Attacks." **Fire Command** 54 (July 1987): 16-20.

Between 1977 and 1986, in the U.S., 612 firefighters died of heart attacks while on duty, according to research by the National Fire Protection Association (NFPA). Five selected, individual incidents are profiled. Author biographical information. 5 figures. 3 photographs. 2 footnotes. Acknowledgements.

2.133 "'Plastic Fires' Create New Hazards for Both Firemen and Public." **Journal of the American Medical Association** 234 (1975): 1211-1213.

Victor H. Esch, Chief Surgeon, District of Columbia Fire Department; Robert F. Dyer, Medical Director, Board of Police and Fire Surgeons of Washington; and Merritt Birky, Fire Research Division, National Bureau of Standards (NBS), comment on the hazards of "plastic fires." 4 photographs.

2.134 "Police Meet to Discuss Protection From AIDS." **Police Stress** 8 (Winter 1987): 22.

The Philadelphia Fraternal Order of Police sponsored a two-day conference in Philadelphia, Pennsylvania. Approximately one hundred officers from across the U.S. attended. Protection from AIDS (Acquired Immune Deficiency Syndrome) was the theme of the conference.

2.135 "Police Occupational Health Questioned." **American City and County** 93 (December 1978): 22.

When a cartridge is fired, lead and lead compounds are emitted into the air. This results in excessive levels of lead oxide in some indoor police firing ranges. The Mount Sinai School of Medicine found elevated blood lead levels in a sample of law enforcement employees. Smith and Wesson developed a bullet which emitts up to 89% less lead and lead compounds. The bullet is nylon-jacketed.

2.136 "Police Physical Fitness." in **The Police Yearbook 1977**, 83-98. Gaithersburg, MD: International Association of Chiefs of Police, Inc., 1977.

Presented at the Eighty-third Annual Conference, International Association of Chiefs of Police, Miami Beach, Florida, September 25-30, 1976. The speakers were: Francis B. Looney, Richard W. Velde, Larry R. Gettman, and Michael L. Pollock.

2.137 Pollack, Alison C. and Horst D. Steklis. "Urinary Catecholamines and Stress in Male and Female Police Cadets." **Human Biology** 58 (1986): 209-220.

The purpose of this investigation was to study urinary catecholamine levels, monthly for five months, in male and female state police cadets. The researchers wanted to relate the findings to occupational stress. Females, consistently for five months, had lower adrenaline levels than males. Two main conclusions: female urinary adrenaline levels are less reactive to stress, and disparities in external stressors or social factors do not account for this difference between males and females. Author biographical information. Abstract. 3 figures. 2 tables. 19 references.

2.138 Radford, Edward P. and Marshall S. Levine. "Occupational Exposures to Carbon Monoxide in Baltimore Firefighters." **Journal of Occupational Medicine** 18 (September 1976): 628-632.

A look at occupational exposures to carbon monoxide (CO) in firefighters in Baltimore, Maryland. The exposures took place between October 1, 1973 and March 31, 1974. Blood samples—519 in total—were taken at 124 major fires, as the firefighters left the fire scene. Fifty-seven blood samples from controls were used for comparative purposes. This study demonstrated that the firefighters developed carboxyhemoglobin levels greater than controls, regardless of smoking habits. Author biographical information. 10 figures. Acknowledgements. 13 references.

2.139 Radnofsky, Matthew I. "Protective Clothing." in **Proceedings of a Symposium on Occupational Health and Hazards of the Fire Service**, South Bend, Indiana, January 11-13, 1971, 75-80. [Washington, DC: International Association of Fire Fighters], 1971.

An examination of prototype structural firefigher suits and prototype proximity firefighter suits. Author biographical information. 1 photograph. 3 attachments (diagrams of firefighter suits).

2.140 Rakestraw, M. Russell. "Reflections on the Death of a Fire Fighter." **Fire Command** 53 (April 1986): 14-15.

Concerns the death, in March 1982, of Mike Goff, a firefighter with the Petersburg Fire Department, Petersburg, Virginia, and the impact of that death on the remaining firefighters and chief. A civilian also died, more than twenty other persons were injured, and monetary loss was estimated at $3.5 million. Author biographical information. 1 photograph.

2.141 Ralph, Robert E. "A Close Look At Fire Fighters' Deaths and Injuries." in **Proceedings of a Symposium on Occupational Health and Hazards of the Fire Service,** South Bend, Indiana, January 11-13, 1971, 12-16. [Washington, DC: International Association of Fire Fighters], 1971.

An analysis of coronary heart disease in active and pensioned firefighters in Toronto, Ontario. Also discussed are back injuries and other related factors concerning death and injuries among firefighters. Statistics are provided for the years 1945-1970. In 1969, for example, one Toronto firefighter died of over exertion, 531 were injured, and there were 4826 days lost time. For that year, there were 16,350 alarms. Author biographical information. 1 photograph. 5 figures.

2.142 Reed, Susan and Mary Ann Norbom. "Nicknamed 'Calamity Jane,' Rookie Cop Anita McKeown Gets Nothing But Bad Breaks." **People Weekly** 24 (August 12, 1985): 51-52.

Anita McKeown is a Santa Monica, California police officer, who has experienced repeated physical and psychological traumas. Two broken ankles, a torn kidney, a broken finger, and a blow to the head are a few of the traumas. The traumas were associated with incidents such as high speed car chases and shootings. 2 photographs.

2.143 Reich, Nathaniel E. "Firefighting and Heart Disease." **Diseases of the Chest** 24 (1953): 304-309.

Heat, cold, burns, smoke, and gases are examples of stressors associated with heart disease in firefighters. Author biographical information. English abstract. Spanish abstract. French abstract.

2.144 Reischl, Uwe, Herbert S. Bair, Jr. and Peter Reischl. "Fire Fighter Noise Exposure." **American Industrial Hygiene Association Journal** 40 (1979): 482-489.

This was a joint venture of the University of California at Irvine (UCI), and the California Department of Forestry (CDF). Firefighter noise exposure was evaluated on board fire truck ladder units, fire engines, and paramedic vans. Noise dosimeters, octave-band analyses, and audiograms were used to measure noise exposures. Noise exposure was found to be excessive. A four-point hearing conservation program was recommended. Abstract. Author biographical information. 6 tables. 4 figures. Acknowledgements. 4 references.

2.145 Reischl, Uwe, Thrift G. Hanks and Peter Reischl. "Occupation Related Fire Fighter Hearing Loss." **American Industrial Hygiene Association Journal** 42 (1981): 656-662.

The Los Angeles Medical Services Division, and Oakland University Center for Health Sciences, collaborated in this investigation, which assessed hearing threshold data of Los Angeles firefighters, in order to determine potential hearing loss. The investigation took place January 1979 through August 1979. Firefighters were administered a questionnaire and audiometric examination. Since hobbies and diseases were not found to be the causes of hearing threshold changes, the changes were attributed to occupational overexposure to noise. A hearing conservation program was recommended. Abstract. Author biographical information. 6 figures. 4 tables. Acknowledgements. 10 references.

2.146 Richard, Wayne C. and Ronald D. Fell. "Health Factors in Police Job Stress." in **Proceedings of Symposium, Job Stress and the Police Officer: Identifying Stress Reduction Techniques**, Cincinnati, Ohio, May 8-9, 1975, edited by William H. Kroes and Joseph J. Hurrell, Jr., 73-84. Washington, DC: U.S. Government Printing Office, 1975.

In this research, which was done in Tennessee, police officers had the third highest suicide rate of the occupations studied. Laborers, accountants, truck drivers, nurses, teachers, and waiters were some of the other occupations. Police admissions to hospitals were mainly for circulatory system problems and digestive disorders. Author biographical information. 6 tables. 16 references.

2.147 Russell, David. "Seven Fire Fighters Caught in Explosion." **Fire Engineering** 136 (April 1983): 20 and 23.

How seven firefighters—Michael Moens, Raymond Bullard, Alan Menillo, Chester Zomzinsky, Charles Young, Charles Zadrovicz, and Robert Edmonds—survived a serious explosion in Fairfield, Connecticut on November 21, 1981. The firefighters were in a second-floor bedroom, when the explosion occurred. Each man's self-contained breathing apparatus (SCBA) and turnout coat helped save him from death. The coat is made of Nomex III aramid, a fiber made by Du Pont. Author biographical information. 1 photograph.

2.148 Sammons, John Henry. "Firefighters Occupational Exposure to Carbon Monoxide." **Dissertation Abstracts International** 34: 2752B-2753B. Ph.D. dissertation, University of Oklahoma, 1973. Order No. DA7331488.

A test population from the Oklahoma City Fire Department was compared to a control group comprised of nonfirefighters. Blood was obtained from each group for five months, at twenty-eight-day intervals. Hemoglobin, carboxyhemoglobin, and indicator enzyme assays were studied. Enzyme levels were studied by using Sigma Chemical Co. standard methods. Changes in enzyme levels indicated myocardial damage, associated with carbon monoxide, in the firefighters.

2.149 Sardinas, Anthony, Julia Wang Miller and Holger Hansen. "Ischemic Heart Disease Mortality of Firemen and Policemen." **American Journal of Public Health** 76 (1986): 1140-1141.

The researchers, using State of Connecticut death certificates, studied ischemic heart disease (IHD) mortality of firefighters and police officers. The researchers studied the years 1960-1978. The Mortality Odds Ratio (MOR) was greater for police officers than for firefighters. Abstract. Author biographical information. 1 table. Acknowledgements. 23 references.

2.150 Scarano, Steve. "EMS Shapes Up." **JEMS** 13 (January 1988): 52-53.

Looks at the benefits of fitness programs. Gives health statistics for police officers and firefighters. California and Ohio are examples of states discussed. Author biographical information. 1 photograph.

2.151 Schenk, John. "Fitness Programs for Emergency Workers Get More Support." **Canadian Emergency Services News** 8 (January/February 1985): 49-54.

Dr. Terry Bates, Toronto Fire Department; David Morton, North York Fire Department; and Dave Forfar,

Markham Professional Fire Fighters Association are quoted. 3 illustrations. 4 photographs.

2.152 Sidor, Reinhard and John M. Peters. "Differences in Ventilatory Capacity of Irish and Italian Fire Fighters." **American Review of Respiratory Disease** 108 (1973): 669-671.

Differences in ventilatory capacity in approximately 1800 Irish and Italian firefighters in Boston, Massachusetts were not attributable to smoking habits in the two groups. The researchers feel, however, that the differences may be related to body build and chest size. Author biographical information. Abstract. 6 tables. 7 footnotes.

2.153 Sidor, Reinhard and John M. Peters. "Fire Fighting and Pulmonary Function: An Epidemiologic Study." **American Review of Respiratory Disease** 109 (1974): 249-254.

A few of the research results reported include: mean height, weight, and pulmonary function by age category of Boston, Massachusetts firefighters; percent of predicted ventilatory capacity of the firefighters by smoking group; and ventilatory capacity of firefighters by objective cough and respiratory symptoms. Author biographical information. Abstract. 7 tables. Acknowledgement. 7 references.

2.154 Sidor, Reinhard and John M. Peters. "Prevalence Rates of Chronic Non-Specific Respiratory Disease in Fire Fighters." **American Review of Respiratory Disease** 109 (1974): 255-261.

Examples of data discussed: criteria for chronic non-specific respiratory diseases; prevalence rates of chronic non-specific respiratory diseases by age groups in the Boston Fire Department, 1970; and age specific prevalence of chronic non-specific respiratory disease in Boston firefighters and police officers, by cigarette smoking history. Author biographical information. Abstract. 6 tables. Acknowledgement. 8 references.

2.155 Siltanen, P., M. Lauroma, O. Nivkko, S. Punsar, K. Pyörälä, H. Tuominen and K. Vanhala. "Psychological Characteristics Related to Coronary Heart Disease." **Journal of Psychosomatic Research** 19 (1975): 183-195.

A study of coronary heart disease (CHD) in Finnish police officers. There were three groups, consisting of a total of 121 officers. The first group did not exhibit any symptoms and had a low risk of CHD. The second group was symptom-free, but had ECG (electrocardiogram) signs of CHD. The third group had symptoms and ECG signs of CHD. Subjects were administered the Personality Inventory Test, Self-Concept Inventory Test, Wartegg's Test, Rorschach Test, and the Sentence Completion Test. A five-year follow-up revealed that the third group had a high mortality rate. 5 figures. 8 tables. Abstract. Acknowledgements. 26 references.

2.156 Skolnick, Max H. and George J. Richardson. **Fire Fighters' Occupational Diseases.** Washington, DC: International Association of Fire Fighters, 1945.

Eleven case histories regarding occupational diseases of firefighters. Most of the case histories are about heart disease and tuberculosis.

2.157 Smalley, James C. "Establishing Physical Fitness." **Fire Command** 52 (June 1985): 50.

Steps to follow in establishing a mandatory physical fitness program for firefighters, and why the program should be mandatory. 1 photograph. 1 cartoon illustration.

2.158 Stapleton, Leo D. "A Program to Design Better Respiratory Equipment for the Fire Fighter." in **Proceedings of a Symposium on Occupational Health and Hazards of the Fire Service,** South Bend, Indiana, January 11-13, 1971, 28-30. [Washington, DC: International Association of Fire Fighters], 1971.

Discusses fire coats, boots, gloves, eyes, and fire helmets in relation to firefighter injuries, then concentrates on talking about respiratory protective devices (RPDs). The air mask, air purifier/filter mask, and "Chemox" mask are examples of RPDs. Author biographical information. 1 photograph.

2.159 Stewart, Richard D., R. Scot Stewart, William Stamm and Richard P. Seelen. "Rapid Estimation of Carboxyhemoglobin Level in Fire Fighters." **Journal of the American Medical Association** 235 (1976): 390-392.

The subjects were 170 firefighters from the Milwaukee

Fire Department, Milwaukee, Wisconsin. Emergency medical technicians (EMTs) from the department were instructed how to collect breath samples, how to analyze the samples, and how to interpret the breath-carbon monoxide (CO) data. The procedure, which can be done in 1.5 minutes, enables a firefighter to rapidly determine carboxyhemoglobin level. Author biographical information. Abstract. 1 table. 2 figures. 19 references.

2.160 Stilwell, J.A. and P.J. Stilwell. "Sickness Absence in an Ambulance Service." **Journal of the Society of Occupational Medicine** 34 (1984): 96-99.

This British study, which spanned two years, examined absence due to illness in the West Midlands Metropolitan Ambulance Service. The reasons for absence were compared to reasons for absence in the post office and fire service. The trend noted by the authors indicated more frequent, but shorter spells of absence. Musculoskeletal injury was the main reason for absence in the ambulance service. Author biographical information. Abstract. 2 tables. 2 figures. Acknowledgement. 3 references.

2.161 Sukay, Lawrence D. "Aerobic Dancing." **Fire Command** 52 (February 1985): 20-22.

A look at the origin and growth of aerobic dancing, as a method of physical fitness, at the Greensburg Volunteer Fire Department, Greensburg, Pennsylvania. Author biographical information. 8 photographs. Profile of the Greensburg Volunteer Fire Department.

2.162 Sultan, Steven Ellis. "The Use of Job Performance, Medical Fitness, Psychological Measures, and Selected Non-Work Factors to Distinguish Stress Disabled Police Officers From Physically Disabled and Currently Active Police Officers." **Dissertation Abstracts International** 40: 1917B-1918B. Ph.D. dissertation, United States International University, 1979. Order No. DA7920534.

The author used a historical-comparative approach in this study. Job performance, home environment, and health of three types of police officers were studied. Stress disabled, physically disabled, and currently active police officers were examined. Poorer job performance, less stable home life, and poorer health was found in the stress disabled officers.

2.163 Superko, H. Robert, Edward Bernauer and John Voss. "Effects of a Mandatory Health Screening and Physical Maintenance Program for Law Enforcement Officers." **Physician and SportsMedicine** 16 (September 1988): 99-102, 104, 106 and 109.

Reports on a program in which approximately 4500 California Highway Patrol (CHP) officers participated. The officers took part—over an eighteen-month period—in the Health and Physical Performance Program (HPPP). Results of the program are discussed in terms of: physiological variables (for example, heart rate, body fat, blood pressure); ergometer test; medical referrals and job actions; sick leave and injuries; body fat and injuries; and coronary heart disease (CHD). Author biographical information. 1 photograph. 4 tables. 3 figures. Acknowledgement. 27 references.

2.164 Takano, Takehito and Hiroshi Maeda. "Exposure of Firefighters to Carbon Monoxide." **Journal of Combustion Toxicology** 8 (May 1981): 89-95.

A Japanese study in which the subjects were 164 firefighters of the Tokyo Fire Defense Board. All the subjects were volunteers and all were male. One hundred and seventeen of the subjects were smokers; forty-seven were nonsmokers. Harmful levels of carbon monoxide (CO) were inhaled by a significant number of firefighters during firefighting. This paper was presented at the Ninth Asian Conference on Occupational Health, Seoul. Author biographical information. Abstract. 4 figures. 14 references.

2.165 Tashkin, Donald P., Michael G. Genovesi, Sawtantra Chopra, Anne Coulson and Michael Simmons. "Respiratory Status of Los Angeles Firemen: One-Month Follow-Up After Inhalation of Dense Smoke." **Chest** 71 (1977): 445-449.

The firefighters in this article had responded to a fire in a high-rise office building in Los Angeles, California on November 12, 1974. They were exposed, at that time, to combustion products of polyvinylchloride. This article reports on questionnaire results and pulmonary function tests administered to the firefighters a month after the initial exposure. A month earlier, nineteen firefighters had exhibited evidence of hypoxemia. Author biographical information. Abstract. 2 tables. Acknowledgement. 21 references.

2.166 Tepper, Allison. "A Follow-Up Study of Chronic

Respiratory Disease in Baltimore City Firefighters." **Dissertation Abstracts International** 47: 1511B. Ph.D. dissertation, Johns Hopkins University, 1986. Order No. DA8616006.

A health survey of approximately 700 firefighters in Baltimore, Maryland was carried out in the mid-1970s. This dissertation is a follow-up to that survey. The author used questionnaires, spirometry, and personnel records. Cigarette smoking, persistent cough, persistent phlegm, breathlessness, and ammonia exposure were investigated. The author concluded that, relatively speaking, disability related to chronic respiratory disease is not common in Baltimore firefighters.

2.167 Terry, W. Clinton, III. "Police Stress: The Empirical Evidence." **Journal of Police Science and Administration** 9 (1981): 61-75.

Examines job-related stressors, physiological effects of police stress (cardiovascular disease and diabetes mellitus), and other effects of police stress (divorce and suicide). Author biographical information. 14 footnotes. 5 tables. Acknowledgement. 67 references.

2.168 Thomas, Donald M. "The Smoke Inhalation Problem." in **Proceedings of a Symposium on Occupational Health and Hazards of the Fire Service,** South Bend, Indiana, January 11-13, 1971, 21-27. [Washington, DC: International Association of Fire Fighters], 1971.

About 80% of fire victims die of smoke inhalation. A table indicates changes in pulmonary function after smoke exposure. Another table gives data about changes in pulmonary function after exposure to pulmonary irritants. Author biographical information. 1 photograph. 79 references.

2.169 Thomas, Phillip C., Lee D. Cady, Eugene R. O'Connell, David P. Bischoff and Rhona Kantor Kershnar. "Heart Disease Risk Factors in Los Angeles County Safety Personnel." **Journal of Occupational Medicine** 21 (1979): 683-687.

Age, sex, family history, blood pressure, cholesterol, weight, smoking, and exercise were studied in over 4000 Los Angeles County safety personnel. Lifeguards, firefighters, sheriffs, and marshals were the safety personnel who participated. The purpose of the study was to develop a cardiac risk index, which could be used to identify individuals likely to develop coronary disease. Author biographical information. Abstract. 1 figure. 6 tables. Acknowledgements. 8 references.

2.170 Tomasian, A., K. Fogarty and K.M. LaFond. "Prevalence of Lung Disease in Cambridge Firefighters." **American Review of Respiratory Disease Annual Meeting Supplement** 125 (April 1982): 164.

Abstract of a paper presented at the Annual Meeting, American Thoracic Society, Los Angeles, California, May 15-18, 1982.

2.171 "Treating Patients Who Might Have AIDS." **Fire Command** 51 (February 1984): 8.

Facts and figures for firefighters and paramedics, regarding patients who might have AIDS (Acquired Immune Deficiency Syndrome). Some of the advice is as follows: avoid direct contact with open wounds, use disposable plastic or rubber gloves, clean blood spills with household bleach, use bag-valve resuscitators for cardiopulmonary resuscitation, and do not eat or smoke until hands are washed.

2.172 Treitman, Robert D., William A. Burgess and Avram Gold. "Air Contaminants Encountered by Firefighters." **American Industrial Hygiene Association Journal** 41 (1980): 796-802.

A personal air sampler was used by firefighters in over 200 fires in Boston, Massachusetts. The contaminants measured were: carbon monoxide, carbon dioxide, nitrogen dioxide, hydrogen chloride, hydrogen cyanide, acrolein, and benzene. Carbon monoxide and acrolein were the most hazardous air contaminants noted. It is recommended that the data in this research not be extrapolated to non-structural fires, since other fires—such as brush—would likely involve different contaminants. Respirators, however, should be worn at all structural fires. Abstract. Author biographical information. 2 tables. 9 figures. Acknowledgements. 17 references.

2.173 Tubbs, Randy L. "Occupational Noise Exposure." **Fire Command** 54 (June 1987): 36-37.

The National Institute for Occupational Safety and Health (NIOSH) has, since 1980, been interested in firefighter hearing loss from noise exposure. Warning devices and power tools can cause firefighter hearing loss. There are a number of ways to reduce noise levels. These ways include: the retrofitting of existing equipment, the use of acoustical sound damping materials, the introduction of new work practices, and the use of vibration isolators. Air horns, for example, should be placed to the front or side of a vehicle's cab. Author biographical information. 3 photographs. 1 figure. 2 footnotes.

2.174 Tucker, D.M. and L.G. Myhre. "Residual Lung Volumes of U.S.A.F. Firefighters in Relation to Age." **Aviation, Space and Environmental Medicine** 57 (1986): 505.

The subjects were 176 United States Air Force (USAF) firefighters, who ranged in age from eighteen to fifty-four years. Abstract of a paper presented at the Annual Scientific Meeting, Aerospace Medical Association, Nashville, Tennessee, April 20-24, 1986. Author biographical information.

2.175 Unger, Kenneth M., Richard M. Snow, Jorge M. Mestas and Warren C. Miller. "Smoke Inhalation in Firemen." **Thorax** 35 (1980): 838-842.

A chemical warehouse near Houston, Texas was consumed by fire. All the chemicals stored at the warehouse were chlorinated hydrocarbons. One hundred and sixty of the 175 firefighters, who extinguished the fire, later reported to hospital emergency rooms. Cough, shortness of breath, and nausea were typical complaints. Thirty firefighters were studied, regarding pulmonary function, immediately after the fire and six weeks and eighteen months later. Predicted values and control subjects were compared to the thirty firefighters. Author biographical information. Abstract. 3 tables. 2 figures. 17 references.

2.176 Violanti, John M., John E. Vena and James R. Marshall. "Disease Risk and Mortality Among Police Officers: New Evidence and Contributing Factors." **Journal of Police Science and Administration** 14 (1986): 17-23.

A study of 2376 police officers in Buffalo, New York, who had been employed for at least five years between 1950 and 1979. Voter registration records, city directories, obituaries, and other information sources were used to obtain data about the officers. A few of the specific results of the research: mortality from specific causes among the police officers between 1950 and 1979, mortality from malignant neoplasms by site, and cause-specific mortality by number of years worked as a police officer. Author biographical information. 5 tables. 29 references.

2.177 Volkamer, Curtis W. and Harold P. Sullivan. "Injuries Sustained by Fire Fighters in the 1970s." in **Proceedings of a Symposium on Occupational Health and Hazards of the Fire Service,** South Bend, Indiana, January 11-13, 1971, 85-88. [Washington, DC: International Association of Fire Fighters], 1971.

Looks at injuries sustained by firefighters from the Chicago Fire Department, Chicago, Illinois. Author biographical information. 2 photographs.

2.178 Washburn, Arthur E. and David W. Harlow. "Multiple Fire Fighter Death Incidents." **Fire Service Today** 50 (October 1983): 11-13.

Nine multiple firefighter death incidents in the U.S. in chronological order: March 10, 1941 (thirteen killed in Brockton, Massachusetts); April 16, 1947 (twenty-six killed in Texas City, Texas); October 28, 1954 (ten killed in Philadelphia, Pennsylvania); August 18, 1959 (five killed in Kansas City, Kansas); January 28, 1961 (nine killed in Chicago, Illinois); October 17, 1966 (twelve killed in New York); June 17, 1972 (nine killed in Boston, Massachusetts); July 5, 1973 (twelve killed in Kingman, Arizona); and August 17, 1975 (eight killed in Philadelphia). Author biographical information. 9 photographs.

2.179 Weber, Kim. "Wellness At Work." **Fire Command** 55 (June 1988): 52-56.

A physical fitness program was started in 1981 in the Jeffersontown Fire Protection District, Jeffersontown, Kentucky. Lieutenant Colonel Randy Lawson and Major Bill Molthop were the originators of the program. Some of the program's requirements are the following: chin-ups, sit-ups, push-ups, treadmill stress test, chest x-ray, and eye examination. Author biographical information. 1 photograph.

2.180 Weiss, S., R.D. Hagan, R.L. Kaman, S.C. Taylor and R.M. Woodworth. "Age-Related Changes of Coronary Heart Disease Risk Factors in Municipal Firefighters." **Medicine and Science in Sports and Exercise** 16 (1984): 195.

Over 600 male members of the Fort Worth Fire Department, Fort Worth, Texas were the study sample. Cholesterol, body fat, and blood pressure were three important variables studied. Firefighters between forty and fifty years of age had increased frequency of ill health indicators. Abstract of a paper presented at the Annual Meeting, American College of Sports Medicine, San Diego, California, May 23-26, 1984. Author biographical information.

2.181 White, Mary Kay and Thomas K. Hodous. "Physiological Responses to the Wearing of Fire Fighter's Turnout Gear With Neoprene and GORE-TEX Barrier Liners." **American Industrial Hygiene Association Journal** 49 (1988): 523-530.

Eight male paid volunteers—mean age of 26.8 years—were the subjects in this research. All were nonsmokers and were firefighters or emergency services personnel. They participated in a double-blind study, in which physiological responses to the wearing of turnout gear, with either a neoprene or GORE-TEX barrier liner, were measured. Heart rate, skin temperature, and sweat rate were a few of the variables measured by the researcher. Author biographical information. Abstract. 4 figures. 4 tables. Acknowledgements. 33 references.

2.182 White, Sydney William. "The Effects of Shift Rotation on Police Job Stress." **Dissertation Abstracts International** 42: 867A. Ph.D. dissertation, Michigan State University, 1981. Order No. DA8117279.

Fourteen stress and strain variables were measured in a sample of thirty-five police officers in a midwestern U.S. police department. A control group consisted of ten officers. Of the fourteen variables tested, there were significant differences between the two groups for only three variables.

2.183 Wilkinson, Charles B. "Aftermath of a Disaster: The Collapse of the Hyatt Regency Hotel Skywalks." **American Journal of Psychiatry** 140 (1983): 1134-1139.

At approximately 7:00 p.m. on July 17, 1981, in Kansas City, Missouri, two skywalk bridges collapsed in the Hyatt Regency Hotel. One hundred and fourteen people died; more than 200 were injured. This article reports on a questionnaire survey of victims, observers, and rescuers. A table lists twenty symptoms experienced by the subjects. Repeated recollections of the disaster was the most frequent symptom. Difficulty concentrating was the tenth most frequent symptom, anger was the fifteenth, and diminished sexual interest was the twentieth. Author biographical information. Abstract. Acknowledgements. 1 table. 6 references.

2.184 Wood, Steven D., Robert Kreitner, Glenn M. Friedman, Mark Edwards and Margaret A. Sova. "Cost-Effective Wellness Screening: A Case Study of 4,524 Law Enforcement Officers." **Journal of Police Science and Administration** 10 (1982): 273-278.

The Health Evaluation and Longevity Planning Foundation (HELP) of Tempe, Arizona evaluated the health of approximately one hundred California Highway Patrol (CHP) officers. The CHP was interested in objective physical fitness standards for its members. This article reports on the variables studied: fatness, blood pressure, cholesterol, glucose, stress, physical exercise, smoking, physician referrals, and general wellness assessment. The article has six conclusions. Author biographical information. 1 table. 10 references.

2.185 Xander, David A. "Body Fluid Replacement." **Fire Command** 54 (May 1987): 44 and 47.

Emphasizes the potential danger to firefighters of hypohydration, the depletion of body fluids. The greater the depletion, the greater the danger to health, thirst being an early indicator of fluid depletion. Other signs of increasing importance are: headache, loss of appetite, impatience, vertigo, spasticity, cyanosis, and inability to swallow. Author biographical information. 1 photograph. 3 footnotes.

2.186 Yankovich, Donald. "A Program to Design Better Respiratory Equipment for the Fire Fighter." in **Proceedings of a Symposium on Occupational Health and Hazards of the Fire Service,** South Bend, Indiana, January 11-13, 1971, 35-41. [Washington, DC: International Association of Fire Fighters], 1971.

The author uses twelve figures in his discussion of the development of a respiratory protective device (RPD) for firefighters. Author biographical information. 1 photograph. 1 reference.

2.187 Zacharewicz, Rick. "Exercise Is Important for Firefighters' Health." **Canadian Emergency Services News** 8 (July/August 1985): 60-63.

Talks about the Eighteenth Annual Educational Seminar, Municipal Fire Department Instructors Association, Toronto, Ontario, June 2-5, 1985. Back strain was described as the number one injury in firefighters. Exercise can eliminate this injury. Dr. Eric Taylor and Dr. Terence Bates were two of the attendees. 6 illustrations. 8 photographs.

2.188 Zatz, Arline. "Is Your Emergency Vehicle a Health Hazard?" **Emergency** 15 (October 1983): 29-31.

The near-death by carbon monoxide (CO) poisoning of John M. Gaughran, Captain, Herbertsville First Aid Squad, Bricktown, New Jersey. Gaughran slept in the back of an ambulance while it was driven sixty miles, after an emergency call. Later, CO test strips revealed the ambulance was loaded with carbon monoxide. Headaches, yawning, and vomiting are a few of the symptoms of low levels of CO poisoning. Twitching, dilated pupils, and erratic breathing are three signs of higher doses of CO. Exhaust systems, rear windows, gaskets, and box corner posts are common causes of CO entry in ambulances. Ten ways to check for CO entering an ambulance are discussed.

# 3

# The Family

3.001 Baldwin, Roger. "Family, Friends, and Neighbors." Chapter in **Inside a Cop: Tensions in the Public and Private Lives of the Police,** by Roger Baldwin, 32-55. Pacific Grove, CA: Boxwood Press, 1977.

Shift work, divorce, suspiciousness, children, and policewomen are the main topics covered. 4 photographs. 12 notes.

3.002 Beegan, Joanne. "Letter to a Rookie's Wife." Chapter in **Handbook for Law Enforcement Wives,** edited by Barbara E. Webber, 91-98. Chicago, IL: L.E. Publishers, Inc., 1974.

Nine things the wife of a rookie police officer should know.

3.003 Brandreth, Dorothy. "Stress and the Policeman's Wife." **Police Stress** 1 (Fall 1978): 41-42.

A nurse writes about the sources of her anxiety, regarding her husband's career as a police officer. 2 photographs.

3.004 Brinegar, Jerry L. "The Family Connection." **Police Stress** 1 (Spring 1979): 19.

Burnout in the police marriage. Author biographical information. 1 photograph.

3.005 Burke, William J., Jr. "The Man's Viewpoint." Chapter in **Handbook for Law Enforcement Wives,** edited by Barbara E. Webber, 109-114. Chicago, IL: L.E. Publishers, Inc., 1974.

States why a police officer can usually communicate

more effectively with his partner, or another officer, than with his own wife. Discusses what an officer prefers to tell his wife about his work, and what he prefers not to tell her.

3.006 Cain, Maureen E. "Interdependence With Family—Marital Integration and Domestic Life." Chapter in **Police Human Relations**, edited by George Henderson, 180-198. Springfield, IL: Charles C. Thomas, 1981.

Compares the views of urban and rural police officers and their wives, regarding police work. Data was obtained through interviews. Information about children in police marriages is also incldued. 11 tables. 3 references.

3.007 Came, Barry, Derek Wolff, John House, Anne Steacy and Lynne Thomas. "A Difficult Job to Take Home." **Maclean's** 102 (January 9, 1989): 36-37.

The Metropolitan Toronto Police Wives Association helps its members learn about their spouses' job. The aim is to help counter pressures responsible for divorce in police marriages. A breakdown in communication between spouses is largely responsible for divorce. 2 photographs.

3.008 Cheek, Frances E. "The 'Stress Carrier' in the Family Setting." Chapter in **Stress Management for Correctional Officers and Their Families**, by Frances E. Cheek, 71-78. College Park, MD: American Correctional Association, 1984.

How correctional stress is carried home, changes in personal style and life habits as a result of working in corrections, denial of stress-related problems, and family stress training. Includes ten things officers can do to reduce personal and family stress, and ten things families can do to help officers cope with stress. 2 photographs.

3.009 Chomiak, Rosemary. "Life in Chicago." Chapter in **Handbook for Law Enforcement Wives**, edited by Barbara E. Webber, 99-102. Chicago, IL: L.E. Publishers, Inc., 1974.

Shift work, time spent in court, and brutality against police are a few of the things this police officer's wife does not like.

3.010 Colson, Diana. "A Wife's Way of Coping." **Police Stress** 1 (Spring 1979): 15-16.

The comments of a police wife to other police wives at the Massachusetts Police Academy. Author biographical information. 1 photograph.

3.011 Danto, Bruce L. "A Study: Bereavement and the Widows of Slain Officers." **Police Chief** 41 (February 1974): 51-57.

Ten widows, whose husbands had, prior to being slain, been police officers with the Detroit Police Department, Detroit, Michigan, were interviewed over a four-month period. Eight of the widows were white; two were black. The youngest at widowhood was nineteen years old, the oldest, forty-six. Eight of the dead police officers were white; two were black. The youngest officer to be slain was twenty-two years old, the oldest, forty-seven. All the widows appreciated the help they received from the Detroit Police Officers' Wives' Auxiliary (DPOWA). Author biographical information. Acknowledgements. 1 photograph. 5 footnotes.

3.012 Durner, James A., Mark A. Kroeker, Charles R. Miller and William R. Reynolds. "Divorce: Another Occupational Hazard." Chapter in **Stress and Police Personnel**, by Leonard Territo and Harold J. Vetter, 251-262. Boston, MA: Allyn and Bacon, Inc., 1981.

Gives police divorce rates for a number of U.S. cities, including: Los Angeles, California; Salt Lake City, Utah; Baltimore, Maryland; and Chicago, Illinois. Causative factors for divorce are discussed. Five recommended programs for dealing with police divorce are outlined. 15 references.

3.013 Giza, Joanne. "A Policeman's Lot." **Newsweek** 96 (November 24, 1980): 31.

The wife of a Baltimore, Maryland police officer describes the changes she saw in her husband from the time he joined the police department and worked in a radio car, until the time he accepted an administrative position at headquarters. She describes how, over a period of time, he told her less and less about his day's work. He became a different person in a number of ways. Author biographical information. 1 photograph.

3.014 Golesh, Russell. "Thank God for a Wife Who Cares." **Police Stress** 1 (Spring 1979): 17-18.

The positive value of being able to talk to one's spouse about stress-related situations at work. The author, a U.S. Customs patrol officer, experienced the stress of seeing a wounded fellow officer, shortly after the officer had been shot. Author biographical information. 2 photographs.

3.015 Hageman, Mary J.C. "Occupational Stress and Marital Relationships." **Journal of Police Science and Administration** 6 (1978): 402-412.

Law officers and their spouses, or spouses-to-be, were asked the same questions, regarding marital satisfaction. This approach enabled the author to control the study population for marital status and length of employment as a law officer. The male participants were attendees at the Providence Heights Conference Center, Issaquah, Washington, where they attended a fourteen-week course of studies. Two types of conflict—intra-role and inter-role—were examined. Detachment, repression, resentment, and job commitment were major variables researched. Author biographical information. 3 figures. 6 tables. 27 footnotes.

3.016 Hanna, Marilyn. "Trooper's Widow Says Thanks." **Police Stress** 6 (Spring 1983): 35.

The text of a letter by Marilyn Hanna, whose husband, Massachusetts State Trooper George Hanna, was shot to death, when he routinely stopped a car. Hanna's widow expresses her thanks to the police officers and other individuals, who gave her support because of her husband's death.

3.017 Hightshoe, Nancy and Robert Hightshoe. "The St. Louis County Department of Police Police Family Program." **Police Chief** 45 (April 1978): 34, 36 and 95.

Describes in detail the three sessions which make up the St. Louis County Department of Police, Police Family Program. The program was designed by the Greater St. Louis Police Academy (GSPA). Author biographical information. 2 photographs.

3.018 James, Pat and Martha Nelson. "Dimension for Survival." Chapter in **Police Wife: How to Live With the Law and**

**Like It,** by Pat James and Martha Nelson, 36-43. Springfield, IL: Charles C. Thomas, 1975.

Work life, marriage and home life, and a third dimension for surviving the police marriage. The third dimension can be any number of activities, ranging from volunteer work to solo activities for either spouse.

3.019 James, Pat and Martha Nelson. "Handling That Anxiety." Chapter in **Police Wife: How to Live With the Law and Like It,** by Pat James and Martha Nelson, 97-109. Springfield, IL: Charles C. Thomas, 1975.

How the wives of police officers can decrease their anxiety about staying at home alone at night. A watchdog, course in self-defense, weapon or police radio can give some wives a greater sense of security.

3.020 James, Pat and Martha Nelson. "It's No Crime to be Married to a Cop!" Chapter in **Police Wife: How to Live With the Law and Like It,** by Pat James and Martha Nelson, 110-115. Springfield, IL: Charles C. Thomas, 1975.

Focuses on the advantages of a police officer's work, and emphasizes the benefits to a woman of being married to a police officer.

3.021 James, Pat and Martha Nelson. "Love Me Love My Work." Chapter in **Police Wife: How to Live With the Law and Like It,** by Pat James and Martha Nelson, 3-12. Springfield, IL: Charles C. Thomas, 1975.

Reasons for becoming a police officer, selection of recruits, training, types of police work, orientation programs for wives/families.

3.022 James, Pat and Martha Nelson. "Make Your Home a Haven." Chapter in **Police Wife: How to Live With the Law and Like It,** by Pat James and Martha Nelson, 59-71. Springfield, IL: Charles C. Thomas, 1975.

Nine suggestions for preparing meals suited for shift work. What to do about the doorbell and telephone. Children and adolescents.

3.023 James, Pat and Martha Nelson. "Public Opinion and How

to Take It." Chapter in **Police Wife: How to Live With the Law and Like It,** by Pat James and Martha Nelson, 85-96. Springfield, IL: Charles C. Thomas, 1975.

Slang expressions for police officer. Neighbors who use a police officer's house as a precinct. Children of police officers and public opinion.

3.024 James, Pat and Martha Nelson. "Sex and the Shift-Work Wife." Chapter in **Police Wife: How to Live With the Law and Like It,** by Pat James and Martha Nelson, 44-58. Springfield, IL: Charles C. Thomas, 1975.

Shift work and irregular hours; male and female police officers working together; and the mystique associated with certain men in uniform can all contribute to sexual/marital problems in police officer marriages.

3.025 James, Pat and Martha Nelson. "Too Much Month At the End of the Money." Chapter in **Police Wife: How to Live With the Law and Like It,** by Pat James and Martha Nelson, 72-84. Springfield, IL: Charles C. Thomas, 1975.

Moonlighting police officers, wives who work, police corruption, and retirement.

3.026 Kelly, Alice. "Big City Police Life." Chapter in **Handbook for Law Enforcement Wives,** edited by Barbara E. Webber, 73-78. Chicago, IL: L.E. Publishers, Inc., 1974.

Remarks by the wife of a police officer, who was with the New York Police Department (NYPD) until his retirement in 1969. After his retirement, he became a professor at the Police Training Institute, University of Illinois.

3.027 Kirkland, Jacqueline Cercek. "Demographic, Occupational, and Personality Variables As Correlates of Reported Satisfaction in Police Marriages." **Dissertation Abstracts International** 48: 1987A-1988A. ED.D. dissertation, University of Nevada, Reno, 1987. Order No. DA8721359.

The Adjective Check List, Pearson Correlation, and Spearman Correlation were used in this study of fifty-five married, male police officers and their spouses (the paired group), and thirty-four male officers and thirty-two spouses (the non-paired group).

3.028 Lester, David and Thomas W. Guerin. "Further Explorations of Police Officers' Satisfaction With Their Marriages." **Psychological Reports** 50 (1982): 608.

The subjects were thirty-one married police officers with a mean age of 31.5 years. They completed questionnaires and a stress test. The purpose of this research was to check the reliability of two previous studies: T. Cherry and D. Lester (1979) and D. Lester and M. Karsevar (1980). Author biographical information. 3 references.

3.029 Lester, David and Michael Karsevar. "Perceived Satisfaction of Police Officers With Their Marriages." **Perceptual and Motor Skills** 51 (1980): 634.

The less stress that police officers reported regarding their work, the more satisfied they appeared to be with their marriages. Author biographical information. 1 reference.

3.030 Leyden, J. Paul. "Police Stress: A Possible Approach." **FBI Law Enforcement Bulletin** 46 (December 1977): 25-29.

A program in which the spouses of police officers accompany their husband or wife during part of his or her shift, in order to better understand police work, and to promote better communication between spouses. Author biographical information. 4 photographs.

3.031 Lowe, Mary E. "The Lowe Family." Chapter in **Handbook for Law Enforcement Wives,** edited by Barbara E. Webber, 67-72. Chicago, IL: L.E. Publishers, Inc., 1974.

Adjustments a police officer's wife has to make, especially because of her husband's shift work.

3.032 Luellen, Nellie C. "One Bird's Eye View." Chapter in **Handbook for Law Enforcement Wives,** edited by Barbara E. Webber, 79-86. Chicago, IL: L.E. Publishers, Inc., 1974.

The wife of a thirty-year veteran of law enforcement recalls what she enjoyed and resented about being married to a police officer. She particularly resented having her husband called back to work, when he was off-duty.

3.033 Lyons, William Kenneth, Jr. "A Police Recruit Family Program for the Anne Arundel County Police Department Introducing the Problem of Stress and Resultant Anxiety in the Police Officer and the Secular and Faith Resources Available." **Dissertation Abstracts International** 42: 1235B. D.MIN dissertation, Drew University, 1981. Order No. DA8119837.

Constant fear of impending danger, alcoholism, possible violent death, divorce, shift work, exposure to severely injured people, and hostility by the public are some of the causes of police stress. The author in his investigation used police stress literature and surveys of police officers and police chaplains. He also visited other police academies to observe police stress programs. The author also discusses stress reaction with reference to the General Adaptation Syndrome (1936).

3.034 Maslach, Christina and Susan E. Jackson. "Burned-Out Cops and Their Families." **Psychology Today** 12 (May 1979): 58-62.

A study of police officers and their families in California and New York. The Maslach Burnout Inventory (MBI) was an important aspect of research in this study. Although police officers try to develop emotional detachment in their work, in order to survive psychologically, they are still susceptible to emotional involvement, when they deal with very young children, teenagers, and the elderly. Having a drink with fellow officers after work is an important social function. The Los Angeles Police Department (LAPD) provides counseling sessions for officers and their families. 1 photograph. Author biographical information. 4 references.

3.035 Maynard, Peter, Nancy Maynard, Hamilton I. McCubbin and David Shao. "Family Life and the Police Profession: Coping Patterns Wives Employ in Managing Job Stress and the Family Environment." **Family Relations** 29 (1980): 495-501.

Forty-two police wives—median age of thirty-one years—were interviewed and completed questionnaires for this investigation. The coping patterns of the wives were of four types: developing self-reliance, adapting to the demands of the profession, building social support, and role maintenance. Author biographical information. Abstract. 2 tables. 2 reference notes. 17 references.

3.036 Maynard, Peter E. and Nancy W. Maynard. "Preventing

Police Family Stress Through Couples Communication Training." **Police Chief** 47 (February 1980): 30-31 and 66.

Reports on the Minnesota Couple Communications Program used at the Rhode Island Municipal Police Academy. The program was established in 1968 at the Minnesota Family Study Center. Drs. Sherod Miller and Daniel Wackman were instrumental in developing the program. The program helps couples to better understand and improve their communications patterns. The program was developed because police officers often have difficulty communicating about work with their spouses. This is due, in part, because of a desire to protect one's spouse and family from the negative aspects of police work. Author biographical information. 2 photographs. 4 references.

3.037 Megerson, John S. "The Officer's Lady: A Follow-Up." **Police Chief** 43 (January 1976): 50-52.

Describes an enhanced, multi-session seminar designed to effectively communicate to police wives the nature of police work, and their importance in the police marriage. Author biographical information. 1 photograph.

3.038 Miller, Chuck and Janice Miller. "Escape From Stress: One Couple's Remedy." **Police Stress** 1 (Spring 1980): 37-38 and 41.

Two separate accounts—one by a husband, the other by a wife—illustrate how these two individuals deal with the stress of police work, as it relates to their marriage. The husband is a police officer in Tulsa, Oklahoma. Chuck and Janice Miller work—in their spare time—at their professional photography service. One of the rewards of this leisure activity has been the opportunity to form new friendships. 2 photographs.

3.039 Mitchell, Sheila. "The Policeman's Wife—Urban and Rural." **Police Journal** 48 (1975): 79-88.

British research in which 582 subjects—urban and rural—participated. Results are reported in terms of: effects on wives of husbands' working hours; effects on wives of living in police houses (official accommodation); effects of police affiliation on wife and children; and effect at work on employed wives. This paper was originally presented at the Meeting, British Association for the Advancement of Science, 1974.

Author biographical information.

3.040 Murray, David C. "**Police Divorces: The Effects, Causes and Prevention.**" Master's thesis, Long Island University, 1977.

Among the topics examined in this thesis are: the effects of divorce on police department and society; the police subculture; psychological and sociological effects of the subculture; stress and its consequences; impact of the police subculture on marriages; and survey of police and nonpolice wives. 40 footnotes. 48 references. 29 tables. 2 appendices.

3.041 Niederhoffer, Arthur and Elaine Niederhoffer. "Children of the Force." Chapter in **The Police Family: From Station House to Ranch House,** by Arthur Niederhoffer and Elaine Niederhoffer, 139-153. Lexington, MA: D.C. Heath and Co., 1978.

How police children, as they grow older, change their attitudes about police work. Reactions of parents when these children become adolescents. Police children who get in trouble with the law. 1 table. 12 footnotes.

3.042 Niederhoffer, Arthur and Elaine Niederhoffer. "The Police Family in Literature." Chapter in **The Police Family: From Station House to Ranch House,** by Arthur Niederhoffer and Elaine Niederhoffer, 7-39. Lexington, MA: D.C. Heath and Co., 1978.

A feature of this chapter is a table which lists twenty-eight fiction books published between 1948 and 1977. The table names the police officer or officers in each book and comments on his or her marriage. 64 footnotes.

3.043 Niederhoffer, Arthur and Elaine Niederhoffer. "The Police Mystique: From Station House to Ranch House." by Arthur Niederhoffer and Elaine Niederhoffer, Chapter in **The Police Family: From Station House to Ranch House,** 59-86. Lexington, MA: D.C. Heath and Co., 1978.

Why many women find police officers in uniform sexually attractive. The opinions of male police officers regarding female police officers as partners. The reaction of police wives to female partners for their husbands. Police wives who know their husbands are corrupt. Efforts by police officers to hide their real identity from neighbors. Why police officers insulate their families from police work. Police officers and their children. Retirement opportunities and problems. 48 footnotes.

3.044 Niederhoffer, Arthur and Elaine Niederhoffer. "The Police Occupation: A Jealous Mistress." Chapter in **The Police Family: From Station House to Ranch House,** by Arthur Niederhoffer and Elaine Niederhoffer, 1-6. Lexington, MA: D.C. Heath and Co., 1978.

What is expected of a police officer by his profession affects his married life considerably, and can easily have an adverse affect on both his work and married life. 11 footnotes.

3.045 Niederhoffer, Arthur and Elaine Niederhoffer. "Policemen's Wives: The Blue Connection." Chapter in **The Police Family: From Station House to Ranch House,** by Arthur Niederhoffer and Elaine Niederhoffer, 87-137. Lexington, MA: D.C. Heath and Co., 1978.

Police wives in the U.S., Britain, Canada, and Australia express their anxieties and uncertainties, regarding their husbands. Shift work, neighbor hostility, sex, career choices for children, female partners, and the confidential nature of police work contribute significantly to the anxieties and uncertainties. 8 tables.

3.046 Nordlicht, Stephen. "Effects of Stress on the Police Officer and Family." **New York State Journal of Medicine** 79 (1979): 400-401.

Presented at the Eighty-fifth Annual Conference, International Association of Chiefs of Police, American Association of Police Physicians and Surgeons, New York, October 9, 1978. Author biographical information. 8 references.

3.047 Norris, Sandra J. "For Some It's Easy." **Police Stress** 1 (Fall 1978): 9.

A police officer's wife talks about her adjustment to police life. 1 photograph.

3.048 Nowell, B.F. "Salute to the Wives." **RCMP Quarterly**

40, No. 4 (1975): 13.

The wives of RCMP (Royal Canadian Mounted Police) officers experience many disruptions daily, because of the nature of police work, and are to be congratulated for effectively handling interrupted family and other routines.

3.049 Parker, Donna. "Be His Anchor." Chapter in **Handbook for Law Enforcement Wives**, edited by Barbara E. Webber, 47-58. Chicago, IL: L.E. Publishers, Inc., 1974.

A former nurse talks about her marriage to a detective with the Champaign Police Department, Champaign, Illinois. She discusses the trauma her husband and she endured, after he shot a man in self-defense.

3.050 Paulson, S. Lawrence. "Orientation Programs for the Police Family." **Police Chief** 41 (March 1974): 63-64.

Highlights of orientation programs for police families in the following cities: Detroit, Michigan; South Bend, Indiana; Seattle, Washington; Orlando, Florida; Dallas, Texas; and Cincinnati, Ohio. The information is from a questionnaire survey of eighty-seven police departments by the International Association of Chiefs of Police (IACP). Author biographical information. 1 photograph.

3.051 "Police Agencies Urged to Help Survivors of Slain Officers." **Criminal Justice Newsletter** 18 (February 2, 1987): 4.

Reports on a study conducted for the National Institute of Justice (NIJ) by COPS (Concerns of Police Survivors). COPS offers emotional support to families and friends of police officers killed in the line of duty.

3.052 Price, Alan A. "Police Marriages: Theoretical Concepts for Selecting Spouses." **Police Stress** 1 (Spring 1980): 31-36.

Relates categories of wives and categories of police husbands to hypotheses regarding levels of marital quality. Author biographical information. 1 table.

3.053 Rafky, David. "My Husband the Cop." **Police Chief** 41 (August 1974): 62-65.

A survey of the wives of one hundred police officers. The detailed results are divided into four categories of information: general opinions; working conditions and benefits; family stress; and public image and social isolation. Author biographical information.

3.054 Reese, James T. "Family Support and Peer Counseling." **Police Stress** 8 (Winter 1987): 8-10.

Edward Donovan, President, International Law Enforcement Stress Association and Al Benner, San Francisco Police Department (SFPD), San Francisco, California are two of the individuals quoted in this article. Author biographical information. 1 illustration. 13 references.

3.055 Saper, Marshall B. "Police Wives: The Hidden Resource." **Police Chief** 47 (February 1980): 28-29.

Talks about the origin of and rationale for the Marriage Partner Program, Kansas City Police Department, Kansas City, Missouri. Includes the remarks of wives. Author biographical information. 1 photograph.

3.056 Siegel, Micki. **Cops and Women.** New York, NY: Tower Publications, Inc., 1980.

Rookie wives, reasons police marriages break up, the women police officers work with, and police widows are some of the topics covered in this book. A psychological profile of police officers, how stress affects them, and stress management are also discussed.

3.057 Simpson, Dave. "A Policeman's Wife Never Knows." Chapter in **Stress and Police Personnel,** by Leonard Territo and Harold J. Vetter, 227-232. Boston, MA: Allyn and Bacon, Inc., 1981.

How the wives of police officers in Charleston, South Carolina live with the anxieties and uncertainties associated with police work.

3.058 Stratton, John. "Pressures in Law Enforcement Marriages: Some Considerations." **Police Chief** 42

(November 1975): 44-47.

Alcohol use and abuse, excessive protection of wives and families, and the venting of anger at home, rather than at work, are associated with law enforcement careers. Police officers have unspoken fears and, at the end of their shifts, have a need to be taken care of. Open communication in a police marriage, an alertness to danger signals in the marriage, and friendships with people not in law enforcement are recommended. Author biographical information. 1 photograph.

3.059 Stratton, John G. "The Law Enforcement Family: Programs for Spouses." Chapter in **Stress and Police Personnel**, by Leonard Territo and Harold J. Vetter, 263-270. Boston, MA: Allyn and Bacon, Inc., 1981.

The Spouses Training Program, developed by Peter J. Pitchess, Sheriff of Los Angeles County, California, consists of eight classes. The sheriff's department training procedures, a tour of the custody division, gathering of evidence, methods of self-defense, and use of the firing range are some of the topics dealt with. 1 table.

3.060 Stratton, John G. "Law Enforcement Spouses Program: Review and Follow Up." **Law and Order** 26 (April 1978): 54-59.

Rationale, program description, findings and results, suggestions for implementing such a program, and future programs. Author biographical information. 4 photographs. 1 figure. 10 references.

3.061 Stratton, John G. "Police Marriages—Determining the Balance." Chapter in **Police Passages**, by John G. Stratton, 149-178. Manhattan Beach, CA: Glennon Publishing Co., 1984.

Discusses, with the aid of statistics, how marriage has changed since the late 1800s. Emphasizes the importance of communication in marriage. States how values, wants, and needs change over the years. Looks at characteristics of police work, which make it difficult or impossible for officers to share various things about their work with their wives. Shift work, inhibition of emotions, and the paramilitary nature of police work can contribute to marital difficulties. Includes case examples of officers with marital problems. 14 references.

3.062 Stratton, John G. "Police Widows—The Forgotten Ones." Chapter in **Police Passages**, by John G. Stratton, 319-332. Manhattan Beach, CA: Glennon Publishing Co., 1984.

The trauma of being a police widow and how to adapt to the loss of one's spouse. How the police department and others can help. Examples of police widows. 12 references.

3.063 Stratton, John G., Barbara Tracy-Stratton and Geraldine Alldredge. "The Effects of a Spouses' Training Program: A Longitudinal Study." **Journal of Police Science and Administration** 10 (1982): 297-301.

The roots of the Spouses' Training Program can be traced back to 1975. At that time, Peter J. Pitchess, former Los Angeles County Sheriff, developed a training and orientation program for law enforcement spouses. The present article is about the effects of a spouses' training program five years later. In studying an experimental group and a control group, it was learned that most officers and their spouses found the spouses' program to be beneficial. The program, however, did not reduce divorce rates. Author biographical information. 4 tables. 10 references.

3.064 Territo, Leonard and Harold J. Vetter. "Stress and the Police Family." in **Stress and Police Personnel**, by Leonard Territo and Harold J. Vetter, 217-225. Boston, MA: Allyn and Bacon, Inc., 1981.

Problems in police marriages are related to: changing work schedules, emotional exhaustion, negative public image of police officers, overprotection by police officers of spouse and family, hardening of emotions, sexual problems, identity problems, and problems with their children. Marital problems, as a police administrative concern, have been dealt with in various ways, including: orientation programs for spouses, interview programs with the spouses of police applicants, ride-along programs, and programs in firearms usage and safety. 9 references.

3.065 Vevera, Patricia. "10-21 Home, But 10-19 Would Be Better." Chapter in **Handbook for Law Enforcement Wives**, edited by Barbara E. Webber, 87-89. Chicago, IL: L.E. Publishers, Inc., 1974.

The importance, to a police wife, of creating her own life—because of the irregular routines inherent in her husband's work.

3.066 Webber, Barbara. "The Police Wife." **Police Chief** 43 (January 1976): 48-49.

The author, who conducts seminars for police wives, talks about the value of a police wife to the police officer, and outlines the anxieties police wives express about their spouses working with policewomen. Author biographical information. 1 photograph. 2 footnotes.

3.067 Webber, Barbara E. "The Police Life." Chapter in **Handbook for Law Enforcement Wives,** edited by Barbara E. Webber, 13-45. Chicago, IL: L.E. Publishers, Inc., 1974.

The wife of a police lieutenant—Urbana Police Department, Urbana, Illinois—talks about her marriage of over two decades. She is employed at the Police Training Institute, University of Illinois. She discusses a number of topics within the context of a police marriage, including: fear, money, unlisted phones as opposed to listed phones, children, and guns.

3.068 Wehrle-Einhorn, Juanita L. "Gender, Stress and Self in the Work-Family Role System: Role Inconsistency Among Police Officers." **Dissertation Abstracts International** 42: 876A. Ph.D. dissertation, University of Kansas, 1980. Order No. DA8115756.

A questionnaire and open-ended discussion were used in this study of 226 police officers—eighty-three female and 143 male. The officers were employed in nineteen U.S. midwestern cities. Population of the cities ranged between 25,000 and one million. Six major findings were reported. One finding was that police work made the female officers more independent and assertive. A second finding was that female officers denied being equated with women's liberation. A third finding was that female officers were not fully accepted in the male informal network.

3.069 Whitaker, Ben. "Police Families' Problems" in **The Police in Society,** by Ben Whitaker, 237-241. London: Sinclair Browne Ltd., 1982.

Problems faced by police officers and their families in England, the U.S., and Scotland. Officers and their families face hostility, curiosity, suspiciousness, and social isolation from neighbors. Rural police officers are subjected to these problems to an even greater degree than their urban counterparts.

3.070 Wilson, Marsha. "The Way We Are." Chapter in **Handbook for Law Enforcement Wives,** edited by Barbara E. Webber, 59-65. Chicago, IL: L.E. Publishers, Inc., 1974.

A wife's mainly positive experiences in her marriage to a police officer.

# 4

# Substance Abuse

4.001 "Are EMTs/Paramedics Turning to Alcohol and Drugs to Cope With Job Stress?" **Emergency Medical Services** 14 (January/February 1985): 12 and 15-18.

Five emergency medical services (EMS) personnel comment on drug/alcohol abuse in their profession: David M. Habben (Grants Pass, Oregon); Diane L. Collins (Denver, Colorado); Guy W. Bull (Santa Barbara, California); Robert G. Nixon (Wellington, Florida); and Victoria L. Countee (Washington, D.C.).

4.002 Bracey, Dorothy. "Police Stress: The American Response." **Police Journal** 52 (1979): 263-266 and 270.

A study by the National Institute of Occupational Safety and Health (NIOSH) found that police officers have serious marital, alcohol, and drug problems, and that they also have high rates of premature death, including a high suicide rate. Some of the organizations which help police officers deal with stress are: the Police Training Division, Federal Law Enforcement Training Center (Georgia); International Conference of Police Chaplains; National Association of Police Chaplains; International Association of Chiefs of Police; and John Jay College of Criminal Justice. Author biographical information. 6 footnotes. 1 note.

4.003 "Cop's Career Was Shot by Use of Narcotics." **Police Stress** 6 (Spring 1983): 32.

An attempt by the New York Police Department (NYPD) to dismiss officer Peter Heron, age twenty-eight. Heron claims his drug addiction is due to job stress, related to violence and death. In one incident, a gunman tried to shoot Heron, but the gun misfired. Next day, Heron shot and wounded a gunman about to shoot another police officer. Heron, a heroin addict, contends the NYPD should have provided him with counseling.

4.004 "Drug, Alcohol Help Offered NYC Fire Fighters." **Fire Command** 51 (April 1984): 9.

Announcement by Joseph E. Spinnato, Fire Commissioner for New York, about a drug and alcohol abuse program for that city's firefighters. It is in the interest of firefighters who have problems to volunteer for the program. Those who have problems and do not volunteer may face penalties.

4.005 "Drug Testing for EMS Personnel." **Emergency Medical Services** 16 (March 1987): 15-16, 18, 20, 23-24 and 81.

Eleven emergency medical services (EMS) personnel comment on drug testing for EMS personnel. The personnel are: June Arbogast, Claire Gavrel and Kevin Kissane (Chicago, Illinois); John Landis (Quincy, Illinois); Richard P. Stabler (West Chester, Pennsylvania); Gary Kesling (Bedford, Texas); Jerry A. Allison (Riverside, California); and Beverly Squibb (Savannah, Missouri).

4.006 Dunne, Joseph A. "Counseling Alcoholic Employees in a Municipal Police Department." **Quarterly Journal of Studies on Alcohol** 34 (1973): 423-434.

The establishment and success of an alcoholism treatment program for the New York Police Department (NYPD). After comparing sickness absences and alcohol-related illnesses before and after counseling, it was learned that there were substantial reductions in both. After four years, 70% of the patients were still abstinent and employed. This article is based on the author's 1971 thesis, a master of public administration, from John Jay College of Criminal Justice, City University of New York. Author biographical information. Abstract. 7 references.

4.007 "Friends Cheer As Leonia Cop Returns to Job." **Police Stress** 1 (Spring 1980): 41.

Anthony Raucci who—because of alcoholism—left his job as a police officer returned to the same position seven years later—completely recovered. Raucci, age forty-nine, had been receiving a disability pension. He had received treatment at Bergen Pines County Hospital, and had joined Alcoholics Anonymous (AA).

4.008 Hepp, Christopher. "Drinking and the Police: It

Seems More Common in Blue." **Police Stress** 8 (Winter 1987): 27-28.

A focus on alcohol abuse among police officers in Philadelphia, Pennsylvania. Charles Loughran, while off-duty, smashed into and killed, while driving a truck, on-duty officer, William D. McCarthy. Officer Frank Stumpo, while drunk, assaulted several people. Frank Selgrath is a former Philadelphia police officer who runs Mustard Seed, Inc., an employee assistance firm. Selgrath is also a recovering alcoholic. 1 illustration.

4.009 Higginbotham, Jeffrey. "Urinalysis Drug Testing Programs for Law Enforcement (Part 1)." **FBI Law Enforcement Bulletin** 55 (October 1986): 25-30.

Elaborates on the basis for a drug testing program, discusses constitutional issues implicated by a drug testing program, and talks about constitutional issues in developing such a program. Related to the latter are a number of factors, including: individual privacy interests, governmental interests, public safety, public trust, potential for corruption, and morale and safety in the workplace. Author biographical information. 1 photograph. 38 footnotes.

4.010 Higginbotham, Jeffrey. "Urinalysis Drug Testing Programs for Law Enforcement (Part 2)." **FBI Law Enforcement Bulletin** 55 (November 1986): 25-30.

Goes into detail regarding when a urinalysis drug test might be required. The emphasis is on: testing applicants; testing trainees and probationary officers; testing at regularly scheduled physical examinations; testing at change of assignment; testing warranted by actions, conduct, or behavior; and unannounced random testing. Author biographical information. 1 photograph. 25 footnotes.

4.011 "IACP Announces Drug Testing Policy." **Police Chief** 53 (October 1986): 22, 24 and 26.

Comments by Jerald R. Vaughn, Executive Director, International Association of Chiefs of Police (IACP), regarding a drug testing policy pertaining to police officers. 1 photograph.

4.012 Iannone, N.F. "Special Problems in Counseling."

Chapter in **Supervision of Police Personnel**, Third Edition, by N.F. Iannone, 147-170. Englewood Cliffs, NJ: Prentice-Hall, Inc., 1980.

A look at problem drinking in law enforcement; options in treating the deviant drinker; counseling problems, procedures, and techniques; referral; the counseling objective; and emotional problems. 33 notes.

4.013 Kaslof, Leslie J. "Natural Preparations Offer New Hope for Stress Relief." **Police Stress** 8 (Winter 1987): 29-30.

Bach Remedies are nontoxic species of wildflowers used to treat individuals with psychological problems. Edward Bach, a British physician, formulated these remedies, which are an alternative to habit-forming drugs.

4.014 Koehler, Richard J. "Drug and Narcotic Screening of Police Personnel." **Police Chief** 52 (March 1986): 74-82.

Focuses on the New York Police Deaprtment (NYPD) and covers four main areas: administrator's responsibility to identify drug use by employees, constitutional issues, drug screening procedures, and post-probation screening alternatives. 45 footnotes.

4.015 Leisner, Kim. "The EMS Addict: Chemically Dependent Providers." **Emergency Medical Services** 17 (September 1988): 12 and 14-16.

Remarks to emergency medical technicians (EMTs) by Harold E. Smith, Ridgeview Institute, Smyrna, Georgia. Smith was an emergency physician who abused drugs for five years.

4.016 McVernon, John. "Drugs, Drink and Duty." **Fire Engineering** 137 (June 1984): 40-41 and 43.

Gives reasons why firefighters can become involved with drugs and alcohol. Discusses marijuana, cocaine, heroin, alcohol, and prescription and over-the-counter drugs. Includes a table which has ten variables in relation to each of the following: narcotics, depressants, stimulants, hallucinogens, and cannabis. Also includes slang terms for drugs. Author biographical information. 2 photographs.

4.017 Nowicki, Dennis E. "Police Officer Drug Abuse: An Issue of Public Safety." **Police Chief** 52 (March 1986): 71-74.

Reduced productivity, excessive vehicle accidents, increased absenteeism, and increased cost of medical benefits are some of the consequences of drug abuse by police officers. In a study of police recruits for the Chicago Police Department, Chicago, Illinois, 25% of those tested for illegal drugs tested positive. Police officer drug abuse is not a victimless crime. There must be a clear, written, and enforced drug abuse policy. Nine principles to this effect are included. Author biographical information.

4.018 Pacer, William P. "The Alcoholic Employee: Recognizing and Treating With Sensitive Firmness." **JEMS** 10 (May 1985): 26-29.

Differentiates between the social drinker, problem drinker, alcohol abuser, alcoholic, and heavy social drinker. Discusses employee assistance programs (EAPs) at the New York Fire Department and the Baltimore County Fire Department, Maryland. Alcohol-abusing employees are convinced to seek help by means of the confrontation technique. Author biographical information. 1 photograph. 1 illustration. 15 notes.

4.019 Smith, Jerry. "Asking for Help Was Hard to Do." **Police Stress** 1 (Spring 1979): 43-44.

A Minneapolis, Minnesota police officer talks about the job frustrations which led to his alcoholism and divorce. He later sought help, became a chemical dependency instructor, and enrolled in the University of Minnesota Program on Chemical Dependency Counseling. He mentions a number of ways of coping with stress. 1 photograph.

4.020 Stewart, James K. "Police and Drug Testing: A Look At Some Issues." **Police Chief** 53 (October 1986): 27, 29 and 31-32.

Reports on a survey about the ways in which police departments deal with police officer drug abuse. The survey was done for the National Institute of Justice (NIJ) by Research Management Associates, Inc. Thirty-three major police departments were surveyed. The Enzyme Multiplied Immunoassay Technique (EMIT) was used to screen urine samples. Author biographical information. 2 photographs.

4.021 Stratton, John G. "One Day At a Time—Alcoholism." Chapter in **Police Passages**, by John G. Stratton, 249-275. Manhattan Beach, CA: Glennon Publishing Co., 1984.

Early, middle, late middle, and late phases of alcoholism. Getting help. 8 references.

4.022 Stratton, John G. and Brian Wroe. "Alcoholism and the Policeman: Identifying and Dealing With the Problem." **FBI Law Enforcement Bulletin** 48 (March 1979): 20-23.

Describes an alcoholism treatment program for active and retired police officers in Los Angeles County. The program, similar to alcoholism programs in private industry, was established by the sheriff of Los Angeles County. Advice to police supervisors regarding what to do—and what not to do—in dealing with alcoholic police officers is included. Confidentiality is a key feature of the program. Author biographical information. 3 photographs. 1 illustration. 4 references.

4.023 Territo, Leonard and Harold J. Vetter. "Stress and the Police Officer." in **Stress and Police Personnel**, by Leonard Territo and Harold J. Vetter, 63-71. Boston, MA: Allyn and Bacon, Inc., 1981.

Covers alcoholism, suicide, and job stress in policewomen. Also includes an article reprinted from **The Times** (Raleigh, North Carolina), Friday, February 17, 1978. The article is entitled "If You Ever Have to Kill a Man, Never Look At His Face." The article is about John Thomas Cursey, a police officer who shot to death two liquor store robbers. Cursey, because of the psychological trauma associated with the shooting, became an alcoholic. His wife left him and he lost his job because of his drinking. He later received a lifetime disability pension—the first ever granted by the city of Memphis, Tennessee for psychological injuries. 19 references.

# 5

# Accidents

5.001 Atwood, Roswell L. "Results of Our Special Survey." in **Proceedings of a Symposium on Occupational Health and Hazards of the Fire Service,** South Bend, Indiana, January 11-13, 1971, 17-20. [Washington, DC: International Association of Fire Fighters], 1971.

Provides statistics about firefighter injuries and deaths, and mentions a number of cities, including: San Francisco, California; Seattle, Washington; and St. Louis, Missouri. Most firefighter injuries are to the back, hands, feet, and eyes. Cuts and sprains are the two most common types of injury. The three most common causes of injury are: lifting and pulling; handling tools and equipment; and falls. Author biographical information. 1 photograph.

5.002 Auerbach, Paul S., John A. Morris, Jr., Joseph B. Phillips, Jr., Scott R. Redlinger and William K. Vaughn. "An Analysis of Ambulance Accidents in Tennessee." **Journal of the American Medical Association** 258 (1987): 1487-1490.

In Tennessee, 102 ambulance accidents involving human injury or property damage over $200 were analyzed. In twenty-nine of the accidents, there were sixty-five injured victims and one death. Darkness, intersections, and passenger restraint devices were important variables studied. Passenger restraint devices were recommended for ambulance attendants and passengers. There should be strict adherence to traffic signals at intersections, and urban speed limits should be obeyed. Author biographical information. Abstract. 2 figures. 2 tables. 2 references.

5.003 "Automatic Safety?" **JEMS** 5 (November 1980): 40.

Opticom, marketed by the 3M Co., is a device which allows the drivers of emergency vehicles, in some cities, to electronically control traffic lights. These drivers have the legal right-of-way through certain key intersections. Since Opticom is meant to supplement a driver's abilities, the driver must still exercise extreme caution when driving.

5.004 Beck, D. "New Study Addresses Ambulance Accidents." **JEMS** 12 (July 1987): 21.

According to a research group at Rensselaer Polytechnic Institute, most ambulance accidents, in New York State, occur at intersections, and are due to the driver of the ambulance not noticing the driver of the other vehicle or the driver of the other vehicle not noticing the ambulance. The Rensselaer researchers recommended that ambulances first stop at a red light, then continue through the intersection. They also recommended that ambulances be painted lime yellow.

5.005 Beck, David. "Ambulance Explodes in Maryland." **JEMS** 12 (February 1987): 15.

A Ford F-350 ambulance, in Montgomery County, Maryland, caught fire and exploded. The two-man crew escaped uninjured, but firefighters suffered minor injuries. The cause of the fire was not known at the time. 1 photograph. Author biographical information.

5.006 Bradish, Jay. "Apparatus Accident." **Fire Command** 51 (January 1984): 47.

Talks about an accident in Buffalo, New York on October 25, 1983, involving a fire engine and an ambulance. Four firefighters and two ambulance attendants were injured. Both vehicles were responding to separate emergency calls, when the ambulance smashed into the side of the fire engine. Author biographical information. 2 photographs.

5.007 Carr, Bennie Lou. "Accident Prevention: A New Challenge." **JEMS** 5 (September 1980): 38-39.

How emergency medical technicians (EMTs) in Georgia teach traffic accident prevention to young drivers and drivers-to-be. Author biographical information. 1 photograph.

5.008 Cooke, Paul L. "Blinded Driver Hits Fire Fighter: Part 1." **Fire Command** 55 (November 1988): 15-17.

Circumstances and investigation of a traffic accident in Denver, Colorado on May 2, 1988. Steven Boudreaux, of the Cunningham Fire Protection District, was injured while on duty, when he was struck by a car. The accident occurred while Boudreaux was attempting to stop traffic for an ambulance. Eight significant findings pertaining to the investigation are outlined. Author biographical information. 1 illustration.

5.009 Cooke, Paul L. "Blinded Driver Hits Fire Fighter: Part 2." **Fire Command** 55 (December 1988): 31-33.

A look at the lessons learned as a result of the accident discussed in the above reference. Major lessons learned are concerned with apparatus positioning, traffic control, lighting, complacency, and supervision of emergency personnel. Training and enforcement of a firefighter safety and health program is the key to preventing future accidents. Author biographical information. 1 illustration.

5.010 Dick, Thom. "Rules of the Road: Some Perspectives on Emergency Driving." **JEMS** 5 (November 1980): 38-40.

A paramedic with an accident-free driving record talks about ten safety practices for emergency drivers. The practices range from checking the vehicle before driving it to using peripheral vision, from being suspicious of other drivers to knowing the geographical area to be traveled in. 2 photographs.

5.011 "A Disturbing Death in Seattle." **Fire Command** 51 (March 1984): 10.

Mary Matthews, a Seattle, Washington firefighter, fell from a ladder truck on January 13, 1984, and died the following day. She was wearing full protective gear, and apparently lost her grip. She had joined the fire department in 1980.

5.012 Estepp, M.H. "Under the Wheels." **Fire Command** 51 (February 1984): 28-29.

Less than thirty seconds after beginning to respond to an emergency call, Barbara Lee, a firefighter with the Prince George's County Fire Department, Maryland, fell off and under the rear wheels of an aerial truck. Her medical treatment involved, in part, fifty operations, 800 units of blood, and an artificial leg. She received extensive treatment at the Maryland Institute for Emergency Medicine in Baltimore. Author biographical information. 1 illustration. 2 photographs. Profile of the Prince George's County Fire Department.

5.013 "Fall From Truck Kills Female Fire Fighter." **Fire Command** 54 (June 1987): 10.

Reports on the death of Winona Lee Crum, a firefighter from Walkersville, Maryland. She was thrown from a fire truck en route to a traffic accident.

5.014 "Fire Fighter Killed During Exercises." **Fire Command** 54 (August 1987): 16.

Daryl P. Wells, a member of the Augusta Fire Department, was fatally injured by a fire engine. Wells was in the parking lot of the Augusta Civic Center. He was photographing training exercises when the incident occurred.

5.015 Gad, Palle. "Traffic Accidents With Personal Injury During Emergency Driving." **Danish Medical Bulletin** 18 (June 1971): 57-60.

This study, which was done in Denmark and which covers the years 1964-1966, provides statistics regarding injury traffic accidents and the Falck Rescue Co. Falck provides ambulance service to most of Denmark. There were forty-one injury traffic accidents during 1964-1966. Author biographical information. 8 tables. Acknowledgements.

5.016 Hanna, James A. "Vehicle Operations in Crowd Situations." **Canadian Emergency Services News** 8 (January/February 1985): 30-34.

Covers: vehicle mechanics, supplies, and logistics; routes and access; staffing; and negotiating traffic jams and crowds. 1 illustration. 4 photographs. Author biographical information.

5.017 Henry, Kenneth C. "I Watched a Friend Die This Morning." **Fire Engineering** 140 (October 1987): 12 and 15.

An account of a traffic accident, in which firefighters at the scene did not know initially that the person killed in the accident was a fellow firefighter, who worked a different shift. Author biographical information. 1 photograph.

5.018 James, D.E. and William E. Ward. "Safety on Four Wheels." **Emergency** 16 (November 1984): 36-37 and 54-55.

Talks about driver training and accidents regarding emergency response units, such as ambulances and police vehicles. Collisions can be reduced and their seriousness minimized. Discusses research by the U.S. National Transportation Safety Board (NTSB), R.A. Whitworth of General Motors, and Dr. John Palmer of St. Cloud State University. An emergency vehicle operator instructor's course is offered in Vermette, Manitoba. 5 figures.

5.019 Lake, Ludwell. "The Driving Force." **JEMS** 12 (March 1987): 58-59.

Describes the EVADE (Emergency Vehicle Advanced Driver Education) program at Southwest Ambulance in Arizona. Dean Erickson is the coordinator and Steve Giardini, the instructor. The Chandler Fire Department, Chandler, Arizona, also participated in EVADE, as did employees of Schaffer Ambulance, Los Angeles, California. Author biographical information.

5.020 Lamm, W.H. "Vehicle Warning Systems." **Emergency** 15 (October 1983): 32-35.

Examines audible and visual vehicle warning systems. Comments on desirable traits in audible devices, including six points about siren selection. Discusses white, red, blue, and amber light. Color combinations for police, fire, and service vehicles, as well as for ambulances, are listed. Signal control systems (programmed route, optical, radio controlled, and siren controlled) are included. 1 illustration. 3 references.

5.021 Miller, Larry Scott. "Police Officer Involvement in Motor Vehicle Accidents Within the State of Tennessee." **Dissertation Abstracts International** 42: 4731A. Ph.D. dissertation, University of Tennessee, 1981. Order No. DA8208986.

A questionnaire was used in this study of 416 Tennessee

police officers and police officer involvement in motor vehicle accidents in that state. Police demographic characteristics, administrative policies, motor vehicle condition, and stress were of special interest to the author. Four major conclusions were presented.

5.022 Minerd, R. "Ambulance Crash Review Exposes Driver Weakness." **JEMS** 12 (December 1987): 20.

Concerns a study by Don Ptacnik, regarding 314 ambulance crashes in North Carolina between 1982 and 1986. The author's recommendations: drive slower, take more time when going through intersections, and always wear a seat belt.

5.023 "Saving Firemen When It Comes to the Crunch." **New Scientist** 74 (1977): 785.

Looks at tests used to determine the level of safety of the Crew Safety Vehicle (CSV). 1 photograph.

5.024 "Shock of Firemen's Worst Fire." **Life** 61 (October 28, 1966): 45.

Death of Jim Galanaugh, a New York firefighter. Galanaugh, and eleven other firefighters, died in a fire in Manhattan, when a floor collapsed in a building which was about one hundred years old. The building in which the twelve men died had not been thoroughly inspected since 1949. 2 photographs.

5.025 Smoke, Clinton H., Jr. "Accidents en Route." **Fire Command** 51 (August 1984): 8.

Letter to the editor regarding fire vehicle accidents.

5.026 Solomon, Stephen S. "Ambulance Accident Avoidance." **Emergency** 17 (January 1985): 34-35 and 44.

Audible warning devices, flashing lights, and vehicle color are discussed in relation to ambulance accident avoidance. Civilian drivers are at fault in approximately 80% of ambulance and civilian vehicle accidents. Mentions research by the National Research Council. Also talks about the psychological effects of different colors. 1 photograph.

5.027 "Study Dispels Longtime Beliefs About 'Line-of-Duty' Deaths." **Police Stress** 8 (Winter 1987): 21-22.

A survey by the National Institute of Justice. Questionnaires and interviews were used to obtain information. The survey was about the deaths of police officers by accident or killed feloniously in action, and how this affected spouses and parents.

5.028 Thomsen, James M. "A Provider's Trauma: Personal Reflections on Pain and Death." **JEMS** 12 (July 1987): 34-37 and 40.

A paramedic describes a car accident in Florida in 1986, involving injuries to himself, his wife, and their two children. Author biographical information. 5 photographs.

5.029 Williams, Lester L. "To and From the Emergency." in **Proceedings of a Symposium on Occupational Health and Hazards of the Fire Service**, South Bend, Indiana, January 11-13, 1971, 81-84. [Washington, DC: International Association of Fire Fighters], 1971.

Contends, with the aid of facts and figures, that going to and coming back from emergencies can be more hazardous to firefighters than fighting fires. Gives examples of traffic fatalities involving firefighters. Emphasizes the importance of and need for seat belts. Colorado Springs, Colorado; Chicago, Illinois; and Denver, Colorado are examples of cities discussed. Author biographical information. 1 photograph.

5.030 Wilson, Amani W.A. "Reported Accidental Injuries in a Metropolitan Police Department." **Dissertation Abstracts International** 41: 1936B. Ph.D. dissertation, Boston University Graduate School, 1980. Order No. DA-8024228.

With the aid of personnel files and Minnesota Multiphasic Personality Inventory (MMPI) profiles, the author studied 338 police officers. He was interested in identifying officers at high risk for accidental injuries. The data examined by the author represented a time period of more than seven years. High accident repetition is discussed with respect to personality and demographic factors.

5.031 Wood, Forrest C., Jr. "Evade: Training for Tire

Blowouts." **JEMS** 12 (March 1987): 56-57 and 60.

EVADE (Emergency Vehicle Advanced Driver Education) is a program introduced in Arizona in 1985. The program also involved the MERV (Multiple Emergency Response Vehicle), which can be programmed to simulate, among other conditions, tire blowouts. EVADE is based on a truck testing program at the Ford Motor Proving Grounds (FMPG) at Yucca, Arizona. EVADE is credited with a reduction in accident rates and repair costs. Author biographical information. 3 photographs.

# 6

# Suicide

6.001 Coleman, Loren. "Police Clusters." in **Suicide Clusters,** by Loren Coleman, 31-33. Boston, MA: Faber and Faber, Inc., 1987.

"Clusters" of police suicides, primarily in 1986 in Boston, Massachusetts and New York. In Boston in April 1986: Edward Foley, patrolman, age fifty-six; Clovis Cobb, patrolman, age thirty-four; Saul Shamjowicz, detective, age thirty-three. In New York in September 1986: Michael J. McNamara, age twenty-eight and Thomas Lucas, age thirty. In New York in January 1987: John Gaggin, a detective lieutenant. Reference is also made to a study in 1986 by Dr. Robert Loo, concerning suicide by members of the Royal Canadian Mounted Police (RCMP).

6.002 Danto, Bruce L. "Police Suicide." Chapter in **Stress and Police Personnel,** by Leonard Territo and Harold J. Vetter, 126-141. Boston, MA: Allyn and Bacon, Inc., 1981.

A study of suicide in the Detroit Police Department, Detroit, Michigan. Twelve officers, all male, committed suicide between February 1968 and January 1976. Seven of the officers were in their twenties, eleven were married, and three were black. Eight officers died of gunshot wounds, two died of carbon monoxide (CO), and one hung himself. Not one officer was in uniform when he took his own life. The author has worked at the Detroit Psychiatric Institute. 8 endnotes.

6.003 Dash, Jerry and Martin Reiser. "Suicide Among Police in Urban Law Enforcement Agencies." **Journal of Police Science and Administration** 6 (1978): 18-21.

Reports on police suicide in New York, London, Chicago, San Francisco, St. Louis, Detroit, Los Angeles, and Wyoming, but primarily focuses on the Los Angeles Police Department (LAPD). The relatively low suicide rate for Los Angeles police officers is partly attributed to the Behavioral Science Services Section. This part of the police department provides psychological and other assistance to officers and their families. The LAPD has had a full-time, in-house psychologist since 1968. This paper was presented at the California State Psychological Association Convention, Los Angeles, California, March 11, 1977. Author biographical information. 1 table. 22 footnotes.

6.004 Fabricatore, Joseph M. and Jerry Dash. "Suicide, Divorce, and Psychological Health Among Police Officers." **Essence** 1 (1977): 225-231.

Suicide and divorce rates may be lower than commonly believed in officers of the Los Angeles Police Department (LAPD). There are three reasons for this: preemployment psychological screening, psychological services—Behavioral Science Services Unit, and personality attributes of individuals interested in a career in police work. Author biographical information. English abstract. 3 reference notes. 22 references. French abstract.

6.005 Gaska, Cass W. "The Rate of Suicide, Potential for Suicide, and Recommendations for Prevention Among Retired Police Officers." **Dissertation Abstracts International** 41: 1402A. Ph.D. dissertation, Wayne State University, 1980. Order No. DA8022754.

A control and sample group were interviewed, a modified form of the Clinical Index of Potential Suicide (CIPS) was used, the chi-square test was used to analyze the results, and pre-retirement counseling for police officers was recommended.

6.006 Heiman, Michael F. "Police Suicides Revisited." **Suicide** 5 (1975): 5-20.

During the six-year period, January 1, 1934 to January 1, 1940, ninety-one New York Police Department (NYPD) police officers committed suicide. Dr. Paul Friedman, in writing about these suicides, attributed them, in part, to the election in 1933 of Fiorello H. La Guardia as mayor of New York, and La Guardia's impact via Tammany Hall on the police department. This paper by Heiman reexamines the police files and case histories, and offers new comments regarding the ninety-one suicides. Author biographical information. Abstract. 2 footnotes. 5 tables. 19 references.

6.007 Heiman, Michael F. "Suicide Among Police." **American Journal of Psychiatry** 134 (1977): 1286-1290.

This article is based on three major sources of information: records of ninety-three New York Police Department (NYPD) suicides between 1934 and 1940, data since 1960 regarding police suicides in twenty-three large U.S. cities, and data pertaining to suicide by members of the Metropolitan Police Department of London. Although handguns were the most common method of police suicide in the U.S., in London it was gas inhalation or drug ingestion. Most police officers in London who committed suicide were married; most police officers in the U.S. who committed suicide were divorced or seeking divorce. 2 case reports. Author biographical information. Abstract. 2 tables. 23 references.

6.008 Labovitz, Sanford and Robert Hagedorn. "An Analysis of Suicide Rates Among Occupational Categories." **Sociological Inquiry** 41, No. 1 (1971): 67-72.

Police officers in the U.S., in approximately 1950, are compared to thirty-five other occupations regarding prestige, income, education, and suicide rate. Author biographical information. Abstract. 2 tables. 9 footnotes. 21 references.

6.009 Nelson, Zane P. and Wilford E. Smith. "The Law Enforcement Profession: An Incident of High Suicide." **Omega** 1 (1970): 293-299.

A study based on suicide in Wyoming during the years 1960-1968. The highest suicide rate per 100,000 was in law enforcement: 203.66 per 100,000. A firearm was used in the suicide of every police officer in Wyoming for the time period 1960-1968. About a third of the officers were divorced or separated. Physicians had the second highest rate of suicide in Wyoming: 132.53 per 100,000. Six reasons for police suicide are discussed. Author biographical information. 2 tables. 4 footnotes. 10 references.

6.010 "Police Alcoholism, Divorce, Suicide Rates Much Higher Than Official Stats." **Behavior Today** 12 (January 26, 1981): 2-4.

Remarks by Edward Donovan, Program Director, Boston Police Stress Program, Boston, Massachusetts. The program, which guarantees officers confidentiality, operates out of a building near the Mattapan Chronic

Disease Hospital. Donovan gives examples of indirect ways in which police officers attempt or actually commit suicide. He also states why officers become cyncal and talks about problems in police marriages.

6.011 Reuss-Ianni, Elizabeth. "A Police Suicide." Chapter in **Two Cultures of Policing: Street Cops and Management Cops**, by Elizabeth Reuss-Ianni, 71-88. New Brunswick, NJ: Transaction Books, 1983.

Police corruption in the New York Police Department (NYPD) before and after the Knapp Commission, including the 1978 suicide of a police officer being investigated for illegal activities. Career and salary, job stress, and integrity and ethics are issues police officers comment on. Police work in Manhattan and the Bronx is contrasted. Ethical Awareness Workhops and the internal affairs division (IAD) are also discussed. 5 notes.

6.012 Ronan, Dick. "The Man on the Roof." **Police Stress** 1 (Spring 1980): 46.

A former police officer in Providence, Rhode Island held a gun to his head, while standing on the roof of that city's police building, threatening to committ suicide. The former officer's supervisor, Lieutenant Donald W. Lawton, persuaded the would-be suicide to abandon his idea of self-destruction. This took Lawton an hour and a half to accompish. The former officer was taken into protective custody. 1 photograph.

6.013 "Stress Leads to Demotion of Policeman." **Mental and Physical Disability Law Reporter** 8 (1984): 460.

A police officer in Pennsylvania, who attempted suicide, was later demoted and prohibited from carrying a lethal weapon. The court did not agree with the officer's claims that marital problems had precipitated his stress and suicide attempt. The case is that of Herman versus the Pennsylvania Department of General Services.

6.014 Yap, P.M. "Suicidal Acts By Occupation (Both Sexes)." Figure in **Suicide in Hong Kong: With Special Reference to Attempted Suicide**, by P.M. Yap, 33. Hong Kong: Hong Kong University Press, 1958.

Data about police officers is included in this figure.

6.015 Yap, P.M. "Suicide and Attempted Suicide By Occupation." Table in **Suicide in Hong Kong: With Special Reference to Attempted Suicide,** by P.M. Yap, 33. Hong Kong: Hong Kong University Press, 1958.

This table includes data about police officers.

# Author Index

Numbers Are Entry Numbers, Not Page Numbers

**E**



**F**



**G**

H

I



J



K



L

S

**T**



**U**



**V**



**W**

**X**



**Y**



**Z**

# Subject Index

Numbers Are Entry Numbers, Not Page Numbers

## D

G

## H



## I

**J**



**K**

O

P

## T

## U

**About the Author**

JOHN J. MILETICH is Reference Librarian at the University of Alberta, Canada. His previously published books include *Retirement: An Annotated Bibliography* (Greenwood Press, 1986); *Work and Alcohol Abuse: An Annotated Bibliography* (Greenwood Press, 1987); and *States of Awareness: An Annotated Bibliography* (Greenwood Press, 1988).

9 780313 266829

Printed by Libri Plureos GmbH in Hamburg, Germany